Secure Software Development: A Security Programmer's Guide

Jason Grembi

COURSE TECHNOLOGY
CENGAGE Learning

Australia • Brazil • Japan • Korea • Mexico • Singapore • Spain • United Kingdom • United States

COURSE TECHNOLOGY
CENGAGE Learning™

Secure Software Development: A Security Programmer's Guide

Jason Grembi

Executive Editor: Stephen Helba

Senior Product Manager: Alyssa Pratt

Development Editor: Jill Batistick

Editorial Assistant: Claire Jeffers

Marketing Manager: Erin Coffin

Marketing Coordinator: Shanna Gibbs

Content Project Manager: Daphne Barbas

Copyeditor: Karen Annett

Proofreader: Wendy Benedetto

Indexer: Alexandra Nickerson

Art Director: Kun-Tee Chang

For product information and technology assistance, contact us at
Cengage Learning Customer & Sales Support, 1-800-354-9706

For permission to use material from this text or product,
submit all requests online at **www.cengage.com/permissions**
Further permissions questions can be emailed to
permissionrequest@cengage.com

ISBN-13: 978-1-4180-6547-8
ISBN-10: 1-4180-6547-1

Course Technology
25 Thomson Place
Boston, MA 02210
USA

Cengage Learning is a leading provider of customized learning solutions with office locations around the globe, including Singapore, the United Kingdom, Australia, Mexico, Brazil, and Japan. Locate your local office at: **international.cengage.com/region**

Cengage Learning products are represented in Canada by Nelson Education, Ltd.

For your lifelong learning solutions, visit **course.cengage.com**

Visit our corporate website at **cengage.com**

Some of the product names and company names used in this book have been used for identification purposes only and may be trademarks or registered trademarks of their respective manufacturers and sellers.

Course Technology, a part of Cengage Learning, reserves the right to revise this publication and make changes from time to time in its content without notice.

The programs in this book are for instructional purposes only. They have been tested with care, but are not guaranteed for any particular intent beyond educational purposes. The author and the publisher do not offer any warranties or representations, nor do they accept any liabilities with respect to the programs.

Printed in Canada
1 2 3 4 5 6 7 12 11 10 09 08

TABLE OF
Contents

CHAPTER NINE
Coding in the Cube: Developing Good Habits   223

CHAPTER TEN
Testing for Quality and Security   255

CHAPTER ELEVEN
Maintain Your Software, Maintain Your Career 281

GLOSSARY 301

INDEX 307

Foreward

Why Secure Code Is Important

You might want to consider what's at stake before reading this book...

A terrorist organization announces one morning that they will shut down the Pacific Northwest electrical grid for six hours starting at 4:00PM; they then do so. The same group then announces that they will disable the primary telecommunication trunk circuits between the U.S. East and West Coasts for a half day; they then do so, despite our efforts to defend against them. Then, they threaten to bring down the air traffic control system supporting New York City, grounding all traffic and diverting inbound traffic; they then do so. Other threats follow, and each are successfully executed, demonstrating the adversary's capability to attack America's critical infrastructure. Finally, they threaten to cripple e-commerce and credit card service for a week by using several hundred thousand stolen identities in millions of fraudulent transactions. Imagine the ensuing public panic and chaos. What makes this scenario both interesting and alarming is that all of the aforementioned [types of] events have already happened, albeit not concurrently nor all by malicious intent. They occurred as isolated events, spread out over time; some during various technical failures, some during simple exercises, and some during real-world cyber attacks (Excerpt from a letter to President Bush from 50 scientists, computer experts, and former intelligence officials, 2002).

What this scenario highlights is the fact that every sector of the global economy, from energy, to transportation, finance and banking, telecommunications, public health, emergency services, water, chemical, defense, industrial, food, agriculture, right down to the postal and shipping sectors, relies on software. Thus, anything that threatens that software, in effect, poses a threat to our way of life. Given those stakes, the obvious question is what is the current situation? The Taskforce sums *that* up in five global statements:

(1)   Cyber incidents are increasing in number, sophistication, severity, and cost.

(2)   The nation's economy is increasingly dependent on cyberspace. This has introduced unknown interdependencies and single points of failure.

(3)   A digital disaster strikes some enterprise every day. Infrastructure disruptions have cascading impacts, multiplying their cyber and physical effects.

(4)   Fixing vulnerabilities before threats emerge will reduce risk.

(5)   It is a mistake to think that past levels of cyberdamage are accurate indicators of the future. Much worse can happen.

The Emerging Threat

In the 1980s and 1990s, a typical cyberexploit was a criminal trespass or Web site defacement. Now our cyber adversaries are motivated by everything from financial gain to terrorism. As a result, the stereotypical image of the kid living on Skittles, while doing 72-hour hacks, has been replaced by a much darker and more complex persona, one who is well organized and intent on trouble.

The statistics from US-CERT make a particularly compelling case for this observation. According to the CERT Coordinating Center, which is the most authoritative reporting agency in the United States, 319,992 security incidents were reported in the 15-year period from the time it began keeping records. Each of these represented a discrete event that entailed one of four attack types: unauthorized access, malicious code, denial of service, or inappropriate usage. The important fact, however, is that 219,623 of these events occurred in the years 2002 and 2003, which means that 69 percent of all known attacks took place in the last two reporting years and there is no indication that that incremental rate of increase has changed in the five years since then.

The same is true for vulnerabilities. Product vulnerabilities are flaws that might allow an attacker to usurp privileges, regulate operation, or compromise data on a user's system. Over the past 16 years, 12,946 product vulnerabilities have been reported to the CERT/ CC. Of these, 7913 were recorded for the years 2002 and 2003. Or, in concrete terms, almost two-thirds of the known product vulnerabilities surfaced in the two-year period *after* September 11th.

As such, the overall trend is clear. America's cyber infrastructure is increasingly under attack and, as a consequence, an effective and continuously evolving response is an absolute necessity. Unfortunately, the evidence so far indicates that this response is not even close to what it should be. The U.S. General Accounting Office has done one of the most complete examinations of the safety of America's information systems and it found significant weaknesses in how we approach the process of software design and development. More-over, it hypothesized that, as the body of audit evidence grows, it is likely that "Additional significant deficiencies will be identified."

Additional Demands on a Historically Faulty Approach

Historically, the track record for software development has always been less than adequate. For instance, a recent Borland study found that approximately 33 percent of all projects are canceled prior to deployment, 75 percent of all projects are completed late, and nearly 50 percent lack originally scheduled features and functions. In addition, it is well documented that depending on project size between 25 percent and 60 percent of all projects are doomed to fail, where *failure* means that the project is canceled or grossly exceeds its schedule.

The reason for this lies in the nature of software development itself. Software is abstract functionality, which is the product of a complex human interaction and communication process. Thus, its structure and the requirements that underlie it are intangible and highly dynamic. Given these conditions, it seems miraculous that anything useful has ever been delivered. But as we have just seen, the problem is just getting started. Now, because of all of the potential harm that could occur from exploitation of coding defects, the product not only has to work right, *but it also has to be secure.*

The black-hat community is very smart. If it can find a hole, it will exploit it and it is always looking. As a consequence, there cannot be any coding defects that would allow easy access. Nonetheless, overwhelming evidence supports the conclusion that America's software is loaded with defects. This is because of our faulty approach to its development. According to the President's Information Technology Advisory Council (PITAC), "commonly used software engineering practices permit dangerous defects, which let attackers compromise millions of computers every year." This mainly happens because "commercial software engineering lacks the rigorous controls needed to [ensure defect free] products at acceptable cost."

According to Capers Jones, who is the chief scientist for Software Productivity Research and something of a guru for the field, most defects arise from design or programming flaws and they do not have to be actively exploited to represent a threat. In fiscal terms, the exploitation of such defects costs the U.S. economy an average of $60 billion a year in 2005 dollars. Worse, according to the Department of Homeland Security (DHS), it is estimated that "in the future, the Nation may face even more challenging problems as adversaries—both foreign and domestic—become increasingly sophisticated in their ability to insert malicious code into critical software."

However, the real concern is that exploitation of a flaw in a basic infrastructure component, such as power or communication, could lead to a significant national disaster. The Critical Infrastructure Taskforce sums up the likelihood of such an event: "The nation's economy is increasingly dependent on cyberspace. This has introduced unknown interdependencies and single points of failure. A digital disaster strikes some enterprise every day [and] Infrastructure disruptions have cascading impacts, multiplying their cyber and physical effects."

Predictions such as this are what motivated the National Strategy to Secure Cyberspace to ask the Department of Homeland Security (DHS) to... "*Promulgate best practices and methodologies that promote integrity, security, and reliability in software code development, including processes and procedures that diminish the possibilities of erroneous code, malicious code, or trap doors that could be introduced during development*" (Clark, 2002, Action recommendation 2-14).

Embedding Secure Coding Practice into the Profession

Given the scope of this directive, the obvious solution is to embed secure coding practice in workforce education, training, and development programs nationwide. The problem is that there has been very little written so far that would guide teachers and students alike in best practice in that area. That is why a book such as this is so important. The outcome of the application of the knowledge it contains produces rational and correct code throughout the life cycle.

These practices are not a panacea; however, they do provide a realistic and viable alternative to traditional insecure programming approaches. Proper application of the secure coding practices outlined in this text will produce an end product that will be trustworthy. A secure coding approach such as this will allow the software industry to upgrade the general reliability of its product, while imposing a practical, systematic perspective on an essentially creative process. And as we have seen, that will help ensure a much more secure society.

Dan Shoemaker, PhD
Professor and Chair
Computer and Information Systems
Director of the Centre for Assurance Studies
University of Detroit Mercy

Preface

THE APPROACH OF THIS BOOK

Secure Software Development: A Security Programmer's Guide is a programmer's guide to developing secure code. It was written from a developer's perspective to help others enter into the dynamic field of software construction. The information and techniques used in the text are targeted to what all developers need to know before they code—regardless of a specific programming language. Although the principles and concepts cross multiple platforms, the examples provided are written in the Java language because of its widespread use in the Web development environment.

When the Web was just starting to evolve, students and other beginners only needed to know simpler languages like Hypertext Markup Language (HTML) and JavaScript to find a great job. Today, students must know how to use and configure an army of programming languages and software tools just to be considered for an interview. This book prepares you for what is needed to become marketable and efficient as a software developer in today's work environment.

Here are some features of the book's approach to the topic of secure code:

- **Chapter Objectives** — Each chapter starts with clear objectives for both software security and quality that you will be able to identify and learn from throughout the book.

- **Chapter Notes and Tips** — Special points of interest and advice from the author's own experience are sprinkled throughout each chapter.

- **Quick Check** — Checkpoint exercises help you to consider an objective from a new angle.

- **Chapter Summary** — At the end of each chapter, a brief review sums up the objectives and highlights major topics of discussion.

- **Chapter Review Questions** — At the end of each chapter, 20 questions test your comprehension of the objectives and other important topics.

- **Hands-On Projects** — At the end of each chapter, hands-on projects provide you the opportunity to research and develop the information learned from the chapter.

- **Case Projects** — At the end of each chapter, additional Case Projects deepen your understanding of the chapter's text and challenge you to more advanced research and development.

ABOUT THE AUTHOR

Jason Grembi developed this text to merge knowledge and expertise from his practical experience from the business world into the world of academic study. Jason is an adjunct professor of information systems in the Computer Science and Information Systems Department at University of Detroit Mercy, Detroit, Michigan. He also teaches at various community colleges and lectures at special events. In addition to his career in academia, he has owned his own IT consulting business for over five years and has worked in the IT consulting community for over ten years as a Web developer. Jason has developed business application software on all platforms and has hands-on experience with quality and security features of software.

STRUCTURE OF THE BOOK

Secure Software Development: A Security Programmer's Guide is structured to follow a typical software development life cycle (SDLC). The book begins by describing current industry standards and trends related to software security and explaining why you need to know the difference between quality code and secure code. The book is written in a somewhat casual, peer-to-peer approach as if the author was assigned to be your mentor. This book walks through each activity of secure software development and provides examples and instructions for each activity.

This book is organized into eleven chapters:

- The opening chapter establishes the need for understanding the field of information security in software development. It provides real-world examples of how malicious attacks can compromise today's software. In addition, it provides a vision of how future software projects will be developed and defines what you need to know to prepare for it.

- Chapter 2 defines current industry standards and frameworks in secure software development and explains how these standards came to fruition. Chapter 2 then examines how those industry standards are being incorporated into organizational policies and practices that produce methodologies used to develop software projects. It also describes the intricacies of a development team and what developers need to do while they're in the cube.

- Chapter 3 lays the foundation to any secure software development process. This chapter explains the essence of secure code and quality code. Security and quality are two separate features of software that need to be defined and designed into the code base even before writing the first If statement. This chapter examines the principles and goals of each coding technique and introduces the common body of knowledge on both security and quality.

- Chapter 4 explains how to prepare yourself for a successful development experience. This chapter introduces the use of an Application Guide in your practice. You will learn how to ensure that every project you work on will be reusable and highly successful.

- Chapter 5 describes how to actively listen for secure software requirements and how to create use cases for quality as well as misuse cases for security. This chapter explains how to understand, analyze, and interpret requirements so that there is a clear correlation of what is being asked to what is being produced. This chapter walks through examples of asset identification and how to list the asset during software requirements; software asset identification includes asset classification and valuation, which helps identify secure requirements for design.

- Chapter 6 explains how to convert secure software requirements into detailed design diagrams so that requirement flaws, such as missing data or undefined data, can be identified before coding. This chapter concentrates on providing techniques and methods that can be used in design to provide a visible, traceable, and reusable process. You will learn how to create design artifacts to ensure that every software feature is accounted for and validated so that quality code is not created only by accident.

- Chapter 7 focuses on taking the design artifacts created from the previous chapter and breaking them down in a very detailed design specification that will be used for coding. Along the way, you will learn how to analyze the design specifications for architecture weaknesses and how to apply the appropriate security mechanism to counter the weakness. This chapter focuses on securing the design up front and early in the development process so that when the time for coding commences, software attacks and defensive mechanisms would have been considered from all angles.

- Chapter 8 discusses why using tools is a major portion of the developer's job. It explains the nature of development tools, the different types and styles that are available, and how to evaluate them. You will also learn how to automatically build and deploy application code so that the deployment process itself is reliable and reusable. This chapter ends with an extensive hands-on project that teaches the student how to use ANT (Another Neat Tool) to reinforce the notion of how a secure development process must rely on the use of tools.

- Chapter 9 dives right into the nuts and bolts of secure code. You will learn how to code software in such a way that it becomes diverse, easy to maintain, and easy to debug. This chapter demonstrates the importance of corrective error handling and application logging, and provides examples of proper code organization. In addition to technical methods and algorithms of how to code secure code, this chapter also touches on the nontechnical aspects of writing code. From developing good social skills to tips on how to create a productive working environment, this chapter focuses on everything a developer does in the cube.

- Chapter 10 covers many of the testing techniques that exist in the industry today. First, you will learn what testing is, how to administer testing to software, and how to think like an attacker and carry out various methods of misuse on the software. As you learn how to carry out software testing, you will be encouraged to test and/or break the software using the various lessons learned from this chapter. This is evident in both the hands-on projects.

- Chapter 11 ends the book by showing the student how to sustain security in software after the project has reached maturity in the maintenance phase. This chapter describes creative ways to actively seek security vulnerabilities in the code and fix them before they happen. In addition, it also provides a blueprint of what to do when an attack has occurred in the software. In closing, this chapter leaves you with a sense of direction on how to maintain your relevance after the glory of a successful software project.

INSTRUCTOR RESOURCES

A variety of teaching tools have been prepared to support this textbook and to enhance the classroom learning experience:

Electronic Instructor's Manual — The Instructor's Manual includes suggestions and strategies for using this text, and even suggestions for lecture topics. The Instructor's Manual also includes answers to the Review Questions and suggested solutions to the projects at the end of each chapter.

Figure files — Figure files allow instructors to create their own presentations using figures taken from the text.

PowerPoint presentations — This book comes with Microsoft PowerPoint slides for each chapter. These are included as a teaching aid to be used for classroom presentation, to be made available to students on the network for chapter review, or to be printed for classroom distribution. Instructors can add their own slides for additional topics they introduce to the class.

ExamView — The ultimate tool for objective-based testing needs, ExamView® is a powerful objective-based test generator that enables instructors to create paper-, LAN-, or Web-based tests from test banks designed specifically for their Course Technology text. Instructors can utilize the ultraefficient QuickTest Wizard to create tests in less than five minutes by taking advantage of Course Technology's question banks or customize their own exams from scratch.

ACKNOWLEDGMENTS

The following people deserve a special thanks:

- Dan Shoemaker for challenging me to go the extra distance. Thanks for the direction, advice, and guidance you have given me.

- Joe Jarzombek, director, Department of Homeland Security. Your organizational leadership and support helped make SwA-CBK what it is today.

- Sam Redwine for your leadership and support on the SwA-CBK. Your efforts do not go unnoticed in this industry.

- Robert Dupuis for your leadership and support that helped make SWEBOK what it is today.

- Gary McGraw and Ken Van Wyk for your efforts to bring software security out into the forefront.

- Jill Batistick, Development Editor, for your leadership, vision, and consistent display of professionalism. I wouldn't have made it this far without you.

- Steve Helba, Executive Editor, and Alyssa Pratt, Senior Product Manager. Thanks for all the support and understanding you have provided me during this endeavor.

- To my editorial team, Daphne Barbas, Nicole Ashton, and Karen Annett. Thanks for all your effort and professionalism you have given me along the way.

- Sondra J. Schneider at Security University for opening a whole new world of issues that I now need to deal with.

- Satya Panduga for the years of professional debate, research, and constant trial and error.

- Ed Tracy at BOH. Thanks for contributing your time and efforts to help yet another generation.

- Jamie and John Rawcliffe for your contribution, peer reviews, and support. Your suggestions really helped guide me in the right direction.

- All of my friends, old and new. Sorry I could not spend as much time with you as I would have liked to in the past two years. Writing a book was a bigger task than I expected.

My Commitment to Excellence

I am committed to serving the needs of the adopters and readers of this book. I would be pleased and honored to receive feedback on the textbook and its supporting materials. You can contact me through Course Technology, via e-mail at jgrembi@gmail.com.

DEDICATION

To Lisa, Danny, and Laura.

—Jason

1

WHY YOU NEED TO LEARN SECURE PROGRAMMING

> **Upon completion of this material, you should be able to:**
> ♦ Avoid career-ending opportunities
> ♦ Understand what you need to know
> ♦ Grasp that the future is better, but more complicated

There are no more heroes in the modern coding environment. Applications are becoming too intertwined with one another, and the number of computer languages you need to know outnumbers the developers on any given project. Businesses do not want hotshot programmers who offer nothing more than their technical talents. Businesses want the all-inclusive team player who is very capable in technology and has the ability to translate business problems into technical solutions. Today's software developer needs to know how to carry out each phase of the application's life cycle, how to create and improve the development process, and how to ensure a secure application. This chapter explains how the development landscape currently looks and defines key industry problems that could open the door to a lot of opportunities for a great, long-term career.

CAREER-ENDING OPPORTUNITIES

Before I explain how to code great software, I thought I would share a few stories of what *not* to do. The following scenarios illustrate how people use applications for malicious intent and how the next generation of application development will need to become smarter and more self-monitoring. In particular, you will learn about the implications of logic bombs, attacking techniques used by bad guys, and how a perfect cybercrime can be committed. When you finish this part of the chapter, you will be able to associate the lessons learned from the following stories to the need for secure software.

When Time Runs Out: The Logic Bomb

In July 2006, a jury found Roger Duronio guilty of computer sabotage for building, planting, and distributing the malicious code that brought down nearly 2000 servers at UBS PaineWebber in March 2004 (Gaudin 2006). Allegedly, the system administrator's motive was that he was unhappy with his annual salary and bonus. Upset, he requested additional compensation and threatened to quit his job if he did not receive a raise. When this demand was not met, he planted a logic bomb that would explode in an application at a predetermined time. In addition, he apparently wanted to cash in on the trouble he was about to cause. Thus, a month before the attack, Duronio purchased $25,000 worth of put options against UBS PaineWebber and planned to sell them for a handsome gain when news of the logic bomb hit the market (assuming a stock sell-off). On March 4, as planned, Duronio's program activated and began deleting files on more than 1000 of UBS PaineWebber's computers. It cost UBS PaineWebber more than $3 million to assess and repair the damage, according to the indictment.

Elvira Maria Rodriguez, an IT manager at UBS PaineWebber at the time of the attack, said the logic bomb had a "catastrophic impact" and the company still suffers from this disruption years later. At the time of the attack, 400 to 500 UBS PaineWebber workers were pulled off their normal jobs to work on the restoration.

The defense attorney for Roger Duronio maintained that there were so many holes in UBS PaineWebber's network security that anyone could have gotten into the system and caused the damage. Moral of the story: Software applications have become the lifeline for most businesses. If any one system is not operating as it should be, companies suffer loss of revenue, customer base, and, in some cases, their reputations. What happened at UBS PaineWebber can happen anywhere. The need for a secure development process, tighter security policies, and user awareness will only increase as more catastrophes like this happen.

1

Bait and Switch: Tricks from Cybercrooks

Imagine how an attacker could trick a complete stranger to get a hold of his or her personal information. Consider the following scenario: A person is sitting alone at a bar working on his laptop. He is dressed in business casual, is well groomed, and seems to be quietly working away on his business. A lady walks up to him and asks if she could use his laptop to check her e-mail and personal Web site. After she enters her username and passwords, the key-logging software that this gentleman has running in the background on stealth mode has just captured everything he needs to cause this person great financial harm.

Everyone can fall victim to cybercriminals without realizing it. In September 2006, a single hacked PC opened the door to a sophisticated criminal attack on E*TRADE, contributing to $18 million in fraud-related costs (Greenemeier 2006). The technique used was an Internet pump-and-dump scheme, in which criminals hacked into an E*TRADE computer and stole customer information, including passwords. The criminals then invested in low-cost stocks and used E*TRADE customers' identities to buy shares of those stocks, driving up the prices of the stock. The criminals then sold the inflated stocks at a profit, leaving their victims holding shares of overpriced stocks.

Moral of the story: Never assume that a user who logs in to an application with a valid password is who he claims to be. Applications should enforce a very stringent password policy, encourage the use of a two-factor sign-on policy such as VPN tokens, or store the user's personal information on an entirely separate server and database so that identity information is separated from business information.

Other Trap Doors: Hackers Will Not Stop

Hacking PCs and applications isn't the only way criminals are stealing sensitive data. Cross-site scripting (XSS), or faking chrome, is another popular method that can be used to dupe just about any user. Faking chrome is a sophisticated **phishing** scheme that involves faking the browser chrome around the Web page. The chrome contains Window frames, menus, toolbars, scroll bars, Secure Socket Layer indicators, and any other elements that make up its borders (Greenemeier 2006). While using the Web, users might not even know that they are using someone else's Web site because of the fake chrome that surrounds the content. Without even realizing, victims give up their identities, passwords, and bank accounts without ever thinking twice.

Moral of the story: Application developers and the entire IT staff are not the only ones responsible for IT security. The user community needs to know what is going on out there. Educate all your end users on pertinent attacks that they could come across while using your system.

GPC: The Perfect Crime

There was once a company that I will call "Great Painting Company," or GPC for short, that had been in business for 20 years. It went to extreme measures to ensure that its records were up to date and that purchasing details such as customers' colors and gallons were well documented. The company soon found itself outgrowing the "off-the-shelf" database used to handle its current business load, and it wanted to bring its business to the Internet.

GPC hired a couple of moonlight contractors, Ken and Lee, to convert all the data into a new usable database with a Web graphical user interface (GUI). When Ken cracked open the old database table, he saw customer names, numbers, and contract prices. He was even surprised to see contact names and side notes from previous jobs as well as current jobs for which GPC was bidding. At first, he thought nothing of it and started to build a relational table while Lee worked on a program that converted the old data into the new table schema. A few weeks into this job, Ken and Lee ran into an old friend, John, and after some social banter they learned that he too was starting his own painting company. Because Ken and Lee were knee-deep into the GPC data conversion, they were able to relate to the types of jobs and projects that their friend was going through. Soon, the three of them exchanged private information about one another's jobs and challenges. The friends exchanged numbers and went their separate ways.

A few weeks passed when Ken and Lee received a phone call from their old friend, John. John offered his friends a handsome sum of money if he could "copy" all the data from GPC. John even threw in a bonus if he could get a copy of that application's GUIs they were custom-building for GPC. Needless to say, Ken and Lee agreed to help. John then came into GPC with his old friends late one evening and simply plugged his 250-GB external hard drive into the USB port. Within minutes, he had enough inside information to outbid GPC on all its current customers, doing so with information that took GPC more than 20 years to compile. No trace of evidence, fingerprints, or log file ever occurred.

Moral of the story: Most cybercrimes go unnoticed and occur from the inside. A secure development process should recognize this fact and separate each application layer (data store, business logic, and GUIs) altogether and design several defensive security mechanisms into the software so that access points to each layer are authenticated. Inside attacks are easy to administer and hard to detect. Software should be developed under the assumption that one of the employees will walk away with the source code. In this book, you will learn how to write parameter-driven software so that not one piece of software alone will give away all of the software's secrets.

QUICK CHECKS

Write an essay on what the stories in this part of the chapter have in common. Name a few systems (Web sites) to which you belong; what kind of personal data do they have on you? How secure are they? How do you know?

AVOID ENDING YOUR CAREER ABRUPTLY: WHAT YOU NEED TO KNOW

If you want to get a great-paying job in the IT industry as a developer, you need to know how to write secure, high-quality code. High-quality code is software that is efficient, simple, and reusable and yet secure so that it would be really tough for an outsider or an insider to take advantage of the application or the data that it holds.

As an example of how important it is that the industry be able to trust developers to write secure, high-quality code, consider that the National Institute of Standards and Technology (NIST) has this to say about application development for electronic voting: "A single clever, dishonest programmer in a voting machine company could rig an entire statewide election if a state uses mainly one kind of system." (Technical Guidelines Development Commitee 2006, p. 8). Notice that they put the onus on the programmer, not the project manager, analyst, or in the requirements gathering process. The programmer is the single most influential person on a development team. The software that gets created will be only as good as the programmers who wrote it. No new tool or best practice will help make the code better if the programmer himself is not trained and equipped to see the big picture.

In the following sections, you will learn why quality and security have become important features of software and what you must do to prepare to be a high-quality programmer.

Know Why You Need Secure Software

It has become increasingly crucial to guard and protect your personal information because there's a lot out there. Hard drives and disk space, with their large capacities, are becoming vital components in our everyday life. Every company, with its products and services, wants to know who you are, where you live, why you bought the product, what type of income you have, and so on. Most Americans now carry between five to 10 credit cards with various banks and department stores. Each of those companies keeps your personal data in some software repository (database or programs) so that it can give you the benefit of loaning you money. Each time you expose your personal information to software (Web sites or other programs), the risk of fraud and theft increases. Information storing has never been as cheap and easy as it is today, and the trend of storing more information cheaply does not appear to be fading any time soon.

So why is all this sensitive information stored? During the past decade, companies have been storing more data about products, people, and resources than ever before. Data mining and data warehousing became a huge trend in the late '90s, and this trend has allowed companies to analyze their businesses more closely, looking for patterns and statistics during certain time frames or cycles. They have found that the more data they have, the better analysis they can provide for future forecasting.

Companies' computer software packages aren't the only ones that want to know who you are. Sensitive information storing has also expanded into TV consoles, gaming boxes, car navigation systems, and other consumer gear. Tomorrow's gadgets and widgets are going to be more custom designed to your personal tastes and preferences, whether it's Radio Frequency Identification (RFID) devices that track the products you buy or the voice-recognizing devices that let you control your music and movies. Someone somewhere has to create a program that logs your personal information into a database and quickly retrieves it at a later time using wireless technologies or standard wires. Any time there is a program containing file I/O, a window of opportunity opens up for **attackers** to do whatever is necessary to get that data.

Items as simple and small as a name and e-mail address provide enough information to cause great harm. Imagine if someone were to hack into Blackboard's database and get a list of students who have read this book and how to contact them. Now imagine the unsolicited mail (**spam**) or potential scams (phishing) that could prey on those people. *Sensitive* information doesn't necessarily mean Social Security numbers or credit card numbers. It could just be a list of names and phone numbers from the targeted group, and that information could lead to disastrous encounters.

Improving business practices through advanced technologies is a goal for most companies. The basic agreement between the merchant and the consumer is that if the merchant can come up with something that makes it easier and more convenient for the consumer to get what he wants, then he will give the merchant his business. Likewise, businesses are always looking for ways to do things quicker, better, and cheaper, and technology provides that very opportunity.

Businesses also feel that if they do not leverage their resources appropriately and buy into the latest technologies, their competitors will, and, thus, they will lose market share and profits. That was the fuel for the whole e-commerce movement in the 1990s that sent all companies large and small to put up a Web site where they could sell their services. Businesses wanted to make their products and services more convenient and available for their customers. But in doing so, some of them exposed their customers' sensitive information to outsiders who might have malicious intentions. The need for software security will strengthen as more of these types of "exposures" threaten the dependability of the businesses' products and services.

Another business practice that is going to change through advanced technologies is the use of "contact-less" payment systems. This system involves waving your payment device around a sensor rather than using the traditional card swipe and sign method. This new method of purchasing products requires just a wave of a small wand and "poof," you now own whatever you want. Although the convenience to this technology is no doubt the selling point, it's scary to think what kind of sensitive information can be exposed through wireless signals wherever you walk, especially because the largest security breach for consumers occurs with credit card numbers being hijacked.

Smarter technology improves business practices. And because businesses have incorporated these technologies with their products and services, sensitive data has been put out in the forefront. Data that may contain your name, PIN, Social Security number, and other personal information can now be viewed by other people or machines with malicious intent. Software security is more than just protecting one's identity. It can also be applied to protecting proprietary code from **physical theft**. A government or business can spend millions on data encryption, secure sockets, and buying certificates, but what if an insider who had access to the code can copy all the source files onto a 6-GB flash drive and walk out?

Know the Types of Attacks

Attackers and **hackers** gain access to sensitive information so that they can steal identities, customers, or secrets for their own gain or to potentially put a company out of business. They launch a series of different types of attacks hoping one approach works over another. Or, they might just use one approach over and over, tweaking and modifying the attack until a hole finally opens. Attacks come from all angles of software development, so you need to know where they come from and the types of attacks associated with each angle.

The following are the most commonly used attacks (Redwine, et al. 2006, p. 50):

- Social engineering attacks
- Attacks against the application's software
- Attacks against the supporting infrastructure
- Physical attacks

Social Engineering Attacks

Have you ever heard of the Jerky Boys? They were a couple of pranksters who called various merchants trying to get services or products while in disguise. The Jerky Boys were actually an early type of social engineering, when not much was at stake. Social engineering tactics have changed from making phony doctors' appointments to stealing identities. Social engineering means acting as an imposter to gain direct access to confidential information. Attackers try to manipulate corporate policy or basic human kindness to get what they want. For example, a person can act like an employee and call the company Help Desk stating that he forgot his password and needs a new one. The imposter will buddy up to the support technician and explain that if he cannot access the network and read a report, his boss will fire him.

Social engineering is easy to carry out by individuals because it is hard to recognize, and has little to no consequences if the plan fails. Attackers can listen in on someone else's phone calls, read someone else's e-mail, or literally look in someone else's garbage for personal data. They will pretend to be a service technician just so that they can log on to a network and copy directories or plant logic bombs.

The following are types of social engineering attacks (Redwine, et al. 2006, p. 52):

- *Organization penetration*: A method of tricking people at work into giving access to company resources. For example, a person in disguise might visit a building as a representative from a vendor wanting to check the systems.
- *IT infrastructure exploration*: A method of obtaining information such as organizational charts and phone numbers by cold-calling under disguise.

- *Phishing*: A technique that involves creating a malicious Web site and dressing it up to look like some other company's Web site. Because these hijacked Web sites look so authentic to the user, without studying the URL, the attack goes unnoticed.

- *Spam*: A method involving unsolicited bulk e-mail. When a user clicks this e-mail to read, the e-mail can install malware or attempt to phish the user to visiting another Web site.

- *Spoofing*: A technique that spammers and virus writers use to change the "From" address in the messages they send. Spoofing users into thinking the spam e-mail is authentic is another attack that is difficult to trace.

- *Man in the middle*: A method involving unauthorized user requests or modified messages between two parties without either party knowing that the link between them has been compromised. This attack is most often used in conjunction with e-mail spoofing, where both parties think they are corresponding to each other when, in fact, the messages are being modified.

Attacks Against the Software Itself

Tools, tutorials, and hacker conventions are just some of the many public sources in which a person can find information on how to attack software. Hacking into networks and accessing application resources was once considered a hobby for the small handful of highly intelligent geeks who lived behind computers. Today, a person with limited computer skills can download free software, follow simple tutorials, and launch sophisticated attacks that were almost unthinkable five years ago. There is an old saying that states, "For every door shut, a new one opens," which is exactly what happens with software attacks. For every countermeasure created, a new attack will be created to one-up the previous. No software will ever be 100 percent completely safe—not for long anyhow.

The following are types of software attacks (Redwine, et al. 2006, p. 52):

- *Cross-site scripting (XSS)*: A type of attack that embeds JavaScript functions into Hypertext Markup Language (HTML) data elements such as text areas for comments. The comment (which includes the JavaScript function) will be stored in the database and redisplayed on the Web page as a hyperlink. When clicked, the JavaScript can send users to other Web sites without the users knowing.

- *Buffer overflows*: An attack on C/C++ code that overwrites the attributes of the object and forces the object to execute native code.

- *SQL code injection*: An attack on Web servers that allows native Structured Query Language (SQL) statements to come into the application undetected and update or delete databases.

- *Time/logic bombs*: An attack involving malicious code that is worked into the program without detection. The logic that is embedded is set to go off under certain events or time restrictions.

- *Back door*: An attack in which the attacker bypasses the application's security mechanism and uses the application resources to view or steal sensitive information.

Attacks Against the Infrastructure

Networks, PCs, and operating systems have their vulnerabilities too. Your application could be very secure and robust, but if an attacker brings down the network, what good is your application? Learning what types of attacks are out there and how they impact your application is a big part of threat analysis and threat modeling. For now, just know that these attacks can affect the infrastructure around the application and bring the application down with it.

The following are types of infrastructure attacks (Redwine, et al. 2006, p. 52):

- *Denial of service (DOS)*: An attack that consumes shared resources and compromises the ability of other authorized users to access or use those resources. Examples are the pop-ups on a browser or the dreaded "Not Responding" status in Task Manager.

- *Virus*: A program or programming code that replicates by being copied or by initiating its copying. A virus attaches itself to and becomes part of another executable program, which is a delivery mechanism for malicious code or for a denial of service attack.

- *Worm*: A self-contained computer program that works its way into other systems, corrupting everything in its path.

- *Trojans (Trojan horses)*: An attack that provides remote access to a system through a back door or open port.

- *Spyware*: Software installed on a machine that secretly gathers information about user activity and reports the finding to its owner in secret data transmissions.

- *Adware*: A program that is unknowingly installed on the PC and produces advertising while it executes. Many adware applications also come with spyware embedded.

Physical Attacks

Physical attacks can be as upsetting to an organization as software attacks. Bringing down a system or blatantly stealing hardware so that attackers can hack into it at their own leisure is just as catastrophic as malicious code insertion.

Theft of mobile devices, code, and information is an enormous expense to the company and provides attackers with the ammo they need to launch a full-scale attack. Traditional theft occurs when a person conspires to sneak (or break) into a secured room and steal computers. Today's modern theft can happen in broad daylight. As we learned from the Great Painting Company (GPC), flash drives and/or external hard drives are a convenient way to copy information and walk out without having to devise elaborate plans.

The following are types of physical attacks (Redwine, et al. 2006, p. 51):

- Cutting critical lines
- Stealing hardware (PCs, tokens)
- Stealing information (data, documentation)
- Stealing resources for personal gain (electricity, server CPU)

Expect the Unexpected: Apply Quality and Security at Every Level

We live in a world where most people are out for themselves. There are a lot of people who will use whatever means necessary to gain a competitive edge against competition or get an easy out from their problems. Malicious intent, which is purposely taking advantage of someone or something for personal gain, is a real problem; people will use your application (for example, your code or your data) for their gain if given a chance. The sooner this assumption is baked into your development process, the better you will be as a developer.

The fact is an attack will happen. Whether for malicious intent or to satisfy their curiosity, people will poke and prod their way into your application if they think it will be of some interest to them. Therefore, as a developer, you have to expect the unexpected from the start.

To prepare yourself and your code from attacks at all angles, you need to know how to include quality and security principles at every level of your job, as discussed in the following sections of this chapter.

Ensuring Quality and Security in the Industry

We have become a society that depends on information to run our business, products, or services. Thus, that dependency has caused a worldwide explosion in the field of information exploitation and software hacking. Those exploitations (**vulnerabilities**) jeopardize everything from consumer trust and business operations to national security.

Driven by awareness of potential disasters that threaten national security and commercial sectors, the U.S. Department of Defense (DoD) and the Department of Homeland Security (DHS) have launched assurance initiatives that will help lead the industry into common best practices and guidelines. In addition to government branches, private sectors also contribute to industry standards by way of councils and nonprofit organizations. They define what the industry needs and how to formalize methods of execution.

Whether from government or private sectors, all software industry standards are published by the Institute of Electrical and Electronics Engineers (IEEE), a nonprofit organization that is the world's leading professional association for the advancement of technology. The IEEE publishes industry standards for technological architectures through the use of an open general acceptance from many experts in one field. It is the central source of standardizations in both traditional and emerging fields, particularly telecommunications, information technology, and power generation (IEEE 2006). Basically, if the IEEE adopts your specification and process, it becomes an industry standard.

Government rules and regulations along with consumer protection policies will provide the need for industry leaders to define new emerging processes. To gain insight into how industry impacts secure software development, you can look at the following examples of the latest trends:

- Industry leaders
- PCI standards
- Sarbanes and Oxley Act

Industry Leaders

We will dive into IEEE standards for software development in later chapters, but first this chapter introduces you to other industry players in the field of information security. As shown in Table 1-1, the industry leaders will be determining where and how you will be spending the next 10 to 20 years of your career. Get to know them and always stay informed with what's going on.

Table 1-1   Industry leaders for standards

Organization	Web Site	Discussion
ISO, International Organization for Standardization	*http://www.iso.org*	ISO sets the standard for all large products or services in a particular business or industry. They provide definition, direction, and examples to international practitioners so that one uniform process can exist. For example, the TCP/IP protocol was mandated by the ISO for network communication. In the earlier days of development, newer protocols were being developed faster than hardware manufacturers could respond. Can you imagine buying products or services without ISO? How many other types of protocols, hardware configurations, and technologies would exist?

Table 1-1   Industry leaders for standards (continued)

Organization	Web Site	Discussion
W3C, or World Wide Web Consortium	*http://www.w3.org/*	W3C primarily pursues its mission through the creation of Web standards and guidelines (W3C 2006). If you ever wondered how to make a Web page dynamic or what the latest trends are in DHTML and style sheets, then W3C is the place to go for examples and guidelines.
NIST, or National Institute of Standards and Technology	*http://www.nist.gov/*	NIST's mission is "to promote U.S. innovation and industrial competitiveness by advancing measurement science, standards, and technology in ways that enhance economic security and improve our quality of life." (National Institute of Standards and Technology 2008, p. 1).

Knowing where the industry is going will help you prepare for what's to eventually come into your organization. The more informed you become, the easier it is for you to prepare for the "next big thing" and not to fear being left behind.

PCI Standards

No other industry takes a bigger loss in software exploitation than the financial industry. Not too long ago, credit cards were for a privileged group whose credit rating was high. Banks were once willing to write off losses related to credit fraud because of the cost associated with tracking, capturing, and prosecuting crooks. Besides, it didn't happen that often and why spend a million dollars trying to recoup $20,000?

In the days of information dependency, however, the game has changed. Credit card companies are giving practically anyone a line of credit, a mortgage, or a loan. On top of that, consumers are using credit cards as a way to pay for their everyday means, from shopping, to entertainment, to paying household bills. We've become so dependent on our line of credit that the financial institutions have banded together to form an alliance (council) to set new standards for merchants, processors, and point of sale (POS) providers. This new standard is called the Payment Card Industry (PCI) Data Security Standard. It will make sure that all participating members, merchants, and service providers that store, process, or transmit card holder data are compliant with their requirements and guidelines.

The following are the new PCI Data Security Standard goals (PCI Security Standards Council 2006):

- Build and maintain a secure network.
- Protect cardholder data.

- Ensure the maintenance of vulnerability management programs.
- Implement strong access control measures.
- Regularly monitor and test networks.
- Ensure the maintenance of information security policies.

So, the financial institutions are cracking down on transactional activities so that they don't lose so much money and along the way they can protect the personal information of their customers. What does this have to do with software developers? A lot, actually, because a big portion of compliancy relies on application developers building software based on industry best practices, which include information security throughout the development process. After reading the subsequent chapters in this book, you will have all the information you need to work in a PCI environment.

Do You Have SOX?

Enron, Tyco, MCI WorldCom, Arthur Andersen, and other leading firms were all caught in corporate accounting scandals from 2001 to 2006 that cost millions of dollars in losses and caused complete devastation to the employees who worked for them. From this devastation, the House of Representatives passed the Sarbanes-Oxley Act, which institutes standards for all U.S. public companies. Typically known as SOX, this act imposes new rules and policies on the way businesses report their earnings. That is, it formalizes methods and practices so that all companies have to abide by the same rules and guidelines as every other public company (Sarbanes and Oxley 2002).

SOX is a great example of how one industry problem (accounting scandals) can pave the way to new and exciting careers. SOX has done so much for raising awareness of secure programming in regard to access rights and approvals that every business owner is concerned with the integrity of his or her data. The moment MCI WorldCom executives were whisked away in handcuffs, SOX became the teeth prosecutors needed to go after white-collar crime. SOX impacted software development because of the automated financial transactions on which we have become so dependent. If your software touched the accounting records, you have SOX!

Ensuring Quality and Security in the Organization

In the workforce, C-class executives (CIO, CEO, CFO) are thinking more about security and quality because they are being held accountable for just about every false report or loss of sensitive information.

Just like the C-class executives, midlevel managers are being challenged to develop efficient systems very quickly with a shoestring budget. Those applications need to be developed so that they can be reused throughout the entire organization with single sign-on authentication. Add in the latest industry compliances and you have yourself one stressed-out management team.

If you can understand the needs of the C-class executive, the organization, and the project, then all you have to do to get the job is fulfill their needs.

Keep the C-Class Out of Trouble

Job number one: Keep the boss happy and out of trouble. Executives who fail to comply with SOX (section 404) do so at their own risk. CFOs without strong internal controls will be held accountable if something goes wrong and could be at risk for jail time. Because of these governing policies, you now have full support from the C-class to implement secure coding best practices. With this support, companies will invest in technologies that focus on automated business processes and embedded systems controls, not on error-prone spreadsheets or late-night phone calls.

Stakeholder Needs

Stakeholders, people with a legitimate interest in a project, also have their own list of needs when it comes to security. If an attack occurs that tarnishes the reputation of the company, then the wrath of Wall Street and/or public scorn could ruin the company. All it takes is one goof-up, lost or stolen data, or malicious attack to put your software out of commission. If that attack gets out into the public, the reputations of the company, product, and you are on the line.

Applications need to ensure that the needs of stakeholders are incorporated. Those needs can be summed up in three categories: confidentiality, integrity, and availability. These qualities are known as the C.I.A. triad:

- Confidentiality is assurance of data privacy.

- Integrity is assurance of data nonalteration.

- Availability is assurance of timely and reliable access to data services for authorized users.

Developers achieve C.I.A. by ensuring that the software addresses certain security properties and principles for the overall dependability of the software package.

The Need for Documentation

Without documentation within the organization, developers wouldn't know what to do or where to look. It is the means of communicating the application's intentions and instructions for all to see.

The act of developing software and all the tasks and activities that embody it need to be as visible as possible. It is easier to manage and improve a development process when activities are clearly defined, complete with step-by-step instructions and time durations. There is no better way to show those activities than to write them down in a supportive documentation, also known as **software artifacts**.

As an example of visibility, consider a situation in which a software requirement called for a field to be validated for a specific rule. In a well-run shop, this rule would have supporting artifacts that would make this requirement visible to the overall development process, as shown in Figure 1-1.

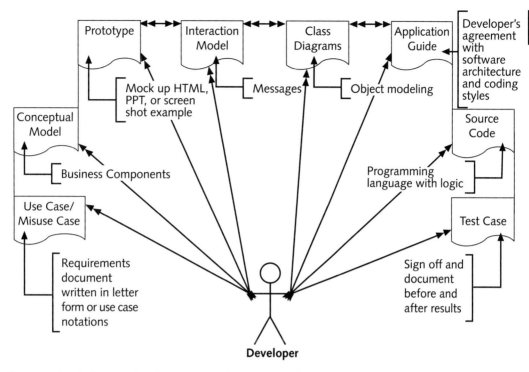

Figure 1-1   Software development artifacts

When software documentation is visible, the application's features, requirements, and access policies will be traced to the design documents, code, and testing procedures. What do we mean by traceable? Well, traceability is when a person can visually associate one use case requirement to design documentation and ultimately the code snippet.

As stated before, an artifact is any end product of software development. Here is a list of common artifacts that you will need to learn how to read, write, and analyze:

- *Software Requirement Specification (SRS)*: The SRS is usually a document that specifies what the system must do. The more critical the project's scope, the more detailed and elaborate these documents get. Typically, a template is created by the management team that includes all the data elements that need to be defined. Business analysts fill out the details that describe those data elements and, in effect, write the specifications for the program.

- *Secure requirement specifications*: This artifact, sometimes embedded in the software requirements, lists what the system must not do. Security requirements are critical for all applications. The developer will need to know what the system cannot authorize, display, or retrieve for the user.

- *Use cases*: A use case describes the system's behavior under various conditions as the system responds to a request from a user called the primary actor (Cockburn 2001).

Each use case provides one or more scenarios that convey how the system should interact with the actor or another system to achieve a specific business goal. Use cases are often coauthored by business analysts, customers, and developers.

- *Threat models*: The process of creating design documents to be used in analysis; threat modeling looks at the application design for weaknesses by listing the types of threats that apply to the particular design. It then prioritizes those threats and defines those threats so that countermeasures can be designed and created before the code is developed.

- *Misuse case*: Written like use cases, misuse cases are meant to depict abuses that the system could incur. Misuse case requirements provide an opportunity for the developers, analysts, and architects to brainstorm events and capabilities an attacker (actor) can deploy.

- *Unified Modeling Language (UML)*: UML is a notation that provides a standard way of communicating system design, architecture, and process flow. It is the information technology industry's blueprint (Boggs and Boggs 2002). As stated previously, the requirement gathering and design process is a two-way communication link that ensures both the developer and the stakeholder understand the system needs. UML is a way to communicate those needs. UML allows members of the development team (leads, programmers, analysts, and so on) to create several different types of visual diagrams that represent various views of the system requirements.

Ensuring Quality and Security in the Cube

All it takes is one bad programmer to make the whole project a complete disaster. The habits and attitude you have toward both quality and security will show in your work. Put your best foot forward and make sure you understand your role within the big picture. The fact is, everyone is responsible for protecting sensitive information and other company assets, but it takes an individual to execute the motions. As you become better at building great systems and identifying software vulnerabilities, so will your team. Success breeds success every time.

Quality and security practices start in the cube. As an individual, your actions and convictions toward your work and with your colleagues will have a direct impact on how well code is written, reviewed, and tested. To raise the level of importance and interest in secure code, practice the following activities:

- Know the enemy.
- Stay away from social engineering tactics.
- Clean up the clutter.
- Stay current.

Know the Enemy

To catch a thief, you must think like a thief. The same is true when it comes to secure development. You have to know who your enemies are and why they would want to exploit your information or application. To think like an attacker, you have to have knowledge in the following patterns:

- Know the weak areas of the application architecture and the areas attackers most likely will target.

- Know who would want to attack your software and why.

- Know what types of resources would be needed by the attackers, such as tools, privileges, and time slots.

- Know how to build countermeasures.

Your attackers could be independent *hackers* seeking to gain recognition among their friends, disgruntled employees trying to seek revenge against the company, or competitors attempting to obtain business/trade secrets. Your enemy has no deadline, no boss to report to, and can fail thousands of times without ever being held accountable. The attacker has all day and night to try, try, and try again to break into the application. Get to know the tricks of the trade so that you can begin to build a defensive team.

Prevent Social Engineering

As discussed, social engineering is when other people pretend to be someone else in disguise. To prevent becoming a victim of social engineering tactics, follow these simple rules in the cube:

- Verify the identity of all callers (for example, caller ID, inter-company phone ring tones).

- If you do not recognize the caller and he or she is asking questions to extract sensitive information, ask for a phone number to return the call.

- Give information only to well-known or clearly identified people.

- Share information on a need-to-know basis.

- Never give your password to anyone for any reason.

- Never type things into a computer when someone tells you to, unless you know the environment and exactly what software is running on the PC.

- For printing confidential or secret information, use only designated printers.

- Watch out for shoulder surfers, that is, people standing behind you who are looking at your monitor.

Clean Up the Clutter

It only takes seconds for someone to steal information from your cube or install malicious programs, such as viruses, Trojan horses, or logic bombs. Do not make it easy for an intruder to gain unauthorized access to your personal domain. Maintaining your workspace is a great starting place for becoming a secure developer.

A clean desk will help organize your notes and force you to file paperwork accordingly (don't just shove it in the drawers). Make sure you follow company policy about shutting off your computers at night or locking the laptop away in a safe place. But most important, you should always lock your workstation before leaving your desk for lunch or bathroom breaks.

No Sticky Notes

Passwords, PIN numbers, answers to "special" questions, and so on—the list of things we have to remember in the modern world continues to grow. But no matter how many usernames and passwords you need to remember, please don't write them on paper and hide them on (or in) your desk. This practice is fairly common in the industry, but with a little friendly snooping, getting hold of your identity is not that hard. SHRED those sticky notes.

If you need to keep track of all those usernames and passwords, store them in a secure place where only you know where they are and what they mean. It is not recommended to store usernames and passwords in an easily cracked computer file such as a spreadsheet.

Lastly, build a strong password by following a formula such as the following:

1. Take two words and put them together, like hoop + ball = hoopball

2. Now uppercase the first letter of the second word = hoopBall

3. Now substitute the letter o with the number 0 = h00pBall

4. Lastly substitute the letter a with the @ sign = h00pB@ll

TIP
By remembering two of your favorite words and your substitute letters, complicated passwords like h00pB@ll become easy to remember.

Record Retention

Record retention is deleting old and unnecessary hard and soft documents and keeping recent, relevant ones on hard drives and in filing cabinets and desk drawers. Record retention also includes shredding sticky notes, and doing good old-fashioned housecleaning in your cube. Be careful not to trust garbage cans; thrown away paper can be easily retrieved and read. If at all possible, use the shredder for all system documentation. If you have old devices like hard drives and/or floppy disks that are on display like relics, make sure you have a reputable source for discarding them. Computer forensics has come a long way and attackers are able to retrieve data on hard drives that was deleted years ago.

Stay Current on Attacks

If software developers do not know what software vulnerabilities are and where they come from, they will never produce secure code. For developers to get better at producing defect-free code, they need to continuously educate themselves.

Stay current by keeping informed of the latest software attacks. Find out where those attacks came from (tool, code), how they got there (browser, installed software), and try to design some ways to prevent these attacks. You can read the following journals and Web sites to stay current:

- *Information Week*: News publication on current events on security attacks; *www. informationweek.com/*

- *Computer World*: News publication on current events on vendor products and tools; *www.computerworld.com/*

- *SD Times*: News publication on current events on vendor products and tools; *www.sdtimes.com/index.html*

- *Cross Talk*: Journal of Defense Software Engineering; *www.stsc.hill.af.mil/index.html*

Build Better Applications

There will always be someone bigger, better, and smarter than you. That's just the way it goes in this field. But that doesn't mean you should stop trying to write foolproof software. We learn how to write quality code by means of process improvements and through trial and error. Time spent on a job or in the field is not a dependable indicator of expertise. If you've been doing a poor job for 15 years, chances are you do a poor job very well. To gain the skill and ability to foresee problems before they happen, you need to have the right experience and exposure to how certain software works. This experience comes with time and motivation to write code. You should always be looking at ways to improve your performance, efficiency, and knowledge.

Building better applications takes time and experience from within. As long as you learn from your mistakes and implement reusable processes or algorithms that prevent those mistakes from happening again, your application(s) will always be better than they were before.

NOTE You could code the most secure application in the world, the guy next to you could write the least secure application, and your application could still be the one to get hacked. If money is at stake, hackers might target the site that will be more lucrative for them. If reputation is at stake, they might intentionally target sites that are more secure. Overall, the more that you build sound security principles and practices into the application in every phase of the software development process, the less likely it is that your application will be compromised.

As you learn how to execute the activities and tasks in this book, your software will encompass all the principles and properties of secure code. These characteristics will help make your application hard for attackers to penetrate. Hopefully, hackers will get tired of trying to make their way through your application and move on to the next one. Obviously, if your application secures the "secret sauce" recipe, then every hacker and attacker around will spend all their time trying to open the holes.

Anticipate the Loss of Mobile Devices

Our working lifestyles have made us more exposed to risk than ever before. We are more mobile and diverse as to where we work and conduct business. We work from home, cars, cell phones, and laptop computers. And as we travel, our personal devices go with us.

Security from physical attacks is a lot harder to provide when users leave storage devices lying around in the public domain rather than inside a locked company building behind secure walls. As a mobile employee, we leave our storage devices in a hotel room, in an automobile, or at home. The more places we go with our devices, the more likely we are to lose them.

Advancing technologies allow people on the go to take more information with them in smaller, less-expensive devices. Flash memory devices and phones that can store all of your office and personal information have been doubling space capacities with every new version. Taking an 8-GB file, such as a database, becomes less of a problem when the storage device fits in your pocket.

The best defense against attacks is to anticipate the loss. Having security policies and advocating awareness will hopefully mitigate most of the potential disasters. Fortunately, you can do three things to anticipate the loss of data:

- Know what data is on the device.
- Protect the data even when the device is lost.
- Expect the device to be lost.

Know the Data on the Device

As you develop software, you will need to become intimate with the data. You need to know what it represents, where it comes from, and where it goes. Team members and users will come to rely on you as the go-to guy for information pertaining to your application.

Get to know directory structures on the servers, PCs, or any other hardware device you find yourself interacting with. Organizing the directories and coming up with logical naming conventions for files and documents will help you better manage the data. That way when someone asks "Where does this come from?" or "What was on that disk?" you will know the answer on the fly and come off looking like a genius. Get to know the data.

Protect the Data on the Device

In secure programming, every transaction and data exposure provides an opportunity for an attack. Knowing what the information is and where it's stored is not enough. You have to protect it from unauthorized users. Make sure privileges and access policies exist and are in place, and do not overload one system. For example, do not place the whole application—and its data—on one server or hard drive. You will learn how to design for these methods in Chapter 7, "Designing for Security."

Expect the Device to be Lost

Those mobile devices are made to be lost or stolen. Don't fight the inevitable—anticipate it. Make your applications so robust and secure that when your users tell you they lost the token or PDA, all you have to do is make sure they get a new one. Of course, the company will need to file the appropriate paperwork for each scenario, but your application should still be as safe as ever.

Here are some general guidelines/policies you can use for your applications:

- Never store data locally on mobile devices.

- Protect confidential or secret data by saving it on a server.

- Work in a system or routine where the mobile device can be deactivated from interacting with the application when lost.

- Place general contact information on a sticker and put the contact information on the device so that people know what to do when the device is found. However, if the contact itself is important, such as Department of Defense, then use some obscure name, like Jay's Coffee House, with a P.O. Box.

QUICK CHECKS Over the next day or two, ask friends or family members what their school ID (Social Security number or driver's license number) is. But before asking, put the disclaimer "For security reasons" in front of your question. For example, "For security reasons, what is your school ID?" Remember to sound sincere and put on your best actor/actress face. Write down your experiences and results. Share these stories with your classmates.

THE FUTURE IS BETTER, BUT COMPLICATED

Gone are the days when one simply needed a text editor and a compiler to code basic functionality. Back in 1996, a developer was able to find a long-term lucrative assignment just by having some lower-level skills such as HTML and JavaScript. Today, however, developing robust and secure applications requires a person to know an army of software development languages, tools, and protocols. He or she needs to know how to configure software and how to protect it from attacks and threats. For example, one simple Web screen that the user sees might interact with over five different types of computer languages and run on multiple platforms on the back end. The development process has become so complex that even at the most entry-level position, a person needs to be knowledgeable and efficient in all areas just to make it through the day.

If you can grasp the information and activities that this book provides, you will have a well-rounded exposure to all things software. You will get a good look from front to back on how software is done.

Tomorrow's applications are going to require security in the development process. You will need to know how to defend your code against all attacks. In fact, it's going to be assumed that you know it before you apply for a job. The next generations of applications are going to be heavily intertwined with other applications and services. In addition, more mobile devices with embedded chips and logic will take over the decision-making processes from the human user. All of the "click Submit button" applications will be replaced by on-demand, real-time execution that is updated while you type or talk.

The following sections discuss examples as to where the industry is going.

Working from Anywhere

With more employees than ever working away from the office, IT departments are supporting more and more remote end users. To address this new reality, a handful of companies (led by Citrix Online, a division of Citrix Systems Inc., and LogMeIn Inc. in Woburn, Massachusetts) are taking a different approach to remote access. This approach doesn't require a virtual private network (VPN) and may make life simpler for IT users and end support. Under the new concept, the user's remote desktop or laptop isn't connected to corporate servers. Instead, the remote user is connected to his PC back at the office, with all the same files, applications, and desktop icons. This is accomplished through a Web browser and screen-sharing technology. Thus, any available remote PC can be used for remote connection without ever leaving a trace of information on the remote PC (Hildreth 2006).

Requirements for Tomorrow's Applications

I recently have been asked to build yet another monstrous application. So far, I have just scratched the surface in understanding the actual functional requirements in the application, but I do know that the data it collects and stores is highly confidential. In fact, if that data were to land in the wrong hands, my client's organization would be put out of business.

FAM, Financial Arm Management, is a financial tool that reports on a monetary activity for its customers. FAM's customers have accounts and holdings in many institutions and are managed by many FAs (financial analysts). FAM consolidates all monetary activities (interest, gains, losses) and allows the user to view the bottom line from anywhere in the world. The FAM system makes it convenient for the members' mobile lifestyles because they get to see their total net worth at any given time. They have the option to drill down for details and even contact the specific FA or broker who is in charge of a specific transaction.

The success of FAM is riding on the privacy and secrecy of its members. Its data is of the utmost importance. Because those members want to access their information using mobile devices (laptops, BlackBerrys, PDAs), I will have to assemble a team of qualified secure developers and start an audit of the architecture and system requirements.

The first security controls that need to be protected are the data in transit and the mobile devices. I have to make sure that no one can access internal tables and that there are no traces of our application if someone loses a mobile device. I will also need to create appropriate response actions within the application if the number of unsuccessful attempts reaches a point of peculiar use behavior. I will have to appropriate application logging activity for audits and appropriate filtering to weed out any other requests that do not come from those mobile devices.

I have to establish security requirements for all the servers (Web and application) that will be spread throughout the world. To guarantee system responsiveness and availability, special listening agents, logging mechanisms, remote access ports, and rerouting capabilities need to be worked in to protect the application from DoS attacks, man in the middle attacks, and various other pesky penetrations.

As for the data to be transmitted, I definitely have to encrypt and decrypt all data, keys, and information. Because the application (code) itself is heavily based on formulas, even the code has to be secure. The application will have to run behind firewalls as well as multiple LAN settings. I'm thinking about storing half the formulas in one LAN and the others in a second. Perhaps I'll even use a VPN link between the two to secure the communication.

Gotcha: An Application That Senses Attacks

One company's application was recently attacked by a hacker who was trying to insert some cross-site scripting (XSS) in a comment section. After quite a few failed attempts in the mission, the hacker's home phone rang from support staff. The support representative just wanted to make sure that the application was working for him and if there was anything he could do. The hacker, now totally surprised and caught off guard, said "no" and that everything was fine. After the impressive response the hacker received from the application's support team, he quickly logged out of that application and never attempted anything malicious to that application again.

So what happened? How did the support team know the application was being hacked in to? The application was coded in such a way that it monitored all user activity. When it detected that a user was trying to insert JavaScript assumed to be XSS, it automatically paged a support team member with this text message: "A:XSS U:(XXX)XXX-XXXX." Because the support guys knew how to interpret that message, they knew what the attack was and who was doing it.

CHAPTER SUMMARY

- ❑ Governments need secure programming to protect and serve the people. Businesses need secure programming to protect and serve their customers. Customers need secure programming to defend their identities from thieves and curious "friends."

- ❑ The latest attacks on software have awakened a sleeping giant. Information security is nothing new, but the way we need to design for it is. Unfortunately, we live in a world where we now have to expect attacks on our applications for someone's personal gain. Security is going to be designed in all software on an ongoing basis and we need to prepare for it.

❑ Developing applications is more than just sitting down and coding from specs. It is about knowing the ins and outs of the profession: industry standards, organizational needs, and what is needed from each and every individual on the project. It takes a lot of time and dedication to stay up to date with the latest trends and methods of software hacking. But by knowing what the offense is going to throw at you, you can build your defensive countermeasures and then sit back and watch what happens. Hopefully, you will do all the homework in the subsequent chapters and you'll come out a winner. From social engineering to XSS, you need to be ready and you need to be secure.

❑ No matter how secure and efficient you build your application, someone, somewhere will crack it. You just don't want to make it easy for them.

❑ No one can predict what hacking tools will be available in the next 10 years, so how can you possibly prepare for that? If you're able to make your application self-sufficient and self-monitoring, you will be able to scare away the majority of hackers out there. Remember, the low-hanging fruit is always picked first.

❑ If and when your application becomes attacked, accept it. In fact, celebrate it (as long as the attack level was low) because you anticipated events like this to happen and you were right. Now, go to your bosses (you will have many of them) and tell them that even though the application was attacked, the data was encrypted, there was nothing of interest in the source code, and the database was behind a firewall on a separate server. Therefore, there is nothing to fret! If you can go to them with this type of response, you will be around for a very long time.

KEY TERMS

attacker — A person who creates and modifies computer software and computer hardware, including computer programming, administration, and security-related items with malicious intent.

hacker — A person who creates and modifies computer software and computer hardware, including computer programming, administration, and security-related items with nonmalicious intent.

malware — A generic term for a number of different types of malicious code.

phishing — Trying to build a Web site that tricks users into giving up their confidential information.

physical attack — Taking a system off-line without authorization or stealing hardware.

physical theft — The loss of an item (computer, flash drive, and so on) because another person stole it.

software artifacts — Support documentation in the software industry.

spam — Unwanted and unsolicited e-mail.

stakeholders — People who have an interest in a project.

vulnerability — A flaw or weakness in a system design, implementation, or operation that could be exploited to violate the system's security policy.

REVIEW QUESTIONS

1

1. Against what are software attacks launched?
   a. the operational systems, software, and physical devices
   b. operating systems, methodologies, and physical devices
   c. standards, methodologies, and policies
   d. people, resources, and CFOs

2. What type of attack fakes a company's Web site and encourages a user to enter personal data as if the application were legitimate?
   a. cross-site scripting
   b. man in the middle
   c. phishing
   d. SQL code injection

3. A bad design within application code could be called a:
   a. bad practice
   b. work in progress
   c. vulnerability
   d. bad requirement

4. _____ is a person who wants to break into an application just to snoop around and show off in front of friends.

5. Physical theft could be when:
   a. servers and/or PCs are stolen.
   b. system documentation is stolen.
   c. copies of database or code are taken.
   d. all of the above

6. A _____ is a hidden piece of code embedded within the system that will cause a malicious attack under a certain triggering event or specified time.

7. _____ makes the development process visible to all members of the project. It also provides the mechanism for traceability between requirements and the code.
   a. Security
   b. Quality
   c. Documentation/artifacts
   d. Social engineering
   e. Code

8. Of the following artifacts, which one does not affect the developer's job?

   a. SRS (Software Requirements Specification)

   b. RFP (Request for Proposal)

   c. UML diagrams

   d. design documents

   e. test cases

9. A software or hardware device that is installed on the network and captures all data to and from the server is called a _____ .

   a. man in the middle

   b. back door

   c. packet sniffer

   d. DoS

10. Software or hardware installed on the network that takes control of the user's processor or prevents requests from hitting a destination is called a _____ .

    a. man in the middle

    b. back door

    c. packet sniffer

    d. DoS

11. The following scenario is an example of a _____ attack: An e-mail is received from a stockbroker with the sender's name as his boss. The e-mail had a question: "Which stock is a good buy?" The stockbroker replies with a ticker symbol. The real recipient takes that information, alters the symbol, and then sends it to the broker's boss with the broker's name as the sender.

    a. man in the middle

    b. back door

    c. packet sniffer

    d. DoS

12. _____ is a person who creates and modifies computer software and computer hardware, including computer programming, administration, and security-related items, with malicious intent.

13. What are the two groups of users who attack software?

    a. authorized and unauthorized users

    b. thrill seekers and curious users

    c. vengeful employees or angry customers

    d. members of software development teams

14. What is the *best* policy for security when it comes to mobile devices?

   a. Do not share the device.

   b. Do not drop or break the device.

   c. Do not store data locally.

   d. Do not take the device out of the office for nonbusiness reasons.

15. Which of the following is the *best* password?

   a. football

   b. footBall1

   c. footB@ll123

   d. F00tB@ll

16. _____ is an example of how to keep current about what is happening in the industry.

17. Software security can be done by anyone. True or False?

18. A clean desk is a secure desk. True or False?

19. You do not have to make an ultrasecure application, just one that is more secure than most. True or False?

20. Developing software will be easier in the future. True or False?

HANDS-ON PROJECTS

HANDS-ON PROJECTS

Project 1-1 Social Engineering

1. Open and listen to the "helpme.wav" file in the Chapter 1 course data. If you cannot listen to the audio, read from the script "helpme.doc."

2. Write an essay of how easy it would be for you to attempt an attack like this. Who would you call? Why? What type of questions would you ask? Who would you impersonate?

Project 1-2 What's Wrong?

1. Look at Figure 1-2. How many discrepancies (problems, security problems, security issues, security concerns, security pitfalls) can you find?

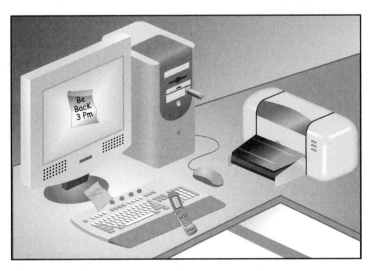

Figure 1-2   What is wrong with this picture?

CASE PROJECT

PCI: How Does PCI Affect Software?

A project manager of an IT department just found out that he needs to be compliant with new PCI standards. His team consists of five Web developers and three mainframe programmers. The application he manages allows customers (users) to purchase merchandise through his application using a credit card. What security measures must he employ to meet the standards?

CHAPTER REFERENCES

Boggs, Wendy and Michael Boggs. 2002. *Mastering UML with Rational Rose 2002*. New York: Sybex.

Cockburn, Alistair. 2001. *Writing Effective Use Cases*. Boston: Addison-Wesley.

Gaudin, Sharon. 2006. Verdict's In: You're Never Too Safe from the Inside Threat. *InformationWeek* 1,099:28-30.

Greenemeier, Larry. 2006. New From Cybercrooks: Fake Chrome, Pump-and-Dump. *InformationWeek* 1,221:26.

Hildreth, Sue. 2006. Making the PC Connection. *ComputerWorld* 40(46):30-31.

IEEE. 2006. About IEEE. http://www.ieee.org/portal/web/aboutus/home/index.html (accessed February 13, 2008).

National Institute of Standards and Technology. 2008. Mission Vision Core Competencies and Core Values. http://www.nist.gov/public_affairs/nist_mission.htm (accessed February 13, 2008).

PCI Security Standards Council. 2007. The PCI Security Standards Council: Frequently Asked Questions - General Information. https://www.pcisecuritystandards.org/about/faqs.htm#q19 (accessed February 13, 2008).

Redwine, Samuel T. Jr., Rusty O. Baldwin, Mary L. Polydys, Daniel P. Shoemaker, Jeffrey A. Ingalsbe, and Larry D. Wagoner. 2007. *Software Assurance: A Guide to the Common Body of Knowledge to Produce, Acquire, and Sustain Secure Software Version 1.2.* Arlington, VA: U.S. Department of Homeland Security. https://buildsecurityin.us-cert.gov/daisy/bsi/940/version/1/part/4/data/CurriculumGuideToTheCBK.pdf (accessed February 13, 2008).

Sarbanes, Paul and Michael G. Oxley. 2002. One Hundred Seventh Congress of the United States of America: Sarbanes-Oxley Act of 2002. http://news.findlaw.com/hdocs/docs/gwbush/sarbanesoxley072302.pdf (accessed February 13, 2008).

Technical Guidelines Development Committee. 2007. Requiring Software Independence in VVSG 2007: STS Recommendations for the TGDC. http://vote.nist.gov/DraftWhitePaperOnSIinVVSG2007-20061120.pdf (accessed February 13, 2008).

W3C. 2008. About the World Wide Web Consortium. http://www.w3.org/Consortium/ (accessed February 13, 2008).

2

CODING IN THE SDLC: NOT A SOLITARY PRACTICE

> **Upon completion of this material, you should be able to:**
>
> ♦ Work with principles associated with software engineering
>
> ♦ Understand the traditional software development life cycle
>
> ♦ Identify standards and methodologies involved in the development of efficient, secure, and reusable code
>
> ♦ Know the roles of the programmer and systems analyst

The nature of software development has changed in the decades since the introduction of the first production-quality devices in the late 1950s and early 1960s. The art and science of software development have evolved through a number of epochs where the machine itself, the programmers' relationships to the machine and to one another, the language, the coding practices, the understanding of the software development process, and our overall capacity for understanding have been subject to a series of paradigm shifts. This trend is set to continue with increasing consumer, business, and legal emphasis on the security of operating systems, end-user applications, and communication systems. This chapter is concerned with establishing the basis for a secure software development life cycle and the implications for the organizational role of the professional programming team member.

SECURE SOFTWARE DEVELOPMENT PROCESS

Today's software has become increasingly more complex. It is very common to find business applications using multiple programming languages created by a development team where the programmers sit on both ends of the world. In addition to the family of programming languages, more and more applications are integrated with other applications through Web services, third-party programs, and off-the-shelf programs. Sharing sensitive information between applications has made writing code more of an orchestrated event than a solitary practice.

Applications that process sensitive information have created a need to apply a standard, secure software development process that can develop reusable and diverse code that maintains a high level of **C.I.A.** (confidentiality, integrity, and availability) to the user community. The industry needs a standard development process so that IT departments can use common assumptions and assurances of how secure code should be written.

Standards make products easier to build because they give direction, and because they are written down as plans and formulas, they allow governing bodies of experts to improve overall processes over time. Today, we are seeing a need for security in software development where security requirements, design, and defensive principles have to be worked into the traditional SDLC (software development life cycle). This includes making smarter code compilers, working security quality gates into the development process, and, most importantly, choosing a development process that embraces this need throughout all the activities of the SDLC.

A secure software development process includes three main ingredients:

- SDLC in the industry
- SDLC in the organization
- SDLC in the cube

SDLC in the Industry

The industry has defined software development as an engineering practice with a "systematic, disciplined, quantifiable approach to the development, operation, and maintenance of software" (Dupuis, et al. 2004, p. 24). For a long time, those approaches to the development areas were focused on making quality code for functionality—*not* security. Now that all our personal information is pushed out into the Web, the software industry is redefining the existing bodies of knowledge to include best practices of security, including the following:

- Standard development life cycle—IEEE 12207
- Capability Maturity Model Integration

The Life Cycle

The **software life cycles** are the various activities, or phases, that software goes through from concept to retirement. The IEEE has adopted the International Organization for Standardization (ISO) 12207 (IEEE and EIA 1998) standard, which specifies and defines the software development activities, which include the following:

- System requirements analysis
- System design
- Software architectural design
- Software detailed design
- Software coding
- Software testing
- Software installation
- Software acceptance
- Software maintenance

The ISO 12207 international standard categorizes the software life cycle into three groups: primary, supporting, and organizational, as shown in Figure 2-1. The primary processes are the main phases that software goes through. Supporting processes are standards that help support the primary processes. Organizational standards set up the environment that endorses the primary and supportive processes.

The ISO/IEEE 12207 standard provides the industry with standard activities each software project *must* follow to be compliant. Each activity is broken out into its own set of tasks that *need* to be done within that activity. Each one of these tasks can be found in its own IEEE standard that plugs into the overlaying 12207. Therefore, the ISO 12207 can be looked at as the standard of all standards.

The IEEE 12207 is an excellent source to see how all processes work together to make a complete, competent IT organization. Even though a security standard does not exist in the current model, the 12207 does a great job in defining all other areas of importance.

CMMI

The SEI (Software Engineering Institute) CMMI (Capability Maturity Model Integration), which is part of Carnegie Mellon University, defines industry standards with government organizations, businesses, and academia to improve the process of software development. SEI CMMI has grown popular in the industry based on the success of its predecessor, SEI CMM (Capability Maturity Model). The CMMI for Development is a model that describes characteristics of effective processes.

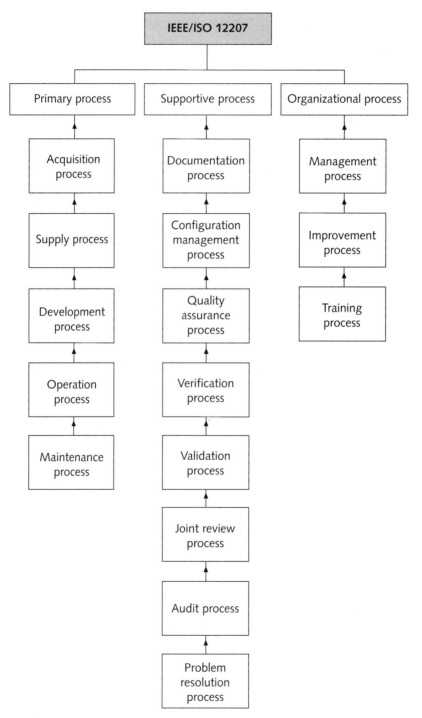

Figure 2-1 IEEE 12207 standard life cycle

CMMI defines how effective organizations are at following a formal development process by classifying the organizations into maturity levels. Each maturity level provides a set of practices and processes that an organization needs to do to advance its level of effectiveness. There are five levels of effectiveness (Software Engineering Institute 2006).

- *Initial*: Processes are usually nonexistent. No standard development process is followed.

- *Managed*: Processes are planned and executed.

- *Defined*: Processes adhere to standards, procedures, and tools.

- *Quantitatively managed*: Processes are measured in statistical terms; detailed measures are taken for performance comparisons.

- *Optimizing*: Processes continue to improve.

CMMI is relatively new to the industry (it came out in August 2006), but if it has the success of its predecessor, CMM, then chances are you'll be working with this model sometime in the future.

QUICK CHECKS

In CMMI, what are the 25 key process areas (KPAs) and how do they relate to software development?

1. Open a browser and use your favorite search engine.

2. Search for CMMI KPS.

3. In CMMI, what are the 25 key process areas (KPAs) and how do they relate to software development.

SDLC in the Organization

Developing software in an organization is no different from creating any other product. A software application is usually initiated with a need or one's idea; that idea is then analyzed for feasibility, cost savings, and usefulness through the use of prototypes. If the results of the analysis are rendered useful, feasible, and affordable, then the project (software) is approved. It takes time, material, and labor to get the job done.

Organizations implement industry standards in their processes, in many different ways, which is called methodology. Standards define the *what* in industry; methodologies define the *how* and *when* in the organization. For example, the IEEE standard for software development requires the organization to produce code, but the related software methodology tells the organization *how* to produce it. A **software methodology** is a set of methods, procedures, and rules that can be repeatedly carried out to produce software.

It has been proven that using a methodology to write code increases the quality of the code produced. But no two projects are alike; therefore, a development methodology needs to be selected that best fits the software requirements and team dynamics. To help determine which methodology is best for the organization, you should first know why you need them and how to evaluate them.

Why Do You Need a Methodology?

Methodology is important because it produces consistency. Teams that follow the *"no methodology"* methodology usually find themselves relying on the heroics of just a few really great developers. And without those great developers, programs are usually riddled with bugs and do not have the characteristics of quality code. Organizations need a consistent process that produces the same results so that it can be reused on several other projects regardless of who is on the team. At ground zero, nothing is done until a methodology is worked out that defines how software will be developed and in what sequence.

Who picks the methodology depends on the organization. It depends on how stringent (or lax) the organization is at following industry standards. Methodologies are very costly because of the resources required to implement them. For that reason, methodologies are usually set by the organization's C class (CIO). There are, however, organizations that will allow the development team to choose their own methodology. If this is the case, then the decision is sometimes made by a lead developer or just an overall agreement by all team members. Talk to your project manager(s) about this to see where they stand on this issue.

Evaluating Traditional Methodologies

In the past, newer hardware and software configurations were hitting the market on a regular basis, replacing the older ones just as fast as the new ones became available. This cycle made it hard for programmers to keep their software up to standards. They found themselves writing and rewriting applications so that they could run on the newer models. This was an arduous task considering that PCs did not exist at the time and programmers had to go to a special machine room to run "jobs." Those jobs were run by using the punch card readers in which a printed message would indicate pass or fail.

As a result of this early-day chaos (imagine dropping all those punch cards and losing their order), many software projects found themselves over budget and under expectations. To improve the overall approach of coding programs back then, methodologies were created so that all the tasks associated with programming could be logically executed in a certain sequence. This sequence of activities allowed the programmer to focus on one element at a time without being bogged down with all the other chaos that surrounded the process. By the early 1970s, programmers started adopting these methodologies as part of their everyday work activity, and these traditional methods still stand today as accepted working patterns in many organizations.

The traditional methodologies include the following:

- Waterfall
- Iterative
- Spiral

Each of these methodologies is discussed in the following sections. It is important to know about these traditional methodologies because many of today's practices still encompass these founding principles.

Waterfall

The waterfall methodology is a way to develop software following through each phase of the life cycle from one to the next in a *very* sequential manner. This methodology is usually best suited when the size and scope of the project is small and generally well understood by all team members on the development team. The waterfall gets its name because of how the process flows down from one phase to the next like a stream of falling water, as shown in Figure 2-2.

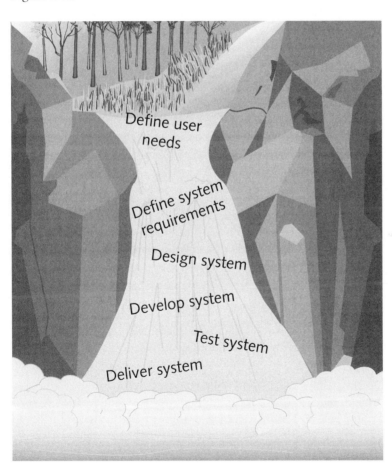

Figure 2-2   Waterfall methodology

In the waterfall method, every phase of the SDLC is conducted in one shot. The analysts will have requirement meetings with the developers to discuss the current business problem and the need for the application. When the developers have had a chance to digest what the needs of the software are, they will design the software components (with the assistance of analysts and users) with the information they gathered from the requirements. Once the design phase is done, the developers can start to code the software program and test for verification and validation.

Drawbacks to this methodology include the following:

- This methodology is too restrictive and forces the developers to complete each phase before moving on.

- It is also very rare that the users know exactly what they want from the start. Usually, people need to see and use the software early on in the process before the "real" requirements actually begin to surface.

- As is often the case with new teams, the co-workers haven't yet established a working "groove." Therefore, poor communication and false assumptions are prevalent in this approach.

Iterative

The iterative methodology, as shown in Figure 2-3, is great for moderate to large applications with varying degrees of complexity. It looks and feels like the waterfall model, but it is based on delivering software in increments (iterations) rather than developing the whole system at once. This methodology allows the users and developers more time to focus on building one requirement/feature at a time. It also delivers a working application to the users early in the development process. By getting the application into the users' hands early, vulnerabilities and bugs can be caught and fixed before developers move on to the next set of requirements.

The iterative methodology is the one most often used in the field. It allows the most time for learning curves, change of requirements, and complete understanding of both system architecture and requirements. It also promotes a type of learn-as-you-go approach so that if a feature or function is not right, the process can always be refined as the project goes on.

Drawbacks to this methodology include the following:

- The iterative process tends to be too constrictive for teams that have been working together closely for years. Experienced teams like to double (or triple) up on requirements and are very good at multitasking. Because the iterative process really concentrates on one feature at a time, some mature teams do not like the pace.

- End users and customers cannot afford to spend the amount of time needed to test each new feature as it's launched. Therefore, feedback and/or discovered problems are slow to filter to the developer's desk.

First deliverable:

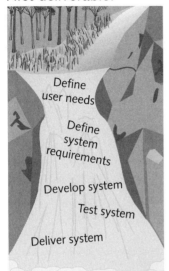

Second deliverable:

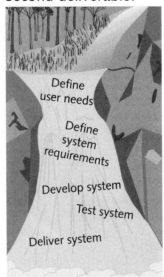

Third deliverable:

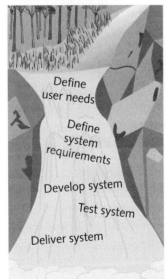

Figure 2-3 Iterative methodology

Spiral

Created by Barry Boehm, the spiral methodology was created for projects considered to be *high risk* (Boehm 1998); the methodology is shown in Figure 2-4. It is a risk-driven process in which each requirement or function is looked at from different types of risk analysis. If the level of risk for that requirement is acceptable, then that requirement will be developed and tested. A new benchmark will be created for that software and this process will repeat itself with each requirement.

Figure 2-4   Spiral methodology

In each phase, or quadrant, the objectives and associated risks are defined and analyzed through the use of prototypes. If the risk is deemed acceptable, the requirement will be designed and developed using a waterfall-like approach and worked into the final product (benchmark). This spiral process allows developers and users to analyze each requirement and apply appropriate *what-if* questions to each functional requirement before the code is actually written. This type of risk mitigation methodology also allows management and/or users to stop projects early before costly overruns and mistakes take place. The *what-if* hook can be used as a security gate to look at each functional and design requirement from a quality and security perspective.

Drawbacks to this methodology include the following:

- It takes a lot of development time to produce and analyze prototypes.

- End users and customers cannot afford to spend the amount of time needed to test each new feature as it's launched. (This drawback is common for many methodologies.) Therefore, feedback and/or discovered problems are slow to filter to the developer's desk.

Considering Advanced Methodologies

Of course, there is no silver bullet. Following a proven methodology alone is not going to produce high-quality, secure code. However, as technologies advance, so do standards. And with new standards come newer tools and methodologies to accomplish and automate tasks. These advanced methodologies will help improve the process of developing code and get us closer to the "silver bullet" dream.

There are many advanced methodologies from which to choose, too many for this book's purpose. But you should be aware of the major ones because it's very likely that these types of processes will be followed on some of your future projects:

- Security Development Lifecycle (SDL)

- Team Software Process (TSP)

- Agile Development: Extreme Programming

- Touchpoints

Security Development Lifecycle (SDL)

Microsoft has adopted Security Development Lifecycle (SDL) as its development methodology. Do not get this confused with the standard development life cycle (SDLC). This methodology, as the name suggests, is really aimed at developing secure software—not necessarily quality software. The goals of SDL are twofold: The first goal is to reduce the number of security vulnerabilities and privacy problems; the second goal is to reduce the severity of the vulnerabilities that remain (Howard 2006, p. 53). SDL is a very adoptable methodology whereas it can be blended in any other development methodology (i.e., iterative). This process is based on 13 stages of activities that are primarily focused on building security into the development in the early stages and throughout the life cycle.

- Stage 0: Education and Awareness. This process calls for ongoing education and awareness on all security issues. It is very important to keep the software engineers (developers, designers, architects) up to date with new threats, tools, and mitigation techniques and managers.

- Stage 1: Project Inception
    - Determine whether application needs SDL
    - Assign security advisor
    - Build security leadership team
    - Evaluate bug tracking process for security and privacy fields
    - Determine what bugs need to be fixed (bug bar)
- Stage 2: Define and Follow Design Best Practices
- Stage 3: Product Risk Analysis
- Stage 4: Risk Analysis
- Stage 5: Creating Security Documents, Tools, and Best Practices for Customers
- Stage 6: Secure Coding Policies
- Stage 7: Secure Testing Policies
- Stage 8: The Security Push
- Stage 9: The Final Security Review
- Stage 10: Security Response Planning
- Stage 11: Product Release
- Stage 12: Security Response Execution

Drawbacks to this methodology include the fact that this process is only as good as the security advisor and leadership team. This drawback, however, is true for any secure development methodology.

Team Software Process (TSP)

The Software Engineering Institute's Team Software Process (TSP), along with the Personal Software Process (PSP), helps the developer to do the following:

- Ensure quality software products.
- Create secure software products.
- Improve process management in an organization.

TSP provides a **framework**, a set of processes, and disciplined methods for producing quality and security principles in software (TSP Software Engineering Institute 2007). TSP and PSP are methodologies that work very well with CMMI. CMMI provides organizations with the *what*, whereas TSP and PSP provide organizations with the *how*. PSP is a training course designed to change the behaviors and viewpoints of software engineers into believing that a newer process (TSP) will greatly improve the overall quality and security of the software.

The TSP process is more of a team event where everyone on the development team can attend training courses, ask questions of TSP coaches, and learn from a variety of subject matter experts.

The TSP process provides guidance on how to accomplish objectives. Those objectives incorporate:

- A secure design process
- A security implementation process
- A security review process
- A security inspection process
- A secure test process
- Security-related predictive measures

Agile Development: Extreme Programming

Agile software development is a conceptual framework for undertaking software engineering projects. Agile methods also emphasize working software as the primary measure of progress. Combined with the preference for face-to-face communication with end users, agile methods produce very little written documentation relative to other methodologies because the actual coding is in small, quick intervals on the fly.

Extreme programming (XP) is an example of an agile development process. XP first hit the mainstream programmer consciousness a few years ago with the publication of Kent Beck's *Extreme Programming Explained*. XP delivers software in rapid, smaller iterations of the software product. This allows for quicker, better customer feedback and time/cost management. Kent Beck describes XP as a "waterfall run through a blender." Iterations typically last for a week or two; there is a high emphasis on code quality via unit testing; and code is integrated "constantly" so that it never becomes out of sync with the rest of the project.

With XP, the developers buddy up next to one another and share the responsibility of coding. As one developer codes, the other one is shoulder surfing, looking for errors or security pitfalls. The idea here is that two heads are better than one and by talking it out, quality and security are taken care of because each developer is watching the next.

XP is a great choice if the development team is split into two groups: experienced and entry/mid level. By pairing up developers, the entry-level team members can attain experience and understanding of the technology and attack types. This methodology also promotes open communication because of the lax environment and proximity of where people sit. Developers may feel more comfortable asking questions or talking about design pattern more freely.

Drawbacks to this methodology include the following:

- If you don't like pair programming, you will not like XP.
- XP does not produce much documentation. As you will find in subsequent chapters, software documentation such as use cases, misuse cases, and design diagrams will be very valuable to a development team.
- It is very rare that the users know exactly what they want from the start. Therefore, creating a working application in rapid speed might be wasted effort. In many cases, simple prototyping would be much more efficient to filter out user requirements. In fact, the developers will spend the same amount of time, whether

writing code that may be thrown out or creating design documents. The drawback is, once objects are coded and embedded into the overall software application, code becomes a lot harder to throw out. At that point, the time is better spent pondering design than code.

Touchpoints

Gary McGraw introduced Touchpoints in his book *Software Security: Building Security In*; Figure 2-5 illustrates this methodology.

Touchpoints are activities that the development team needs to do during a particular phase of the software development life cycle (McGraw 2006, p. 84). The Touchpoints methodology strictly focuses on security designs, principles, and features of a software application rather than the functionality. For example, instead of focusing on *what* the software requirement is supposed to do, the Touchpoint method will focus on *how* that software requirement can make the application vulnerable to security risks if implemented (abuse case).

Because the Touchpoint method focuses strictly on security issues, it can blend right in with any other software methodology used for quality measures and functionality.

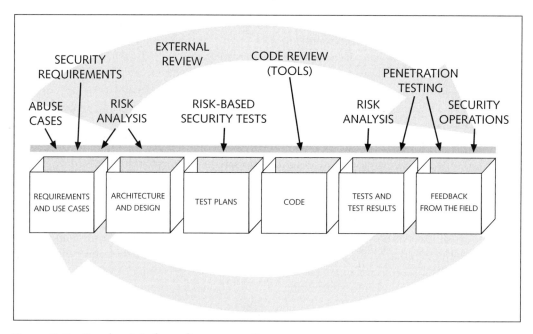

Figure 2-5   Touchpoints for software security

The Touchpoints for software security that can be applied during each phase of a standard software development life cycle process. Using the Touchpoint method provides security activities in every phase and forces security to be worked into the software package from concept to implementation.

Be Ready for a Hybrid Situation

Like every other software project out there, development time is always tight and the budget doesn't allow room for mistakes. Choosing to go from one methodology to another as the team develops has always worked for me. It's kind of like the best of both worlds. Don't get me wrong; I'm not saying that sticking to one methodology won't work. It's just my opinion that using only one approach for the complete duration of the software development life cycle is not very flexible. This does not account for the team's increased experience level as it gains knowledge and intimacy with the application.

If you're going to work on a project where the development team is *required* to stick to *one* process or standard to maintain compliance or assessment, you are not ready for a **hybrid methodology**. However, if you're on a team that uses methodologies to improve their overall process but the project manager is allowing the development team to "stretch their wings," then perhaps a hybrid methodology will work.

First ask your project manager (PM) if he or she cares to follow a methodology (some explaining might be required). If so, ask the PM if a specific one is mandatory or if you can choose one that fits the software development life cycle and team dynamics. If you still have the green light, then you're in the driver's seat.

In a hybrid methodology, you might start with an iterative methodology and as time goes on and familiarity with the system and requirements sets in, you might switch to a waterfall methodology. Don't be afraid to switch gears if the development team is hitting on all cylinders. After the team is in the groove, do anything to keep the synergy going. Hybrids make a good choice.

As Figure 2-6 illustrates, a development methodology could start off on a very rigid, step-by-step process. This detailed start-up process allows the development team members time to get to know one another's styles and strengths. It also provides time needed to digest the application properties: goals, assets, requirements, and database table definitions. As the team settles down into a normalized work flow and a solid communication foundation is established, the rigidness can ease up and allow for a more fluid approach. Over time, the application properties will become well known and normal software development life cycle activities will be accomplished much faster. Therefore, at the end of a three-year run with the same team on the same application, a software requirement could be executed using a waterfall approach and still have the same quality and security attributes as one executed using a spiral.

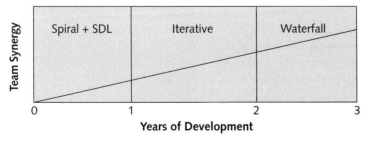

Figure 2-6   Hybrid solution

Time is not the only factor to look at when judging when to change the approach. You also need to look at the overall quality and security of the code and the comfort level of the team in these areas.

SDLC in the Cube

All development methodologies share one common element: people. People are the biggest factor in software quality and security. The people whom you code with, talk to, and associate with can bring you down or make you famous. If software quality and security are not high on their list of objectives when they work, chances are their product won't be secure or high quality. I don't want to sound like a greeting card, but if your heart is not in your coding, you risk buggy code. You must have the desire and motivation to make great software because it takes more than just a structured methodology—much more.

Sometimes it seems that no matter how structured the methodology is, one person can write defect-free code and another cannot. Make it your personal goal to learn why. What were the contributing factors (environment, skills, and so on) that made the code defect free? Can they be replicated? Try to document that knowledge and share it with the rest of the development team. If no one is interested, keep it in your back pocket for later use. What makes one developer better than the next is not natural talent (although naturally gifted people make it look easy). What makes a great developer is the endless ambition to constantly learn in this field and grow stronger in technology.

The developer is the one who will be going through all the SDLC activities and methodology procedures in the cube. The developer is the one who can make or break the whole process. How's that for responsibility? If you want to make a difference and become the go-to person on the team, you need to learn the art of:

- Communicating effectively
- Encouraging discussions

Each of these traits is discussed in the following sections.

Communicating During SDLC

The art of communication is lost in this field. This could be because of language barriers, cultural differences, lack of understanding, fear of public speaking—the list goes on. Developers like to work with computers, not people. If you want to improve the software development life cycle on your team, learn how to communicate. That includes all those wonderful **active listening** skills you didn't think you needed for this field. You need to be able to convey your thoughts and ideas very clearly. Likewise, you need to be able to paraphrase and summarize someone else's thoughts and ideas.

You can practice these techniques daily with your coworkers, family, or friends. The more you do it, the better you get. You might even want to enroll yourself in one of those Dale Carnegie courses. As you communicate more with your colleagues, the requirements and design become clearer and more defined. By the time you sit down to code, all your thoughts, ideas, and meaning should already be worked out through proper communication.

Encouraging SDLC Discussions

We all hate criticism, even when it's constructive. It's human nature to want to do well the first time and hit that walk-off home run. But fantasy is not reality. Even Babe Ruth set a record for the most strikeouts, while at the same time holding a record for the most home runs. Learning from our experiences in software development is another great way to improve the process and then change what doesn't work. Encourage discussions with your co-workers about the development process, methodologies, and what works versus what doesn't. Tell them how they're doing with requirement gathering or design. If an analyst or lead developer is writing meaningless verbiage in the SRS (software requirements), tell him so. Let the analyst know what type of information is really useful and what is not. That way, the next SRS should be better than the first.

Discuss work flow and how processes will reinforce understanding. Your colleagues will start to understand what your needs are as a developer. They will also learn how to do it better the next time around through these discussions. That is how great teams start to form, and those attitudes will spill into the SDLC methodology.

THE DEVELOPMENT TEAM

Team dynamics are important when looking at a secure development process. In fact, it's one of the reasons why I chose to write this book. I believe that no one individual can possibly know and do all things with software. Because of the vast knowledge and skills needed for secure programming, it is too complex of a job for one person. A secure software development process should have the appropriate team structure with qualified personnel to make the work flow as it should.

A good team structure includes:

- Key players of a development team
- Defined roles and responsibilities for the team
- Defined ways in which team members interact with each other

Makeup of a Development Team

Like the phrase "the right tool for the job," the right development team can make or break the success of a project. Like a jigsaw puzzle, all team members have to play their individual roles so that the whole group can benefit from their work. Because people are the cornerstone of all successful (and not so successful) software projects, you should know the players on a development team. The lineup includes:

1. Project manager (PM)

   This person has strong management skills and is keenly aware of the SDLC. He or she is likely **PMP** (project management professional) certified to manage an IT project. An effective PM is one that has good people skills, communication skills, and interpersonal skills.

   The PM is fully aware of the security needs and policies of the current project. This includes privacy needs, asset protection, and vulnerable spots of the program. In addition, it is *useful* if the PM is also familiar with the business—how it works, the daily operations, and new business practices. This person interacts with everyone involved on the project.

2. Business analyst (BA)

   A business analyst is someone who knows and understands the business side of the application. This person takes customer requests and translates them into software requirements. Writing software requirements using UML, conducting analysis, and testing are required. This person needs to be aware of the security needs and policies of the project. This includes privacy needs, asset protection, and vulnerable spots of the program. This person must be able to demonstrate good communication skills and interpersonal skills.

3. Tech lead (lead developer)

   This person is very efficient in the technology used on the project, is aware of the security needs of the application, and ensures sound design is used throughout the application. As a technical lead, this person is required to know secure design principles and methodologies and how to apply threat modeling and threat analysis. A technical lead has a willingness to learn, follows directions, and is a good problem solver.

4. Testers

   A tester is someone with a thorough understanding of the system's requirements and how the system was designed and developed, and knows how to break software. This person also needs to be aware of the security needs and policies of the project. This includes privacy needs, asset protection, and vulnerable spots of the program and how those vulnerabilities might be attacked.

5. Customer/user

   An end user is someone with a thorough understanding of the system's requirements and knows how the software will be used by the masses (for example, number of users, busiest times, reporting features).

NOTE The team players, in my opinion, make up the core group of a development team. Please do not think that I am discounting the importance and hard work of other team members, such as technical writers, coordinators, and network architects. Also, bigger projects can and will have more than one manager, lead, and programmer.

Accountability: Roles and Responsibilities of the Team

The complexity of team dynamics in communication, knowledge base, and experience makes it imperative for all team members to play their part in software development, as shown in Figure 2-7. Like an orchestra, all individual instruments make a unique sound, but when playing together they create beautiful music. The most successful projects I have been on were the ones that required individual team members to play out their role on the team even when it required them to take a "backseat" approach on certain topics or areas. I've also experienced projects that went horribly wrong because of the "too many cooks" syndrome. One element that all those failures shared was the lack of roles and responsibilities.

Figure 2-7   Everyone plays his or her part

It is the job of the PM to define roles and responsibilities, but all too often, the roles and responsibilities are *assumed* instead of *defined*. The problem is that not everyone draws the same conclusion. When failures occur, and they will occur, it is important to hold people accountable. Accountability can be anything from being called out in a meeting for not following directions to being fired. The PM will have to come up with some accountability plans, but the team members need to know where they stand and who's in charge, or team breakdowns will happen. Roles and responsibilities are a *must* on any team so that everyone knows how he or she fits into the team's pecking order.

The tricky part about assigning roles and responsibilities is that it's not your responsibility as a developer. Only the PM can assign duties, and unless the PM understands the importance, it won't happen. Surprisingly, roles and responsibilities are *assumed* on a lot of projects. And like many assumptions, some of them can be false.

Team Interaction

Everyone is going to be your boss—your customers (they pay the bills), the project manager, and, if you're a contractor, employees of the organization will be your boss as well. You are going to have to deal with many people wanting status reports, updates, and basic project information. You need to know how to interact with everyone.

As a developer, your main interaction should be with other developers and business analysts. They are your primary source of information. Project managers tend to place business analysts (BAs) ahead of developers in the pecking order. If that's the case, you have to report to the BAs and treat those people as if they were also your boss. You might find yourself reporting to many people. That's just the way it is, and you need to know how to manage this. The best way is to interact with the right people with respect and a positive attitude. Other colleagues will pick up on this and start to respect you and treat you with the same level of professionalism.

Team interaction with other colleagues is a great career booster. If done correctly, you will be considered a valuable asset on the team—not only as a technically strong person, but also as someone with whom everyone *wants* to work. As long as it's done genuinely, getting in valuable face time with the boss(s) or going out after work with the "gang" often strengthens the team as a whole. With a good team comes good software.

While on the topic of team interaction, the following are some pitfalls you need to be aware of and avoid:

- Cliques
- Office politics

Still "Cliquing" after School

Talking to the same "gang" of people day in and day out forms alliances. If everyone on the team is included in that alliance, great. If not, this could cause a breakup in the team dynamics. Just like in high school when all the cool people hung out in one group and did not include you (or did that happen only to me?), cliques are bad and not appropriate at the office. It creates an *us versus them* attitude that can spill into the quality of the code. Perhaps your arch enemies will sneak in little logic bombs or sabotage your work. Most often, people who feel threatened by you will hide information from you. For example, instead of telling you about a patch or corrective fix to an error, they might just say, "Let him figure it out on his own." This is a common response in cliquing and it will kill the synergy that a group of people need to work together.

Include all team members in group activities. Either during lunch, after work, or general water cooler talk, the development team needs to have an open invitation for the rest of the team. Nothing hurts the team dynamics more than cliquing—don't do it.

Politicking to Stay Out of Politics

Office politics: bad to participate, impossible to avoid. To be successful, you not only have to code great software, but you also have to be seen and heard. Be savvy with your communication and socialization. People at work may use sensitive information to their personal advantage; if you try to keep secrets around the office, it will get around. People use sensitive information to gain position or to achieve some personal goal. Be mindful about what you disclose and whom you tell and why. Have a purpose and meaning with all information you disclose.

Chapter Summary

- ❑ A secure software development process encompasses industry standards, development methodologies, and best practices.

- ❑ Industry standards define *what* needs to be done in software development. The ISO/IEEE defines the primary phases of a traditional software development approach to software engineering.

- ❑ Software methodologies provide the development team with a set of directions on how to carry out activities within each phase of software development.

- ❑ Software methodologies and standards play a key role in how efficient, secure, and reusable the code is because they focus the activities and tasks that need to be carried out on a daily basis.

- ❑ At the end of the day, it all comes down to people. No matter how defined the process is, or how rigid the procedures are, if the development team is not working together as a whole, the project can fail.

Key Terms

active listening — The process of listening in a structured way for meaning. It includes summarizing, paraphrasing, and evaluating body language.

C.I.A. — The three main principles in secure code: confidentiality, integrity, and availability.

framework — A predefined process or structure which another software project can use or plug into.

hybrid methodology — Interbreeding two or more development methodologies so that the process that is ultimately followed adapts to the dynamics and knowledge base of the team members.

PMP — A project management professional who holds a certification from the Project Management Institute. The PMP designation following your name tells current and potential employers that you have a solid foundation of project management knowledge that can be readily applied in the workplace.

software life cycle — The official phases that software goes through while being created from start to finish. Those phases are requirements analysis; design; architectural design; detailed design; coding; testing; installation; acceptance; and maintenance.

software methodology — A governing process that defines and rationalizes the set of procedures and processes that are followed while coding.

REVIEW QUESTIONS

1. The main goal (objective) of a secure software development process is to:
   a. get the overall project done quickly
   b. develop code in uniform
   c. write quality code that handles known security flaws
   d. encourage teamwork and bug-free code

2. Of the categories that make up a development process, which one would help improve the following scenario?
   "The developers are not following a similar pattern for designing and writing code."
   a. development methodology
   b. software standard
   c. Security Development Lifecycle
   d. Personal Software Process (PSP)
   e. team roles and responsibilities

3. Of the categories that make up a development process, which one would help improve the following scenario? "The developers are not filling out the required ISO 'sign-off' forms when completing the code reviews."
   a. development methodology
   b. Security Development Lifecycle
   c. standards
   d. waterfall methodology
   e. team roles and responsibilities

4. Of the categories that make up a development process, which one would help improve the following scenario? "Because we are performing at the same level, we can use whatever methodology we want without any one person dictating over us."

    a. development methodology

    b. Security Development Lifecycle

    c. organization standard

    d. CMMI

    e. team roles and responsibilities

5. Which of the following team members is considered to be the liaison between the programmer and the customers/users?

    a. project manager

    b. tester

    c. business analyst

    d. technical lead

6. The various phases that make up software development are commonly referred to by what name?

    a. software development

    b. software architecture

    c. software systems

    d. software life cycle

7. A _____ is a repeatable practice that uses the same tools, worksheets, and design patterns to produce similar results from one requirement to the next.

8. When software development goes through all stages from start to finish in one swoop, it is said to be coded using what methodology?

    a. waterfall

    b. object oriented

    c. procedural

    d. spiral

    e. iterative

9. When software development goes through all stages in increments rather than the whole system at once, it is said to be coded using what methodology?

    a. waterfall

    b. object oriented

    c. procedural

    d. spiral

    e. iterative

10. When software development goes through all stages, one requirement/function at a time, it is said to be coded using what methodology?

    a. waterfall

    b. object oriented

    c. procedural

    d. spiral

    e. iterative

11. A _____ is a set of mandatory criteria that states how to carry out a particular activity.

12. The ISO/IEEE _____ is referred to as the industry standard for the software development life cycle.

13. Of the following team members, who should be certified from PMI?

    a. project manager

    b. tester

    c. business analyst

    d. technical lead

14. Of the following options, which one will help you determine your role and responsibility on the team?

    a. Join the team and figure it out as the project evolves.

    b. Just assume what they are and complete tasks that you assumed.

    c. Ask during the interview.

    d. Ask the technical lead or project manager.

15. Taking a straightforward set of engineering best practices and working in security checkpoints is an example of what methodology?

    a. CMMI and TSP/PSP

    b. IEEE ISO 12207 and waterfall

    c. Touchpoint

    d. spiral and SDL

16. A strong developer can work independently and not interact with the rest of the team and still produce high quality, secure code. True or False?

17. A drawback to XP is that the developers waste time developing unnecessary code. True or False?

18. One of the first things to consider before developing code is choosing a methodology. True or False?

19. A drawback to using SDL is that security is sometimes overlooked or forgotten. True or False?

20. Socializing can be good for the team. It can strengthen the team dynamics and cement long-lasting professional relationships. True or False?

HANDS-ON PROJECTS

HANDS-ON PROJECTS

Project 2-1 Draw It!

During the SDLC process, many important artifacts (software documents) will be produced from the team. Knowing what artifact should be produced from each phase and from who will reinforce your understanding of the SDLC process.

1. Draw a detailed diagram of each phase of the software development life cycle process and list the types of activities and artifacts (documentation) that are produced with each phase.

HANDS-ON PROJECTS

Project 2-2 Research Some Issues

Writing software is more than engineering practices and specifications. In fact, the human element of software development is just as important as the technical side of the equation. The following questions were created to reinforce your understanding of certain character traits of a software developer.

Write answers in short essays for the following questions:

1. From the information given in this chapter, which attributes of a developer will you need to sharpen? Why?

2. What are the various agreements, both professional and casual, that you have with people in authority (for example, teachers, bosses)?

3. Have you ever had a mentor or coach? How did that person encourage teamwork? Explain how things turned out.

4. Why is socializing essential to a development team's success?

CASE PROJECT

Look It Up!

In your own words, how can the CMMI model be used on a software development project?

CHAPTER REFERENCES

Boehm, B.W. 1988. A Spiral Model of Software Development and Enhancement. *Computer* 21(5):61–72.

Dupuis, Robert, Pierre Bourque, Alain Abran, James W. Moore, Leonard L. Tripp, and IEEE Society. 2004. Guide to the Software Engineering Body of Knowledge, Version 2004. http://www.swebok.org (accessed February 14, 2008).

Howard, Michael and Steve Lipner. 2006. *The Security Development Lifecycle*. Redmond, Washington: Microsoft Press.

Institute of Electrical and Electronics Engineers (IEEE) and Electronic Industries Association (EIA). 1998. *International Standard ISO/IEC 12207:1995 - Software Life Cycle Processes*. New York: The Institute of Electrical and Electronics Engineers, Inc.

McGraw, Gary. 2006. *Software Security: Building Security In*. Boston: Addison–Wesley.

Software Engineering Institute. 2006. *CMMI for Development, Version 1.2, Improving Processes for Better Products, CMU/SEI-2006-TR-008, ESC-TR-2006-008*. Pittsburg, PA: Carnegie Mellon.

TSP Software Engineering Institute. 2007. The Team Software Process (TSP) and the Personal Software Process (PSP). http://www.sei.cmu.edu/tsp/ (accessed February 14, 2008).

3

PRINCIPLES OF SECURITY AND QUALITY

Upon completion of this material, you should be able to:

♦ Understand principles of security and quality in the industry

♦ Work with principles of security and quality in the organization

♦ Identify principles of security and quality in the cube

Writing secure software takes certain repetitive, precise, coding styles that must consistently produce desired results. These styles need to be so ingrained in your everyday programming discipline that coding any other way is not even an option. These disciplines come from a personal obligation to ensure the code you write is of the best quality and security that you can possibly design and develop. Just like learning how to golf, the very first step is to learn how to swing a club. If you do not address the ball correctly, you're in for a long, hard day. If security and quality principles are not in the code, your programs might never be at par with today's development demands.

PRINCIPLES OF SECURITY AND QUALITY IN THE INDUSTRY

The foundation of software applications and the development processes that produce them are based on common best principles of quality code and secure code. These principles are the driving force behind the concepts and designs of industry **best practices**. To produce secure code that will stand the test of time, you must learn how to incorporate these principles into the development process. That can be accomplished by knowing the following facts:

- Secure code is not quality code.
- Quality code is not secure code.

Goals of Secure Code

A developer can write very efficient code that is easy to maintain and reusable; however, if that code allows an **unauthorized** user to access the application's **assets**, then that code is of no use. Unlike software quality, software security is not subjective. Sensitive information is either exposed or it's not, and there is no second chance of getting it right. Samuel T. Redwine Jr. and Noopur Davis define secure software this way: "Secure software means highly secure software realizing—with justifiably high confidence but not guaranteeing absolutely—a substantial set of explicit security properties and functionality including all those required for its intended usage" (Noopur, et al. 2004, p. 12).

The definition of secure software that Samuel T. Redwine Jr. and Noopur Davis published at the National Cyber Security Summit in 2004 is the same definition that this book follows throughout all subsequent chapters. In that definition, the terminology "substantial set of explicit security properties" is directly targeted at the goals and principles of secure code.

C.I.A., confidentiality, integrity, and availability are the three primary goals that the industry considers to be of the utmost importance in any secure software development process. What the developers do to protect, enforce, and ensure C.I.A. will equate to the "justifiably high confidence" part of the secure code definition. The properties are defined in the following sections. To find out what C.I.A. is and how to achieve it, read these sections:

- Confidentiality
- Integrity
- Availability

Confidentiality

Confidentiality is attained by keeping unauthorized users (humans or software) from accessing confidential information. The goal of confidentiality is to ensure that no user other than the owner(s) can see or access the data.

Authorization and authentication are the two properties that support confidentiality:

- *Authorization*: Ensuring that the user has the appropriate role and privilege to view data

- *Authentication*: Ensuring that the user is who he or she claims to be and that the data comes from the appropriate place

By maintaining confidentiality, the software will be trustworthy for the user community. An example of authorization and authentication is the username and password. As with most applications, the username and password are not only the most critical data elements required, but they also happen to be one of the weakest links in the application's security architecture. To help strengthen usernames and password policies, application architecture can rely on tokens as one more defensive layer to help authorize and authenticate user requests. Figure 3-1 shows two examples of items that the user would have to carry with him every time he wanted to use the application.

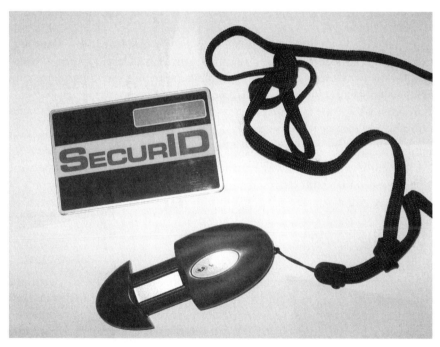

Figure 3-1   Security tokens

Integrity

The integrity of the application is defined by the way in which the application accepts, transmits, and stores data. From the point of entry all the way to the database and back, the data must remain unchanged by unauthorized users and remain very reliable. Data encryption, digital signatures, and public keys are just some examples of how to maintain integrity (and confidentiality), and are covered in Chapter 7.

Availability

Availability refers to the percentage of time a system is available during its normally scheduled hours of operation (excluding any scheduled downtime). Availability is the one goal of secure software that will make your application very dependable and, thus, users will start to rely on the application for their needs. If your application is not available at the time users need it, good luck trying to win them back! A good reputation is hard to gain and very easy to lose.

Quality Code Is Not Secure Code

A developer can write very secure code that authorizes and authenticates every user transaction, logs the transactions, and cancels out all unwanted requests; however, if that code does not return the expected results, then this very secure code might never see the light of day. Quality software is **efficient**, easy to maintain, and, most of all, satisfies the needs of the original requirement. You must know how to write quality code before you write secure code.

If the code you write is inefficient, buggy, or complex, you make it easier for attackers to launch attack; acquire secrets hidden in log files; or simply gain access. Developing quality software must be approached in a systematic effort that embodies requirement gathering, development methodologies, and best practices in a way that is repeatable, visible, and reliable. Quality characteristics of software are not the same as security. It is not measured in terms of C.I.A. but rather in terms of ease of use and whether it's reusable and maintainable (to name a few).

Achieving software quality is accomplished by knowing what needs to be done, how to do it, and how long it will take. Having quality code simply means that it was developed by professionals who understand what software development is and how to carry it out. It does not mean that it is also secure.

Goals of Quality Code

SWEBOK, Software Engineering Body of Knowledge, is an all-inclusive standard that describes the sum of knowledge within the profession of software engineering (all phases). The goal of SWEBOK is to define a clear set of boundaries and materials that make up software development from an engineering perspective. SWEBOK sees software construction as an "engineering process that creates working, meaningful software through a combination of coding, self-validation, and self-testing" (Dupuis, et al. 2004, p. 64).

 NOTE

This definition is sometimes debated within the user community because of the use of the word *engineering*. The debate is "just because a person writes code does not make him a software engineer." There is a distinction between a *software engineer* and an *application programmer*. A **software engineer** comes from a school of computer science and math, whereas an application programmer can be anyone from any background who writes code.

Quality principles include the following:

- Total automation
- Manage complexity
- Software diversity

Total Automation

There are just two techniques used for software development: manual and automated (Dupuis, et al. 2004, p. 4-3). Manual techniques are the human ability to logically break down complex problems into smaller, easier-to-manage problems, and then develop automated solutions to handle each problem. Total automation is a tool-intensive process designed to move as much of the overall software development process from the human factor to an automated process.

Humans are very creative and good at thinking up solutions to problems. In fact, great logicians are able to foresee problems in design *before* they even get coded. The main problem with humans, however, is that we are forgetful and error prone. However, we complement a computer's weakness because it lacks creativity and problem solving (for now, anyway). So, there is a dependency between humans and computers, and total automation is the act in which a developer can write software to convert manual, repetitive activity to an automated, flawless system.

If you were to analyze the tasks and activities that developers go through on a daily basis, you could easily come up with automated solutions for those tasks. Computers are getting smarter by the day and are really taking over everyone's daily activities. Gathering requirements, designing, coding, testing—there is an automated tool that can do all of just that. It is the goal of total automation to have tools configured with other tools so that they can communicate instructions to one another and do all the work.

Manage Complexity

No matter how reusable or understandable the code is, complexity will always be a factor that you have to deal with. You will be creating algorithms in nested "If statements" while looping through collections of objects—all the while making your code more complicated. Quality code, however, should manage this complexity so that it is not so intimidating to other developers. Remember, all code has to be maintained, even if it's a line or two. SWEBOK gives three great steps to follow while dealing with complexity and organizing code: removal, automated, and localized (Dupuis, et al. 2004, p. 88).

1. *Removal of complexity*: This might seem too easy, but the best way to handle complexity is by not having it. End users usually want it all, but if the analysts really dig into the requirements and get to the core functionality, a lot of bells and whistles can usually be dropped, making the software less complex. Good coding habits also remove complexity. If programmers learn to code efficient methods and functions, a lot of duplicate code could be mitigated.

2. *Automation of complexity*: If the complexity cannot be removed, try to automate it. Just like automating developers' activities, try to automate software activities. For example, triggers on a database can be set up to execute a routine when certain columns are updated. Or, perhaps code compilers and other software can be used to scan other code for quality and security issues.

3. *Localization of complexity*: The complexity that can neither be removed nor automated needs to be localized. Create small units or modules that off-load the work for other programs. That way, the complexity of such logic is encapsulated and hidden from other programs as well as contained to one area. This localization principle works very well with object-oriented code and it allows for a more plug-and-play development approach.

Software Diversity

Change is inevitable, and your software must change with it. **Software diversity** is the ability to "*anticipate* change in the software so that it becomes flexible and self-maintaining" (Dupuis, et al. 2000, p. 4-2). It's the anticipation of change that will make your code timeless and reusable as long as you design and code for it up front. The challenging part about diversity is coding for future changes while you are supposed to be coding for the requirements at hand. Therefore, software diversity needs to be part of who you are and how you code because if you don't include this principle in your development process, your code becomes obsolete even before the ink dries.

Here are some helpful tidbits to consider when looking for ways to code for diversity:

- Use **CONSTANTS** throughout all source code. Never hard code values. When you catch yourself hard coding in the source code, *stop* and replace with a constant.

- Use objects as input arguments to methods or functions instead of individual variables. This allows you to add additional properties for input variables without needing to change the signature of the method (number of input fields).

- Do not embed business logic with presentation requirements. For example, multiple GUIs such as Web browsers, mobile devices, and mainframe screens can share the same business logic on different platforms.

- Design the application to be driven by parameters. All options, setup activities, and instructions should come from a database table (CONSTANT files or external XML files) rather than from source code.

PRINCIPLES OF SECURITY AND QUALITY IN THE ORGANIZATION

All organizations need software. To some companies, the software produced is their main product and to other companies, software enables them to create products. Whichever is the case at your company, one thing is for certain—each company has its own view(s) of what the goals of C.I.A. and quality software should be for its organization. CIOs (chief information officers) and/or CTOs (chief technology officers) bring knowledge and experience to the company and make strategic decisions for use of information systems and leading technology. Their vision and leadership will affect how software development processes are carried out and how principles of secure code will be incorporated.

Because developing secure software takes time, money, and human resources, the process alone cannot be done without the support of management. VPN tokens, data encryption, and tools all cost money, and the rules and guidelines that you must work with depend on the types of policies and principles that the organizations have regarding secure software. The following sections will talk about principles and concepts aimed at achieving C.I.A.

The Principles and Concepts of Secure Software

To achieve C.I.A., organizations rely on generally accepted security principles that are produced and published by active researchers in the information technology field. The Information Systems Security Association (ISSA) is one such resource whose main purpose is to "promote practices that will ensure the confidentiality, integrity, and availability of organizational information resources" (ISSA 2007, para. 1). ISSA provides guidelines, publications, skills, and provides the industry with lessons learned, common best practices, and other educational material that organizational leaders can use in their practices.

Other generally accepted principles and concepts of secure software can be found in books, in magazines, and from government agencies. For example, the DHS (Department of Homeland Security) partnered up with software security professionals from the private sector, academia, and other government agencies to improve the software development practices regarding security issues. The result of this partnership created a guide of best practices for educators, trainers, and practitioners (organizations) for secure software called Secure Software Assurance Book of Knowledge, or CBK for short.

CBK's primary role is to provide a framework for sound practices and procedures that is relevant to the security of software by defining terms, concepts, and principles that are needed to code securely (Redwine, et al. 2006). This guide is a work in progress and will continue to advance as more knowledge is gained and realized in this dynamic field.

Secure the Weakest Link

The "weakest part of the system will most likely be attacked first" (McGraw and Viega 2002, p. 93). As the saying goes, you are only as strong as your weakest link; the same applies to application code. Analyzing and evaluating the weakest application layers and defensive layers is a principle that needs to be practiced at the beginning stages of software development (requirements) all the way through the maintenance stage.

There will always be a weaker component of the system; the idea is to have the weakest link be risk tolerant or acceptable. For instance, in a typical example of a username and password, security tokens are added to the architecture to secure the weakest link (password). The VPN token itself does not eliminate the problem of someone stealing a password, but it does add a layer of risk acceptance because the attacker would then have to steal both the password and the token.

Defense in Depth

Defense in depth is designed on the principle that "multiple layers of different types of protection from different vendors or software provide substantially better protection" (Bradley 2007, para. 2). The goal is to limit access to certain features of the application, making them available on an as-needed basis. For example, if the attacker is smart enough to break through the firewall on the router, then the attacker will have to intercept encrypted data. Basically, add as many filters and layers of security as possible, especially if the information that needs to be protected is highly sensitive.

Fail Securely

No matter how well designed and coded an application is, all systems go down for a variety of reasons. Power failure, server crashes, and other network problems are reasons beyond the control of the application programmers. **Fail securely** is simply what happens when the system goes down. Failure is an activity that *will* happen and should be planned for. The problem is that when systems do fail, there are typically security problems related to the failure process.

To address failing securely, it is imperative that the software do the following:

- Address error-handling issues appropriately. The application developers should design a common method for dealing with applications issues, capture errors appropriately, and log the necessary data so that the development team can respond quickly. (Graff and Van Wyk 2003).

- Degrade gracefully—the application should detect when a critical feature or Web service has stopped working and should operate with very limited capability rather than just end abnormally (Graff and Van Wyk 2003).

Least Privilege

This principle states that you should give users the least amount of privilege required to perform their use case functionality (OWASP 2006). This principle is targeted at protecting application resources, access to databases, log files, and other file-network permissions. Applications that need access to other system resources, such as files, cookies, or other software, should be granted within restricted areas and should not provide administration privileges or root access to all directories.

Keep It Simple

Keep security simple and keep the application simple. Simplicity is easy to understand, analyze, and enhance. If the code is written using quality principles in an easy-to-understand architecture, code reuse and availability would be more prevalent because everyone on the development team would know how to code the software modules and maintain them if needed.

Secrets Are Not Kept

This principle, a.k.a. keeping secrets is hard (McGraw and Viega 2002) or security by obscurity (OWASP 2006), states that the application can not secretly hide data from the user. Binary code is not secure because it can be easily decompiled, and hidden values in HTML screens can be seen by right-clicking and then clicking View Source. Do not try to hide secrets because they will be found. Instead, place secrets in external resources, such as databases, separate applications, or a blend of both.

The Saltzer and Schroeder Principles

In 1975, the published work of two authors became highly regarded in the software industry as sound software principles. Jerome H. Saltzer and Michael D. Schroeder, members of IEEE, created the classic paper, "The Protection of Information in Computer Systems," which spoke of desired functions and design principles for system protection and authentication. This paper is the most referenced throughout the industry because of its timeless information of basic techniques that deal with application security. The paper discusses techniques that can be used to protect information stored on a computer from unauthorized use or modification. It was created in three main sections.

TIP Even though the paper was published in 1975, the principles still hold true today. You can read it by visiting the following link: http://web.mit.edu/Saltzer/www/publications/protection/index.html

The security principles that Saltzer and Schroeder introduced have become the basic principles of any generally accepted concept of secure software. Two principles that I consider to be the most important are complete mediation and separation of privilege:

- **Complete mediation**: Every access to every object must be checked for authority, as shown in Figure 3-2. This principle, when systematically applied, is the primary underpinning of the protection system. It forces a systemwide view of access control, which, in addition to normal operation, includes initialization, recovery, shutdown, and maintenance. It implies that a foolproof method of identifying the source of every request must be devised (Saltzer and Schroeder 1975). Overall, security is a two-way street. Authentication and authorization of data must be verified and validated at every entry point into the application. A person who has permission to view and update data at the start of the transaction might not have the same permission granted by the time the data makes it back to the user. Therefore, constant checkpoints along the way of the system architecture should be set up for each and every request going to and from the user to the application and the application to the user.

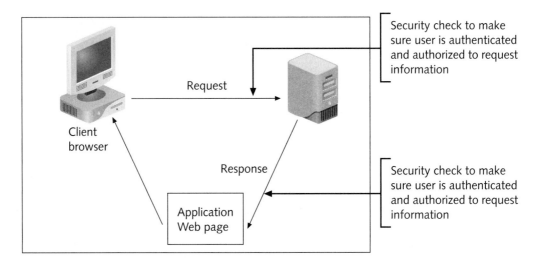

Figure 3-2   Security in complete mediation

- **Separation of privilege**: Where feasible, a design that requires two keys to send and receive data is more secure than a design that allows access to the information with only one key. This principle, when implemented, should not grant access solely based on one condition but rather a sequence of events and conditions (Saltzer and Schroeder 1975). Note that this principle supports the validation of certain conditions to be true before any access is granted. For example, consider a certain Web screen that allows a user to update personal information based on certain authentication and authority. If the code assumed that the person was identified before making it to this logic, the update would be granted, as shown in Figure 3-3. The code snippet updates a database for anyone who calls the method. The programmer just assumes that the system authenticated the user and the request is valid.

```
private static void updateData(double salary, String userId)
            throws ApplicationException (

    final String METHOD = "updateData()";
    debug(CLASS + "." + METHOD + "==>Begin");
    try (
        // Load the database driver
        Class.forName( "sun.jdbc.odbc.JdbcOdbcDriver" ) ;

        // Get a connection to the database
        Connection conn = DriverManager.getConnection( "jdbc:odbc:Database" ) ;

        // Get a statement from the connection
        Statement stmt = conn.createStatement() ;

        // Execute the Update
        int rows = stmt.executeUpdate( "UPDATE Emp SET Q_SALEMP_NO = '"+salary+"' WHERE EMP_ID = '"+userId+"'");
        // Print how many rows were modified
        System.out.println( rows + " Rows modified" ) ;

        // Close the statement and the connection
        stmt.close() ;
        conn.close() ;
    ) catch( SQLException se ) (
        System.out.println( "SQL Exception:" ) ;
        ErrorFormatterUtil.formatApplicationException(CLASS,METHOD,errorMsg,errorMsg,se);
    ) catch( Exception e ) (
        System.out.println( e ) ;
        ErrorFormatterUtil.formatApplicationException(CLASS,METHOD,errorMsg,errorMsg,e);
    )
)
```

Table is updated

Figure 3-3   Before separation of privilege

Now, let's apply the separation privilege to this code and add another key. We will call this key passApplicationID, as shown in Figure 3-4. In this example, the key passApplicationID is passed into the method for simplicity. Of course, the passed key could come from the session and the other half of the key could come from a database. This key serves as a system identifier that holds the name of the application screen the user is coming from. Therefore, an attacker would not only need to know what method to call and which parameters to pass, but would also need to know the secret screen name that only allows such requests to pass through. See Figure 3-5 for the query to retrieve the key from the database.

The Principles and Concepts of Quality Software

All organizations want quality software and they want a development process that will foster and produce such software. ISO and IEEE have published many resources regarding this matter and yet, even in today's world of top IT talent, I still see code that looks like a ten-year-old wrote it. The challenge that organizations face with incorporating quality standards into the development process is that very few people from top management actually go to the code-level detail where the quality standards are found. Unlike security, where access is either granted or denied, quality is like vaporware—easy to proclaim but hard to prove.

Working quality principles into the code takes a lot more skill and ability than adding encryption or digital signatures. Coding for quality is a disciplined practice where constant improvements are applied after each review and iteration until certain techniques become second nature to the developer. After these quality principles are ingrained into the software developer's daily habits, the developer wouldn't want to code any other way.

```
private static void updateSecureData(double salary, String userId,String passApplicationID)
throws ApplicationException {

    final String METHOD = "updateSecureData()";
    debug(CLASS + "." + METHOD + "==>Begin");
    DBConnectionManager dbConnMgr = null;
    Connection conn = null;
    String appID = getAppID(userId);
    if (passApplicationID!= appID) {
        return;
    }
    try {
        // Get Connection from DBConnectionManager.
        dbConnMgr = DBConnectionManager.getInstance();
        conn = dbConnMgr.getConnection();
        // Get a statement from the connection
        Statement stmt = conn.createStatement() ;
        // Execute the Update
        int rows = stmt.executeUpdate( "UPDATE Emp SET Q_SALEMP_NO = '"+salary+"' WHERE EMP_ID = '"+userId+"'");
        // Print how many rows were modified
        System.out.println( rows + " Rows modified" ) ;
        // Close the statement and the connection
        stmt.close() ;
        conn.close() ;
    } catch( SQLException se ) {
        System.out.println( "SQL Exception:" ) ;
        ErrorFormatterUtil.formatApplicationException(CLASS,METHOD,errorMsg,errorMsg,se);
    } catch( Exception e ) {
        System.out.println( e ) ;
        ErrorFormatterUtil.formatApplicationException(CLASS,METHOD,errorMsg,errorMsg,e);
    }
}
```

New method added to get application ID from database

If the IDs do not equal, do not execute

Figure 3-4   After separation of privilege

```
public static String getAppID(String userId) throws ApplicationException{
final String METHOD = "getAppID()";
debug(CLASS + "." + METHOD + "==>Begin");
Statement stmt = null;
ResultSet rs = null;
StringBuffer query = new StringBuffer();
String appID = new String();
DBConnectionManager dbConnMgr = null;
Connection conn = null;
try {
/     Get Connection from DBConnectionManager.
    dbConnMgr = DBConnectionManager.getInstance();
    conn = dbConnMgr.getConnection();
    query
        .append(" SELECT DISTINCT I_APP   ")
        .append(" FROM APPTBL ")
        .append(" WHERE ")
        .append(" I_USER_ID = '"+ userId + "'")
        .append(" AND I_APP = 'SCLLC' ");
    stmt = conn.createStatement();
    rs = stmt.executeQuery(query.toString());
    while (rs.next()) {
        appID = rs.getString(1);
    } //end while
    rs.close();
    stmt.close();
    conn.close() ;
} catch (Exception e) {
    String errorMsg = "==>Exception occurred processing ResultSet." +query +  e.getMessage();
    debug(errorMsg);
    ErrorFormatterUtil.formatApplicationException(CLASS,METHOD,errorMsg,e);
}
return appID;
}
```

Select the application ID from the table; compare the result to the one in session from the user

Figure 3-5   Retrieving the key from the database

1. Open the "SecurityCheck1.java" file from the Chapter 3 course data.

2. Read the following code snippet and look for areas of improvement from the security lessons learned from this chapter.

3. Using Notepad or your favorite code editor, can you re-write this logic with security improvements?

1. Open the "SecurityCheck2.java" file from the Chapter 3 course data.

2. Read the code snippet and look for areas of improvement from the security lessons learned from this chapter.

3. Using Notepad or your favorite code editor, can you re-write this logic with security improvements?

Understandability and Portability

Are variables given meaningful names and do the names of the variables represent the actual value that they represent? Are method names created to represent the logic that the method encapsulates? Is the code commented correctly? Are the logic and loops coded in a way where you can easily understand the programmer's intent? Can other programs plug into your code with seamless integration?

Maintainability and Testability

Can the application run itself? Are all the mechanics and logic run based on parameters? Are there user-friendly administration screens that can change those parameters without a whole lot of manual intervention? Can the code be deployed automatically?

Is there adequate debugging logic built into the code to work out complex problems employed in a production environment? Can these debugging techniques be turned on and off on the fly? Are there application logs or behind-the-scene warnings for internal problems that need to be addressed without the end user knowing?

Flexibility and Reusability

Can the code be modified easily without affecting a lot of modules and programs? If an enhancement is needed, does the code need to be changed in only one spot or throughout all modules?

Can the code be reused for other purposes or services? Is there a good separation of logic where reusable methods are not embedded with surrounding methods that are not reusable? Have repeatedly used blocks of code been formed into subroutines?

Readability and Capability

If I were to print the method, would I be reading a short book? Can a person get lost reading the many statements and method calls? Are the methods built for optimization? Are arrays and other collections checked for any memory leaks or overflow? Are the input variables validated before use?

Usability and Reliability

Is a GUI used? Is there adequate online help? Is a user manual provided? Are meaningful error messages provided? Will the software perform when needed? Can it handle concurrent users? When will it fail? Is exception handling provided?

QUICK CHECKS

1. Open the "QualityCheck1.java" file from the Chapter 3 course data.
2. Read the code snippet and look for areas of improvement from the quality lessons learned from this chapter.
3. Using Notepad or your favorite code editor, can you re-write this logic with the quality improvements?

QUICK CHECKS

1. Open the "QualityCheck2.java" file from the Chapter 3 course data.
2. Read the code snippet and look for areas of improvement from the quality lessons learned from this chapter.
3. Using Notepad or your favorite code editor, can you re-write this logic with the quality improvements?

APPLYING PRINCIPLES OF SECURITY AND QUALITY IN THE CUBE

They say in life that *character* is what a person does when he is alone. For developers, how you code programs when no one is watching over your shoulder is a true test of your dedication to quality and security. If your determination in this field is to produce great software and to become the best developer you can possibly be, your everyday decision making needs to be based on the beliefs that quality and security need to come first.

Quality Is an Art Form

Software quality can mean many things to many people. Depending on who you are and which domain you're looking from, you will have your own areas of interest to gauge. For example, an end user might view software quality from a perspective of usability, ease of execution, and responsiveness, whereas someone from operations might be looking for overall CPU efficiency, network traffic, and memory leaks (heap management). Project managers (PM) might define quality code as that which works in a timely matter, correlating functionality with costs. All these viewpoints and characteristics are valid and they are all areas that you will have to deal with while developing software. Software quality is more of an "art form" because of the many ways in which it can be defined.

As you now know, following a software methodology includes everyone on the team, from the PM down to the entry-level programmer. All members on the team should be involved with the quality of the product in their own way because of their own perspective. From requirements gathering, to design, to development, to testing, all activities need some sort of quality process that ensures certain capabilities. But no one is more responsible for the quality of the code than the developer. The developer is the one who produces code; he or she alone types in the characteristics that make the quality code.

Quality code means writing software for an intended purpose that must work when needed. This very simplified definition encapsulates two critical and sequential rules of coding:

1. Code software to the *best* of your abilities.
2. Keep that software running at all times.

How you carry out these key attributes will define just how good you really are. Great developers spend hours writing code, improving each statement, and challenging themselves to one-up their previous program. This constant inner battle is what's going to give you the edge over everyone else. The benchmarks and other quality factors used to measure how good your code is can be learned, but the skill and passion to do it lies in your hands. These things cannot be taught in a textbook or weeklong boot camp. This is where art meets science.

I will tell you what quality factors are and show you how to work these factors into code, but the bottom-line factor of quality will be measured by your desire to make it as good as it can possibly be. By adopting a disciplined approach to writing software, you will master the two above disciplines. Then, writing quality code will become second nature and you won't want to do it any other way.

Would You Know Quality If You Saw It?

You can tell if someone knows what quality really is by looking at his or her code. Otherwise, it's just a big game of buzzword bingo. At the end of the day, when all the requirements and design meetings are done, it's just you and the computer. The console is your canvas, the keyboard is your brush—do you have what it takes to make quality code?

Would You Know Security If You Saw It?

Security is an ambiguous term. It means a lot of things to a lot of people. As a developer, it means securing the application and its assets by making the code strong enough so that it is hard to penetrate, trick, guess, and deceive. Software security is hard to measure, detect, and test, and, worst of all, it's hard to prepare for the unknown. So, how do you know if you're secure?

Building *smart* code is a great way to advertise your skills as a secure developer. When you build software that can counter attacks, you should advertise the code's ability to sense danger by sending out messages to the user. I did this on a project where I could tell that the user was "playing around" with my HTTP query data on the application's URL. Naturally, my code sensed something wasn't right and was able to sanitize the query data; it then threw out a JavaScript message, as shown in Figure 3-6.

Figure 3-6   Smart code message

This message made a huge statement to the end user. It said, "Don't mess with me because I'm watching you and I'm ready." Remember, the low-hanging fruit is picked first; make your application as intuitive as possible so that attackers move on to the next application.

 Advertising the software's ability to counter attacks can sometimes provoke unwanted fights. Attackers and hackers like a good challenge. If you don't know who your users are, don't advertise.

Chapter Summary

- In this chapter, we covered two key attributes of software: quality and security. These two attributes must be dealt with as separate entities when developing code but with the same level of importance.

- You cannot have quality without security or security without quality. These two attributes complement each other very nicely, and both make the overall software product really great. Good developers should be able to identify what quality factors are in software and how to code them. Likewise, good developers should know how the software they develop can be attacked and what the weakest areas are in their software.

- "Good enough" is no longer good enough. Because of the many views and definitions of software quality, no one really had a good measuring stick for how "good" is "good." But now with software plug-ins from Web 2.0 technologies (for example, SOAP, RSS) and security, the measuring stick has just been shortened to either Pass or Fail. Your code is either reusable or it's not; it's either secure or it's not. There are no more prizes for "close enough."

❑ Quality and security are nothing new to software development. As you have read from Saltzer and Schroeder's principles, which date back to 1975, it's evident that security was always an issue. What is new, however, is the way information is being used and exchanged. The Internet and mobile devices have required everything to be executing in real time and at lightning speeds. This change in end-user activity has created a much bigger demand and focus on quality and security.

❑ We've learned what quality and security are and how to implement them. By now, I hope you realize the importance of following some type of methodology. Methodologies help the overall process by making everyday development activities predictable, continual, and, most of all, visible. You need visibility so that you can measure how well you're doing and improve the weaker areas. You also learned what the 'ilities' are and how they can enhance your software with quality factors.

❑ Software quality is an art form and it takes talent and ability to create software that can live beyond the test of time. Use lessons from this chapter as your foundation in both quality and security. If you can do this, you will be able to compete against the world's global talent.

KEY TERMS

asset — A valued resource that the application has to protect.

best practices — The handbooks of practice, which include administrative rules, guidelines, policies, and procedures that explain the best possible way of doing something.

CONSTANTS — A fixed value in a programming language.

efficient — Making use of application resources and programming logic with optimal performance and speed.

fail securely — How the software reacts when the system goes down.

software diversity — The ability of software to *anticipate* change of requirements, end usage, functionality, or definition.

software engineer — One who approaches the construction of software from an engineering discipline and calculated approach.

unauthorized — The validation process in which requests are denied the permission to use or view an application resource.

REVIEW QUESTIONS

1. The absence of _____ in the development environment would explain a statement like the following:

   "The developers are not following a similar pattern for designing and writing code."

   a. development methodology

   b. reusability

   c. flexibility

   d. usability

2. The underlying difference between the CBK and SWEBOK is:

   a. One uses best practices and the other lists standards.

   b. CBK is for managers and other security personnel and SWEBOK is for developers.

   c. CBK is for software security and SWEBOK is for engineering software.

   d. CBK is for software security and SWEBOK is for software development.

3. The absence of _____ in the development environment would explain a statement like the following:

   "The developers are using different tools and techniques to accomplish the same task."

   a. portability

   b. total automation

   c. capability

   d. flexibility

   e. reusability

4. According to Saltzer and Schroeder's design principles, what are the three categories that classify as a security breach? (*Hint:* You need to read their research paper.)

5. Into which of the eight design principles by Saltzer and Schroeder does the following design fit?

   "The developers should design their code so that proper authorization is checked when the initial request is sent to the server and when the response is sent back to the client."

   a. fail-safe

   b. complete mediation

   c. least privilege

   d. keep it simple

6. If a developer were to break down code into smaller modules that were easier to read and understand while at the same time rewriting simpler and more efficient "if conditions," the developer would be doing what?

   a. KISS

   b. performance tuning

   c. refactoring

   d. coding for reusability

   e. coding for usability

7. Into which one of the eight design principles by Saltzer and Schroeder does the following design fit?

   "The developers designed their code so that no update transaction can execute unless the request comes from a security administrator who is using the update screen from application xyz."

   a. fail-safe

   b. separation of privilege

   c. least privilege

   d. keep it simple

8. The _____ is an area of a computer system that most likely will be attacked first.

9. _____ is a secure principle that limits the amount of comments and other hard-coded or hidden data elements in system documentation and application code.

10. Building software that uses CONSTANTS for every value and depends on parameters to drive logic is an example of:

    a. secure code

    b. nature of danger

    c. software diversity

    d. refactoring

11. According to SWEBOK, what three things can be done to manage complexity?

12. According to SWEBOK, what are the two techniques used in software?

13. To address failing securely, what should be built into the code?

    a. Proper error handling

    b. Parameter-driven input values

    c. Self detection of failure

    d. Separate GUI requirements from business requirements

3

14. Which element is not a property of secure code?

    a. Confidentiality

    b. Integrity

    c. Error handling

    d. Availability

    e. Ensuring that the user has the appropriate role and privilege to view data.

    f. Ensuring that the user is who he or she claims to be and that the data comes from the appropriate place.

15. What is gained by keeping data unchanged by unauthorized users from the point of entry of the program all the way to the database and back?

    a. Confidentiality

    b. Integrity

    c. Error handling

    d. Availability

16. What is gained by keeping the service or transaction alive for the duration of the request?

    a. Confidentiality

    b. Integrity

    c. Error handling

    d. Availability

17. Where can you learn more about generally accepted security principles?

18. What is CBK's primary role in the coding industry?

19. You can have quality code that is not secure code. True or False?

20. A tester can easily test for the quality principles in code. True or False?

HANDS-ON PROJECTS

HANDS-ON PROJECTS

Project 3-1 Find the Weak Links

1. Open up the "Find the weak Links.doc" file from the Chapter 3 course data.

2. Create a list of "weak links" and explain why they are weak.

3. Provide a list of design alternatives that would improve this design.

Project 3-2 Find the Achilles' Heel

1. Open up the "Application Diagram.doc" file from the Chapter 3 course data.

2. If you wanted to attack this application, where would you start? Which server looks like the Achilles' heel of the architecture? What would you do differently?

3

CASE PROJECT

Look It Up

What are the 10 Knowledge Areas (KAs) that SWEBOK recognizes as "disciplines" that define the process of software engineering? Explain how SWEBOK's process improves the software quality.

CHAPTER REFERENCES

Bradley, Tony. 2007. Network Security: In Depth Security. http://netsecurity.about.com/cs/generalsecurity/a/aa112103.htm (accessed February 15, 2008).

Dupuis, Robert, Pierre Bourque, Alain Abran, James W. Moore, Leonard L. Tripp, and IEEE Society. 2004. Guide to the Software Engineering Body of Knowledge, Version 2004. http://www.swebok.org (accessed February 14, 2008).

Graff, Mark and Kenneth Van Wyk. 2003. *Secure Coding: Principles and Practices*. Sebastopol, CA: O'Reilly.

ISSA. 2007. ISSA Code of Ethics, Information Systems Security Association. http://www.issa.org/Association/Code-of-Ethics.html (accessed February 14, 2008).

McGraw, Gary and John Viega. 2002. *Building Secure Software: How to Avoid Security Problems the Right Way*. Boston: Addison-Wesley.

Noopur, Davis, Samuel T. Redwine, Jr., Michael Howard, Watts Humphrey, Gary McGraw, Gerlinde Zibulski, and Caroline Graettinger. 2004. Processes to Produce Secure Software: Towards More Secure Software. http://www.cigital.com/papers/download/secure_software_process.pdf (accessed February 15, 2008).

OWASP. 2006. Least privilege. http://www.owasp.org/index.php/Least_privilege (accessed February 15, 2008).

Redwine, Samuel T. Jr., Rusty O. Baldwin, Mary L. Polydys, Daniel P. Shoemaker, Jeffrey A. Ingalsbe, and Larry D. Wagoner. 2007. *Software Assurance: A Guide to the Common Body of Knowledge to Produce, Acquire, and Sustain Secure Software Version 1.2*. Arlington, VA: U.S. Department of Homeland Security. https://buildsecurityin.us-cert.gov/daisy/bsi/940/version/1/part/4/data/CurriculumGuideToTheCBK.pdf (accessed February 13, 2008).

Saltzer, Jerome H. and Michael D. Schroeder. 1975. The Protection of Information in Computer Systems. http://web.mit.edu/Saltzer/www/publications/protection/index.html (accessed February 15, 2008).

4

Getting Organized: What to Do on Day One

Upon completion of this material, you should be able to:

- Understand the Application Guide
- Know how success breeds success
- Define coding conventions

What makes some developers better than others? Can a developer produce secure code on one project and not be able to replicate those results on another? If so, why? This chapter addresses these questions and explains the secret to creating a software development process that produces consistent results in how the code looks and acts in any application. After reading this chapter, you will be able to identify what an Application Guide is and know the benefits of such a guide.

THE APPLICATION GUIDE

Organizations are realizing how inefficient the duplication of data is while they struggle to do more with fewer resources. Organizations want to leverage what they already own so that new software applications do not start from scratch; instead, they want the applications to use information and business rules from other applications. To do this, however, developers have to write code that is well defined, easily integrated and reused. The first steps in producing any such software are to plan and then define the context in which the software will be written.

When an application receives a "green light" from sponsors, the project managers allow the business analysts time to interface with the customers and gather as many requirements as possible before the developers arrive. This approach to building a development team is very common and considered to be acceptable in the industry. After all, why would you hire developers before the software requirements are documented?

When developers arrive on a project, they usually come from different hiring sources. Some are employees of the organization that sponsors the project and other devlopers are hired as contractors who are brought in for their particular skill sets. To complicate matters, those contractors might even be from different contracting houses and some of those might physically be in other countries. After they are selected to join the team, they are given the dime tour of the building, told when usual business hours are, and then shown to their cube. After arriving at their cubes, they are given a manual full of system documentation and told to work with a business analyst for their specific assignment. Sounds reasonable enough, right?

There is just one missing link in this approach to building a development team that is often overlooked. The missing link here is the creation of an Application Guide that connects developers to other developers and applications to other applications. The Application Guide is overlooked because many project managers do not recognize the need and most developers are protective of their work and territory.

I have used Application Guides and they have proven to be overwhelmingly successful in all of my projects. Although the Application Guide isn't part of a standard ISO/IEEE SDLC artifact, it will be just as useful and, in some cases, even more critical. To have a secure development process that produces quality code with security built in, you need an Application Guide. The following is what you need to know about starting this guide:

- Defining the Application Guide
- Creating an Application Guide
- Risks of not using an Application Guide
- Risks of using an Application Guide
- Why you should not hoard secrets

Defining an Application Guide

All software applications do the same thing: manage data. Therefore, common procedures and decisions need to be worked out before writing the first line of code. One of the most important documents on a software development project is the Application Guide. This guide is actually a tool that provides the blueprint of how a developer codes software on a specific application. It provides working "how-to" instructions for developers so that they can build a development environment with the same tools and configuration as other developers on the same team. It also documents project details, such as standards, rules, and coding conventions that the developers need to follow while creating code.

When developing code in a team environment, it is critical that the modules and artifacts created by each team member share common look-and-feel characteristics. This is hard to do when the developers themselves come from different backgrounds, companies, and/or countries. If each developer's code is not created in the same manner, chances are the application will be harder to manage, maintain, and debug. For example, if two developers on the same team use different tools and methods, the end product will not be the same. The Application Guide is the tool that holds the team together and ensures that all code is created equal.

After the guide is created, it will be treated as a contract agreement among the developers that states the standards and rules of developing code for a specific application. This agreement will be enforced during development and peer reviews. In as much detail as possible, the guide needs to state all the design patterns and coding styles that the developers should implement in the software. The more detailed the document, the easier it is for people to follow and work with. The goal here is to make all of the software components look very much like one another within the same application(s). The only way to do this is by enforcing boundaries and rules that the developers need to follow during software development.

The Application Guide documents step-by-step instructions on how to create the development environment and process. Where do you (developers) acquire the development software tools? Where are the tools located on your hard drive? How do you configure them (environment variables)? How should the application be designed? This type of information is critical to capture because of the army of tools and numerous programming languages you will be using to create only one application.

Not only is this information useful for keeping track of your current tool set, but also it is useful when you have to reimage your PC and you need these instructions to help you get "code ready" again. This is what guarantees that one development machine is set up and configured like all the others and that anybody can set his or her own machine with minimum downtime.

The type of information that is documented in the Application Guide includes the following:

- Where to get specific software (for example, URL addresses, servers)
- Where to install software (directory structure, hard drives, servers)
- Where to find license information
- Where to find deployment instructions
- How the software is tested and what tools to use
- Where to push code into production (server names, IP addresses)

Creating an Application Guide

Creating the Application Guide requires detailed specifics of the project, such as programming languages, choice of tools, and other plug-ins. Some of these specifics might not be defined at the time that the document is initially created. That's acceptable and is somewhat expected. In fact, it normally takes several iterations of "trial and error" before an Application Guide starts to work for a team. The creation of an Application Guide starts on day one and never finishes until the software is fully matured and in maintenance mode. This living document will continuously be refined, amended, and changed as the application itself changes. This guide is created so that those changes and their impact on the application can be documented in a single artifact. Therefore, when the need arises to re-create a development machine or just remember how you installed a certain tool and got it to work, it will be easy.

In this section, you will learn:

- When the Application Guide is created
- Who creates the Application Guide

When the Application Guide Is Created

The Application Guide is a living document that is created *before* the development phase of SDLC by the technical lead and it is maintained on an ongoing basis as the project evolves. The goal of this document is to provide a current snapshot of how the software is put together and how it currently interacts with other construction tools or third-party software modules. It lists the types of tools and skills that are needed to develop software for the application and what an individual developer will need to know to support it when the application moves into the maintenance phase. The guide serves as a recipe book on how to build the developer's environment quickly with little or no help so that all developers can build software using the same environment, tools, and standards.

The Application Guide is created after the software requirements and design are complete but before any code is written. This guide starts off as a simple Microsoft Word document that introduces the application's name, provides an empty table of contents, and gives a placeholder for revision information.

Who Creates the Application Guide

It is the lead developer's responsibility to initiate and maintain this guide. The Application Guide is a written agreement created by the developers for the developers. Because every developer has to write code for the project, every developer should have his or her concerns and suggestions voiced democratically in a collaborative meeting. The team decides which tools to use, which conventions to uphold, and any **frameworks** that need to be followed. Even though this is a collaborative effort, the lead developer has the final say in the event the team cannot reach an agreement.

Because the guide is created in a democratic fashion and the team members have had a chance to voice their opinions, the Application Guide will serve as the rule book for any future disagreements. For example, code reviews can be a somewhat subjective process. One developer reviews another developer's code looking for errors and poor design. This sometimes creates an environment that is not team-oriented. The Application Guide forces everyone to have the same opinion and work toward the same design. There is nothing subjective about it.

Risks of *Not* Using an Application Guide

You don't have to create an Application Guide. There are millions of developers out there right now who create software without one. Likewise, there are millions of developers who waste too much time reinventing the wheel. A lot of time goes into reading software white papers and APIs trying to reinstall software that you already had working. It takes a developer an average of 12 hours with an Application Guide to successfully install and configure all the tools he needs to start coding. Without one, it's common for an individual developer to slowly build his PC for a week and still not have it 100 percent.

 NOTE You can build an image in a development machine using software like VMWare or Norton Ghost and then distribute it to developers who just start it up and go. You can even have multiple images that all run inside a virtual environment independent of the PC settings. All of the development software is already installed in the image, so if your PC explodes, just get a new one and fire up the development image, sync with version control, and you're good to go. You still need the guide so that the underlying process is documented, but then you also document the "quick restore" process in the guide. This type of imaging could also be done on a regular basis (or even automated) to keep the image up to date.

Wasting time isn't the only risk you take in not following through on an Application Guide. Without an Application Guide to hold the team to certain guidelines and standards, it's easy to lose control over the whole process. Nothing is holding the team members accountable. This can decrease quality as well as increase the likelihood of security vulnerabilities falling through the cracks. If the team gets lax in the development methodology, their motivation for coding defensively (for attacks) is lost and they just want to get the job done as quickly as possible without any further thought on the matter.

How Chaos Can Creep into Methodology

The main risk that projects face when not using an Application Guide is having no control over how software is written at the microlevel of bits and bytes. Even well-managed projects that follow standard methodologies can have **organized chaos**.

As more developers are hired onto the team, it's easy to lose control over the standards and principles that you want to incorporate in the development process and software. For example, if there are a total of six developers, with three reporting to one analyst and the other three reporting to another analyst, it is possible that those six developers will be working on separate assignments in parallel to one another. If you do not follow an Application Guide, you might have six separate programs that do not look anything alike. This type of unstructured code can lead to quality issues and make it harder to handle security features.

It's All in the Details

If the code does not look the same, it will not act the same. As soon as one or two programs go astray from the team's original design and set of standards, a few bad apples will spoil the bunch. You see, after you have one or two bad programs (or modules), you cannot stop other developers from using those programs as templates, or starting points, for newer programs. After this happens, two bad programs turn into four, then eight, and so on.

It is important to have all code look the same, act the same, and be written using the same tools and standards so that future changes can be applied with little or no effort. You do not want to spend all of your development time reading someone else's logic of crazy programming techniques. In addition, if the code was not cut from the same material as yours, how do you know it's secure?

 I have run across situations where I'll be looking at a class and find some code that doesn't perform any useful function. Often, this is code that is being executed, but either has no output or produces some sort of output that is never used. More often than not, there is no useful function because the code was either carelessly copied from another program where it was in use, or the developer did not fully understand the code he or she was copying and left it in because he or she didn't want to take chances with removing it.

Risks of Using an Application Guide

The Application Guide is not a silver bullet and deciding to use it isn't going to make the code error free. There will still be problems, either with requirements, design, or just simple logic mishaps; an Application Guide is not a cure-all.

In addition to not solving logic problems that are going to exist in the software project, there are other risks that you take when deciding to use an Application Guide:

- More documentation
- The owner's manual effect
- The possibility that developers might give up on it
- The idea that it's just another artifact to babysit

More Documentation

Here it is, the dreaded word: documentation. No one likes to create it, read it, or maintain it. It seems like the mere mention of it makes eyes roll. But guess what? It's a necessity on software projects and you have to learn to love it because it's the only way to communicate effectively within a team.

TIP   Here's the key to documentation. Make it useful and relevant. After a document, such as an Application Guide or use case, is proved wrong, the reliability and trustworthiness of that document and all others like it is lost. After being lost, the trust might never come back. If you're on a project that requires documentation, make sure it's filled out completely and that it satisfies the need; everyone hates worthless documentation—and there is a lot of that out there. Don't add to it.

Granted, it's hard to write detailed how-tos. If one or more steps are skipped or assumed, the users might have trouble following the instructional guide. If the Application Guide abuses its trustworthiness, developers might shelve this document and try to figure out things on their own. Thus, you get a double dip of inefficiency: wasting time trying to figure out software configuration and wasting time filling out an Application Guide that no one follows.

Don't Let Your Guide Fall Victim to the Owner's Manual Effect

As stated previously, an Application Guide must be accurate and up to date for it to provide any value. This is not a glamorous task after the code has been written. The Application Guide's role is a lot like the owner's manual of that new 64-inch flat screen High Definition DLP that just got delivered. At first, the owner's manual is the thing you rely on for all the bells and whistles and operations. But, after you get used to channel surfing and plugging in all your media, you might never open up that manual again. Like an owner's manual, the Application Guide is very critical during the start-up phase of a software project. There are standards to define, coding styles and conventions to create, and after the project is in full swing, implementation and peer reviews to conduct. However, when all is said and done and the dust settles and the glory is over, the role of the Application Guide might fade into the sunset as well. Make sure it stays accurate and up to date because, sometimes, the sun has a way of coming back to shine very brightly on your team.

Why People Give Up on the Application Guide

When organized chaos breaks out in the development team, egos come into play. People start to wonder, "Why am I trying so hard when others don't?" Or, one developer might put in the extra effort to follow the methodology and stick with the Application Guide while another developer doesn't, and at the end of the day, no one cares. In fact, it's possible that those developers who do not comply might get an "award" from management because they might have coded more quickly. When these scenarios start to pop up on the development team, other developers will start to give up.

Methodologies come and go. Certain managers make high-level decisions, force certain standards on development teams, and then after some time, they leave. And when they leave, the "force" goes with them and development teams go back to the usual, organized chaos they started with. It takes discipline and support to use an Application Guide, but after people start seeing results and benefits, it sells itself.

Babysitting a Project

As a developer, you are going to have to keep track of many software artifacts. Business analysts will be handing you requirement use cases and misuse cases. You will also need to create design documents for yourself as well as status reports and issue logs for the management team. As important as the Application Guide is to you, some feel that it is just one more document that they need to maintain and keep track of.

Maintaining Current State

Another risk of maintaining an Application Guide is the babysitting process you have to do over an application. For example, if you are the controller of an Application Guide, you need to know the "ins and outs" of that application. Over time, tools will change, software versions will be upgraded, and deployment processes will be enhanced. As the controller, you have to watch for these changes constantly and update the document accordingly.

Keeping Track of Where It Is

Application Guides can be Microsoft Word documents, which are easy to print, e-mail, or copy. Keeping track of who has what is almost impossible. Therefore, make sure you have a good version control software package such as Microsoft SourceSafe, or an **open source** tool such as CVS to keep track of changes. Maintaining one Application Guide is going to be hard enough; don't complicate it by storing it on every developer's hard drive and sending out a new edition when it is updated.

 Occasionally, I get asked, "Because the Application Guide documents how the software works and is deployed, doesn't that give away all our secrets to would-be attackers?" The short answer is yes. As we learned in Chapter 3, keeping secrets is hard and we should have an open design. However, the best defense is a good offense. The Application Guide will not help a hacker attack the software alone. A security problem is a security problem. Your Application Guide could make it easier to find, but you have to assume that if it were there, it would be found in time.

Don't Hoard Your Secrets

So, why would you want to document all of your secrets? After all, this is a highly competitive field, and if someone else can easily replicate what you do, aren't you giving away your job? All of these are good questions, but the bottom line is that someone else will figure it out. And when this person does, he or she will share it and take credit. You grow in this profession by mastering your craft, keeping current, and implementing newer technologies where and when they make sense. You also become very valuable to your current employer if you're a team player and are willing to share your secrets and help others.

There are a lot of smart people in this field. Don't think that you can make yourself valuable by writing complicated code in four different computer languages using 20 different open source frameworks. That is not the key to longevity. Businesses need developers to solve business problems and share that knowledge with other areas or departments to reuse and leverage a solution so that they can concentrate on other problems. If you spend your time reinventing the wheel, your job will be the next to be outsourced.

TIP

As a developer, you are going to need to know how to use and configure many software tools. Each tool does come with its own API and configuration instructions and you do not need an Application Guide to regenerate the same instructions. But, did you know that you would burn weeks of development time if you depended on reading hundreds of white pages and researching how-to information on the Internet every time you had to re-create your testing PC (yes, it happens often)? Besides, there will always be some necessary, but undocumented tweaks or changes to files to get everything to work seamlessly. Quit wasting time and write that stuff down for later reference.

You want to be that person who solves problems (business or technical), documents the solution, and then publishes that document for the rest of the team, the departments, and the organization. That is how you become efficient and valuable.

QUICK CHECKS

Open up the Application Guide located in Chapter 4 of the course data. Review it for familiarity, and then answer the following questions:

1. Explain why you think or why you don't think this guide provides enough information to configure your development PC.

2. Do you think this guide clearly defines what is expected in your code?

SUCCESS BREEDS SUCCESS: THE BENEFITS

Getting that first successful project under your belt is the hardest. It takes practice and trial and error to get a successful Application Guide up and running. However, after you do, the project will run itself. The developers will communicate more effectively with one another as well as with the business analyst. This cohesion between the two groups will form a better development process that makes them work together as a whole, rather than as isolated individuals who might otherwise feel threatened or intimidated in a competitive environment.

This cohesion will produce better results both in the quality and security aspects of the code. When team members work together instead of against one another, the sum of the results is always greater than the two parts. This positive cohesion will spill out not only into the code that is produced, but also into the long-lasting working relationships you will develop with your colleagues.

Other project managers will take note on how well your team works together while theirs do not. They will ask, "What is it that makes your team successful, and how can I implement some of that into my project?" The Application Guide itself will not make everyone hold hands and sing "We Are the World," but it will eliminate all the fighting and disagreeing that usually pits worker against worker in a highly competitive, stress-filled environment.

A successful implementation of the Application Guide will have:

- Benefits for the industry
- Benefits for the organization
- Benefits in the cube

Benefits for the Industry

The **SDLC documentation** is everything about software development except for the code itself. The Application Guide is the document that gets to the granular level of detail that the developer needs. The Application Guide can be used as an industry standard guideline if accepted by the IEEE or ISO; for that to happen, more and more developers would need to use it and publish their results. This is the first publication that I am aware of that addresses the Application Guide, and I hope you learn from it and take it with you.

If an Application Guide works on an individual project, then it is transferred to other projects within an organization and continues on with success. Where should this success stop? If one organization uses it with success, would it work equally as well for other groups? The network of software developers is surprisingly small considering how many people are involved. Hiring IT talent on a contract basis is very common in this industry, so it is very common to see the same individual in many companies. Don't think those developers are leaving their experience behind. We all take what works with us—and if the Application Guide works, then we'll reuse it on our next assignment.

Benefits to the Organization

Over time, you will find other developers, managers, and organizations will be interested in what made your process so successful. After all, if the technology is similar, chances are what worked for you will work for others. As each application uses an Application Guide and a standard approach to software development, all code will start to look and act the same. As each project evolves, the same software characteristics (quality and security) will be propagated to the next. Over time, you will have a complete family of software products that can be maintained and managed by anyone in your IT organization. The Application Guide is a powerful mechanism that can be used to streamline a lot of redundant processing.

Organizations (big and small) have limited resources for technology. Their budgets are only so big and the C-class folks are always looking to leverage what they currently have. Therefore, the available software (for example, operating systems, programming languages, tools) and hardware (for example, servers, mainframes) are going to be limited. One organization will have many departments, and each department will have many projects. Each project across the organization will be using the same technology and computer languages because that is what is called "company standard."

Figure 4-1 demonstrates how one company can have multiple departments, with each department having multiple applications. Chances are high that those applications share the same technology (programming languages and operating system). Therefore, a proven Application Guide can be used as a template for each application, saving thousands of dollars in start-up costs.

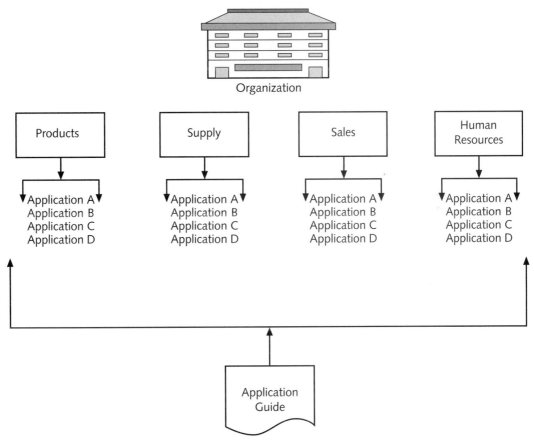

Figure 4-1   Application Guide inside an organization

If an Application Guide is proven to be successful on one project, chances are very high that the guide can be copied and reused throughout the department and even in other areas of the organization. That is a powerful little document that can save $50,000 per project each time it's used (this dollar amount is the result of calculating the cost of one developer working about three months to lay the groundwork at an average hourly rate of $65.00).

Code Reuse

If all the code on a given application was created with the same characteristics and design across all modules, there would be a lot of reusable components. Enterprise wide, the application share the following reusability for every software module developed:

- Database connections
- Capability to log user activity
- Capability to handle errors
- Start-up processes (user log-on procedures)
- Security (roles and privileges)
- Administration (parameters and metadata)

All these common components can be reused across many applications: the source code, the frameworks, and the naming conventions. The Application Guide is the key to software reusability. It forces all developers to use the same components so that all their code will look and act the same, which can then be reused.

Cross-Training

It is every organization's goal to ensure that there is adequate manpower to support its operations. That includes both business knowledge (requirements) and technical knowledge (how the application is coded). If an Application Guide is used across all projects within an organization, a developer will be able to move from one project to another with little to no learning curve. Cross-training developers on multiple projects will have already occurred with the Application Guide and all the developer will need to do is focus on the requirements at hand and not on the overall surrounding technical architecture.

4

By using the same technology, methodology, and tools, we are creating similar applications across the board within the organization. In addition, we increase the knowledge base so that our top 10 percent helps the bottom 10 percent through the use of an Application Guide. We no longer rely on the heroics of individuals. After the Application Guide is created, that tool becomes the technical lead used to enforce rules and behaviors.

So, what if a problem arises with a tool? For example, if you chose to use a particular script in your code and that script is no longer supported, what happens if that script is in 10 separate applications across the organization? This is called the "thousand-eyes effect." You hope with all those talented developers using the same tools, someone in the organization can find a work-around or a fix and share it with the rest of the projects. Because we use the same tools, we have the same problems. This is not necessarily a bad thing.

TIP   I once was told that using an Application Guide eliminates the "hotshot" developers and merely makes all developers on the team average. I say average is not a bad thing as long as average is producing secure code that is very efficient and built to last. If average produces software that is secure, efficient, and proven, organizations will embrace it.

Awareness

Knowing how the application's code is written, what the code can do, and what the code cannot do is half the battle on analysis. If all the developers are fully aware of the intricate designs, complex algorithms, and security features that the software offers, then just think how efficient future requirements meetings will be with end users and customers. Instead of concentrating on how the code will be created during these meetings, the developer is free to concentrate on the requirement itself and make sure he or she understands everything that is being asked for instead of how to code it.

Just the mere fact that there are software standards that will be upheld and enforced on a particular project is enough awareness to keep developers cognitive of their designs. They know that they will be held accountable if they do not follow the application's rules and that those rules are created to uphold security and quality features within the code.

Anything the team does to raise awareness for quality and security is a benefit to the organization. The Application Guide will enforce quality and security principles and guidelines, which, in return, will raise the awareness and importance of such features.

TIP   The Application Guide raises awareness in security because the project team will determine what data elements need to be encrypted, what security tools to use, and what security testing techniques need to be followed. These types of security-related design considerations need to be addressed and upheld in code, and the Application Guide will tell the developers what to do.

Quality Awareness

Secure code starts with quality, and the Application Guide definitely strives for quality. Producing software with quality designs, tools, and patterns will equate to efficient code—guaranteed. The guide forces developers to follow strict rules of software for every feature from data access to error handling; all application activity will be dictated by the guide. Because every developer on the team has to follow the same rules and guidelines, the group dynamics will start to produce synergy, which produces a quality team.

Benefits in the Cube

Using an Application Guide will bring many benefits to you and to the development team. Not only will it get all developers working from the same page, but it will also provide them with one common vision of how the code should be, where it's going to be, and what it's going to be. The main benefit is a formal, uniformed code structure, but other benefits include team building and the provision of accurate estimates.

The Application Guide will do the following:

- Improve the code review process
- Create a common language and understanding

Improving the Code Review Process

The Application Guide lays out the *where* and the *how* of the developers. It leaves no room for guessing or assuming. Each developer will know where to store certain source files (package or directory) and how to name objects, data, and methods. All coding instructions will be documented and enforced.

Eliminating guesswork saves the developer time and energy from analyzing rudimentary items. That time and energy needs to be spent on the specific requirement, not on what to call a field or where it should be stored.

Eliminating guesswork also improves the peer review process because every developer knows exactly what reviewers are looking for. The peer review process can have a negative connotation associated with it because of the subjectivity that goes into such an event. Typically, two (or three) developers sit in a conference room with a person's code printed out. All reviewers read the code and try to look for coding mistakes, bad coding practices, poor quality, and security vulnerabilities. An Application Guide eliminates all the subjectivity because all that should happen is checking to make sure that the code is written per spec and that it conforms to the rules in the Application Guide.

We All Speak One Language

Geek speak can be cute and funny, but to people who are not in the know, it can be annoying. By collaborating together and working from the same rules and standards, your everyday verbiage will begin resembling that of the other developers on your team. Names like "Worker Beans" and "Presentation Layers" will start to have meaning. Other developers will soon be speaking (and meaning) the same jargon and references.

These common notations will spill over to the business analysts who can then relate to you in terms of time and effort. They will get to know what those terms mean and relate to how you code software. The more they understand about your workload and obstacles, the more they can help in requirements and timelines.

4

COMING TO TERMS: DEFINING THE CODING CONVENTIONS

Your coding conventions define how the code is written and how it looks. After you make your decisions, you will live with these choices for the rest of the project's life cycle. Be careful and be thoughtful when filling out the Application Guide for these areas.

Because the developers will be using these conventions daily, it's only logical that they lend a hand in defining them. If the group helps decide, it is more likely that the group will cooperate. The following activities will have to be addressed by the team so that the Application Guide can help foster a secure, repeatable development process:

- Defining the look and feel of the guide
- Versioning the code
- Creating test data
- Governing standards
- Agreeing to disagree
- Maintaining the guide
- Testing the guide

Working It Out: Defining the Look and Feel

Every developer brings creativity and individuality to the overall project. Although uniqueness is good when it comes to designing neat little algorithms to complicated problems, it does not lend itself well to writing code. This is because the developers should be writing code that conforms to the same styles and constraints as the other modules in the same project. To develop code that will stand the test of time, one must use secure methods and principles as well as build for diversity (ability to change the behavior of the software with little or no manual work). To do that, it helps if the code was developed with the same design principles, conventions, and policies as other software modules that are being used within the same application. A project's coding rules set the boundaries for an individual developer.

Coding rules state what a developer should do and how a developer should do it while developing code on a specific application. It directs the developer on specific tasks and methods. For example, it directs him or her on:

- How to write loops and algorithms
- How to create input variables
- How to validate input variables
- How to look for software vulnerabilities

The more detailed you get in the Application Guide with project standards, the more uniform and secure the software will be. Before any programming commences, the developers need to meet together and discuss this subject. They need to decide which standards to follow and also any specific rules that they need to follow while developing. This decision will become more of an agreement of terms that they can hold each other to while conducting peer reviews (code walk-throughs) or system testing.

If this section is done correctly with very precise rules and standards, then every individual developer will be aware of how to develop code that looks and acts the same as every other module. Do not expect to get it right the first time. It can take months before a solid, proven set of rules and principles is worked out so that it supports the needs of the application and the developers.

The conventions the team needs to decide on are:

- Naming conventions
- Tools
- Coding conventions

Naming Conventions

An example of a naming convention could be a common field, such as a user ID, that is referenced in the code throughout the application. There could be various variable names that reference this field if the conventions are not defined up front in the Application Guide. Figure 4-2 shows how the same variable can have many names.

```
private String userId = "";
private String logOnID = "";
private String uId = "";
private String user = "";
private String id = "";
```

Figure 4-2   Many ways to code a User ID variable

Now imagine if you had to change the definition of this field to a different length or delete all instances of this variable out of the code. It would be very hard to find or maintain because of the loosely defined naming conventions. When developers code software, they tend to be focused on a particular task or problem and they forget about other elements that affect the application. Defining standard naming conventions helps keep all code uniform.

TIP   Using the same naming conventions with the same look and feel also makes it easier for others to read when looking for software vulnerabilities.

Naming conventions influence the naming of objects, files, and plug-ins.

Object Names

What do you call your software modules and the packages in which they reside? What are the method names? What are the table names? All software programs have names. And your method of determining what a name is could help categorize the code so that when you need to look at something, at least the code is somewhat organized for quick analysis. For example, in my applications, all the programs that access tables via SQL are called DAO (Data Access Objects). Therefore, if I need to look at a particular query, I can quickly review the DAO objects and not have to read through the other 20 or so objects that make up that program.

TIP   Object names are important and need to be meaningful. Follow a separation-of-duty architecture that separates business logic from presentation (HTML, ASP, JSP). Then name your objects accordingly.

Files

The directory structure of where each file type is stored also needs to be defined and documented. On any given project, there are many file types that make up the application: filenames such as .doc, .class, .sql, .java, or .asp. It is important to direct the team where to put each file type so that similar files can be stored together and not scattered throughout the application. Having a standard place for all similar file types will make maintenance a lot easier when making changes to the application. They will be easy to find and it makes for a more organized application.

Not only does having the same directory structure make sense from an organizational stand-point, but it also makes other tools more automated and integrated. For instance, if we were to create an automated process that used **File Transfer Protocol** to send all files ending with the .java notation to another server, we would need a physical directory to look in. However, if some developers placed their .java files in one directory while other developers chose different directories, then our scripts would not be that reusable across the project.

Certain files require certain security principles. For instance, files ending with the extension name .html *might* be okay to store on a different type of server (sometimes out of our security jurisdiction) and other files ending with the extension .class or .php might require more secure privileges. Therefore, standardizing the directory structure for the application is good for the developers and the tools, and it makes it easier to enforce security policies.

Third-Party Plug-Ins

Open source tools, frameworks, and code are becoming very common these days. The plug-and-play mentality is how you need to develop your software. Therefore, you will use third-party plug-ins for a lot of your data processing. For example, FOP is an Apache open source code base that can be used to produce PDF files. If your application needs to produce PDF files, you want to name one tool (provider) that does this service for you. If you do not mandate one, then each developer might choose his own open source tool or, worse, write a homegrown solution.

Tools

How the tools were installed should be documented because the intent of a standard tool set is to have each developer's entire PC set up the same as the others. This includes installing software on the same drives, paths, and directory structures. By following the same file directory structures, the developers' local testing environments will look and act the same. This mitigates integration issues, whether the developers are sitting next to one another or on the other side of the world.

Documenting why the tool was chosen is also good information that might need to be referenced in the future. While going through the tool selection process, you will gather a lot of information about which tool to use under certain conditions. If those rationales are not captured somewhere, it is easy to forget why you chose a specific tool over another, and you might have to defend that decision later on during the project.

TIP

By documenting the rationale, you're saying to the reader, "I looked at alternative methods, but I chose this tool because...." This type of rationale will justify your decision while proving you did your homework during the selection process.

Developers often make design decisions that have a lasting impact on the software. It is important to document the rationale that was used to make that decision so that no one else can criticize or question your development process.

In the end, the Application Guide is all about documenting decision making: why you chose one tool over another, one software version over another, or one procedure over another. If the rationale for your decisions is not documented, it might be difficult to defend them in the future. It's easy to forget why we decided to use a particular design or tool over others even though a lot of time and effort was spent researching and comparing. All too often we make decisions and move on without documenting our rationale. Then later we have to redo that research to figure out why we decided that in the first place. If the reasons for your decisions are not documented, you could waste valuable time on the same task months later. Or even worse, you could be challenged by other developers on different teams. You want to say, "I chose this tool for this task because..."

Coding Conventions

Documenting coding conventions will help keep the code uniform across multiple developers. Coding styles include rules such as where to place the brackets in the "If" statements and what naming conventions should be used. Figures 4-3 and 4-4 show how two different developers can have unique approaches to coding the same task.

```
public class SampleIf1 {
    public final static boolean DEBUG = true;

    public static void main(String[] args) {
        if (DEBUG){
            System.out.print("some message");
        }
    }
}
```

Figure 4-3   First approach

```
public class SampleIf1
{
    public static void main(String[] args)
    {
        if (DEBUG)
        {
            System.out.print("some message");
        }
    }
    public final static boolean DEBUG = true;}
```

Figure 4-4   Second approach

In the figures, each piece of code produces the same result but with two different approaches. How the code is structured should not depend on who coded it. All developers should follow the same design. This makes the code look more like all other code within the project, which makes it easier for other developers to read and analyze.

As you get more comfortable with coding conventions, you will want to become a master at using the conventions with style sheets, CONSTANTS, and bookmarks.

Style Sheets

Style sheets, or **CSS** files, in a Web application make all of the graphical user interfaces (GUIs) look the same across all screens within the application. Defining which style sheet to use and where to use it gives all the developers the direction they need.

CONSTANTS

There are always constant values that exist in every program within an application. Take those constant values and create a common module that holds all of these in one place. When it is a class all by itself or a common file that is included in all programs, CONSTANTS will save hours when reviewing code.

Using CONSTANTS will enforce the same spelling in all programs, enforce consistency, and make efficient use of server memory. In Figure 4-2, you saw many ways to code a variable named User ID. Using CONSTANTS will eliminate the problem of having many variations so that each developer isn't making up his or her own design or investigating how someone else did it.

As Figure 4-5 illustrates, you can tell a constant variable by looking at it. The spelling will be in all uppercase, which is the standard spelling convention. As long as every developer uses the same CONSTANTS per use case, the code will all inherit the same conventions.

```
public static final String USER_ID                          = "";
```

Figure 4-5   Using a CONSTANT

Bookmarks

Some people can remember URLs and others can't. I can't and, therefore, I rely on bookmarks to take me to those API instructions or favorite JavaScript how-to sites. There are way too many Web site addresses for me to remember—and I'm sure you have other things to worry about as well. As a software developer, you will often be helping out your colleagues (and using someone else's PC) and you will need to recall one of your favorite URLs that tells you the information you need. Keeping all the developers' bookmarks in sync across all development boxes (computers) is a great way to find information quickly and efficiently while you travel from box to box helping others.

Treat bookmark exports just like any other source code file. After you have a complete and organized listing of tools, APIs, and how-tos, check that file into your source code repository and have everyone on the team import it into their browsers.

TIP   I currently work from a variety of development machines from my home laptop and desktop to my company's workstation. I use software like E-Capsule Private Safe on my thumb drive so that I can carry my bookmarks with me and always find the information I need when I *need* it.

4

Code Versioning

Version control software should be a major consideration on any software project. It allows team members to safely store source files and other related documentation in a software repository other than the developer's PC. Version control software plays a major role in how software is developed. Construction tools should be selected and configured to automatically interact with the version control software used on a project.

Be sure to select a version control software product that allows for third-party plug-ins so that automated tools can interface with the versioning software. This greatly enhances the development process by eliminating all common deployment problems that are created by manual processing. Some of the problems that can be eliminated include the following:

- *Stepping on code*: This occurs when one developer overwrites another's code.

- *Not deploying all components*: This occurs when newer modules are left behind on the developer's PC and they never make it to the test or production servers.

- *Not deploying the right version of code*: This occurs when a source file goes through multiple versions and the earliest version accidentally gets deployed instead of the latest upgrades.

By the way, what is the method of your madness? What is the difference between version 1.2 and 2.0? How you version your software needs to be addressed in the Application Guide. Otherwise, you will have all kinds of labels and no one to keep track of the chaos.

TIP

I like to keep at least four characters in my algorithm, such as V. 2.1.3.1. If the first number is the major version, the second is an upgrade to that version, followed by minor enhancements to the upgrade, followed by enhancements to the enhancements.

In the end, you need to appreciate that versioning and deploying code are not team events. One person should control these activities and they should not be a shared responsibility. Work it out with the team and your project manager.

Creating Test Data

Creating test data is another task that developers need to work out and document as a group. How and where do you get valid test data? Which servers do you test on? How do you rebuild the development process on the fly? These are all important questions that need to be answered.

Creating valid test data is something all developers need to do to test their work. Hopefully, programs can be created to automate this task, and those programs need to be stored in some common code library to which everyone has access. Written instructions and sequential steps need to be written down so that there can be a standard, set way of building the test data. Otherwise, every developer will have his or her own unique way of creating test data that makes for inconsistent test cases.

Governing Standards

The Application Guide governs which standards are used while the code is being built. Standards reinforce the notion of a universal understanding across a broad range of developers, languages, and tools, and the implementation of standards is the key for software diversity and code uniformity. Therefore, a controlling mechanism such as the Application Guide will not only help keep track of which standards are being used on any given project, but also will hold each developer accountable for using them.

The three standards the Application Guide (and code) needs to incorporate are as follows:

- Industry standards
- Organizational standards
- Project standards

Industry Standards

Industry standards set the stage for how code should be developed and what types of design patterns or frameworks to follow. Look to the industry to see how other organizations are coding or how vendors create their tools.

J2EE is a good example of industry standard. Back in the day when JSP was just coming out (pre-1999), all we had was JSP files and servlets to code in. Then, industry standard frameworks such as Apache STRUTS started to pop up, and Sun Microsystems developed a standard called J2EE. All J2EE really means is that you're using a web XML to register and deploy with. However, if you are coding a new Web application in Java, it is best to use the J2EE architecture because that is what has become industry standard and that is what new servers will depend on.

Organizational Standards

Company standards might include which browser to code for, which code libraries to use, and/or how to promote code in the production environment. The development teams need to be aware of any and all company policies that might have an impact on the way the code is developed. The implementation of organizational standards will impact the code the most because it tends to narrow the available list of options as far as standards are concerned. For example, a development team may want to build in the use of new web 2.0 technology like webcasting, but if the company prohibits the use of any video files on the server then webcasts would not be a viable option.

Project Standards

Project standards are rules and guidelines that the development team wants to enforce in their code. Perhaps it is a common file that is included in all code, such as a footer or header that they want to use across the application. Or, it could be what tools and frameworks to use for specific use case requirements. There are a lot of alternative techniques, tools, and frameworks one can use for coding a particular task, which is why it is imperative that the development team use one standard way. When the code base uses the same technique across the board and throughout the application, it is easier to implement code reuse, debugging, and security features.

Agreeing to Disagree

After an Application Guide is created, all development tools are defined, and rationales are documented, project managers and other executive decision makers can use their authority to help enforce the guidelines and encourage the use of peer reviews. Otherwise, without the encouragement from management, such an arduous task of getting the whole development team on the same page will not happen. If an individual developer feels that their management does not think the Application Guide is mandatory, that person might not work together with other team members and might develop code using a different set of principles or none at all. When this occurs, major problems with teamwork start to unfold.

I've always maintained that if a person has an issue with the Application Guide (for example, if he or she thinks some governing rule is wrong), I would rather replace that rule with one that makes sense and continue working as a team. But, if a person has an issue with uniformity and using a standard guideline, I would rather replace the individual.

However, enforcing rules and standards isn't the easiest thing to do, especially with talented and creative people, such as developers, who do not want to give up their individuality and style just to become mere "typists" or "programmers." Most developers do not want to conform to certain styles or frameworks because they see it as a way of not growing or learning. Although this is true to some extent, the benefits of having a standard way of developing code certainly outweigh any individual developer's goals.

Managers and/or team leads need to explain very clearly how the Application Guide is a benefit to the team, other projects, and even the company as a whole. If the individual is still reluctant to change or conform to the team's style, the managers need to investigate and understand why.

Dealing with issues regarding the Application Guide can be a sensitive situation because it's usually created through a democratic process, meaning not everyone gets his or her way. If certain developers are adamant about not wanting to code using a certain framework or design pattern, the managers or leads need to understand their reasoning. This task requires qualified people with the skills and knowledge to know whether the individual developer has valid reasons. Hopefully, the developers can work through their issues before it comes to this, as they are very logical people, but sometimes "enforcers" need to step in.

If management and/or leads still find pockets of resistance to change after listening to reason, only one of two scenarios can happen:

- Change the Application Guide.
- Allow the individual developer to leave the group.

Each scenario has a direct and dramatic effect on the rest of the group. On one hand, it announces to all team members that managers are serious about making the project successful and they have the authority to enforce change. On the other hand, removing individuals who are reluctant to change allows the rest of the group to move on and grow as a whole rather than having the individual stifle growth and damage the team's dynamics.

Maintaining the Guide

As stated, the Application Guide is a living document that is updated as the development process becomes refined and improved. It is up to the team lead or the architects to make sure this document is maintained with up-to-date information. When the developers feel that they have enough direction and information necessary to begin coding, they will put all of the documented rules and standards into practice. When the guidelines are actually put into practice, issues and oversights are usually found and design flaws are uncovered very quickly. Common issues found with the Application Guide include the following:

- Rules that are not defined in great detail are sometimes documented with ambiguous statements such as "The team will follow industry standard coding conventions." Make sure all rules are well documented and supported with specific examples.

- Rules that needed to be defined did not get discussed or documented This sometimes happens during development, especially when requirements change. For example, when the Application Guide was created, generating reports in PDF format might not have been a requirement. When new tools or technology get introduced to the application, be sure to update the Application Guide and add new rules and/or delete the old rules.

- The rules, standards, or tools that are defined do not apply to the project. Perhaps these rules were just on someone's wish list or maybe many developers thought they would use it, but as the code was developed, that tool or rule was never applied. Remove any irrelevant directions, rules, or examples from the Application Guide. No one wants to scroll through pages of material that are of no use.

Whatever the issue is, there should be a process in place that handles changes to this document. Figure 4-6 provides a process flow that will help you decide when to make changes to the development process and when to document those changes in the Application Guide.

When an issue is brought to the attention of either the team lead or the architect of the project, there needs to be some formal investigation of whether the issue is valid, and then the Application Guide might need additional clarification. That clarification should answer the following questions:

- How did this issue come up?

- Should the rationale be updated with these findings so that these types of issues do not come up again?

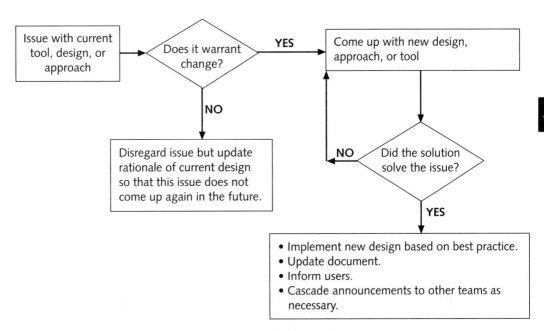

Figure 4-6 Defining a maintenance process for the guide

Testing the Guide

The Application Guide needs to be tested from time to time to ensure that all the supporting documentation is still accurate. I've found the best and easiest way to test this guide is to have the new developers build their own development PC from this guide using the step-by-step instructions. If your project doesn't have any room for new hires, another way to test this guide is to give a developer's PC a fresh install of the operating system and rebuild it from scratch using the instructions from the guide.

Testing the Application Guide is not a very exciting phase to carry out. It takes a lot of time and requires detail. If something doesn't work as documented, you have to investigate and figure out what is wrong. What were the missing steps? Does the installation process need more detail and clarification? One slight overlook or mistake (for example, stating "click Cancel" instead of "click OK") and development tools might not get configured the same across all developers' machines.

Also, if standards and rules are not specific enough, developers will not know exactly how to implement them into their code, which can cause integration issues. Taking the time to write detailed specs and then testing them for accuracy makes the overall development process easy to implement and reuse.

Table 4-1 is a checklist to help ensure that the Application Guide is complete.

Table 4-1   Application Guide checklist

Key Area	Data Elements	Complete?
Tool maintenance	• Are all the tools currently used on the project listed? • Does each tool have step-by-step, detailed instructions on where to get this tool? Are there details on how to install this tool? • Are there any tools documented that are no longer used on the project? • Are the same versions currently available for a specific tool? If not, does the newer version have the same functionality and feature that is used on the current project?	☑
Standards and frameworks	• Are standards documented in a way that new people know how to apply them in their code? • Are frameworks listed and defined? Would a new developer know to interact with a specific framework under certain conditions? • Does the document tell the developers to use a certain design pattern or standard over another one?	☑
Coding rules	• Does this document give specific instructions on how to code statements or loops? • Is the use of CONSTANTS enforced? • Does it mention which coding and naming convention to follow?	☑
Rationales	• Does the guide explain why the project chose one tool over another or one style over another?	☑
Directory structure	• Can a new developer build the directory structure exactly like everyone else's PC? • Are there filename rules that need to be documented and explained in this project?	☑

If an identified issue is valid and a problem with the current process does need to be addressed, then the issue goes into a solution–finding mode. Is there a tool, standard, or rule that can be created to resolve this issue? Do you need more time for investigation? Does this issue impede the development process? Does development need to stop before this issue can be addressed? Finding a solution to a particular problem can be quite time consuming. Investigating new tools, applying new algorithms, and interfacing with new third-party plug-ins can take a lot of trial and error. After it is solved, however, the problem is solved for the whole group and the application (and any other application using the same guidelines) instantly inherits the solution.

TIP

After a solution to the issue is found, it must be implemented into the application and tested. The Application Guide must be updated with the latest information. An audit trail of this document is handy to keep so that all team members can view the different types of updates that have occurred to this document. Most version control software has features that keep a running list of changes so that you know what was added and deleted. If you are not using version control software, a revision log in the document itself is strongly suggested.

4

CHAPTER SUMMARY

- ❏ The Application Guide is a tool that provides the blueprint of how the software application is written.

- ❏ The guide serves as a recipe for how to build the developer's environment on the fly with little or no help so that all developers can build software using the same environment, tools, and standards.

- ❏ It's common to overlook certain aspects of development that you won't even realize until you actually sit down to code and realize that you have an issue that needs to be discussed.

- ❏ The Application Guide is a living document that should be created by the developers for the developers.

- ❏ The Application Guide will go through different iterations of changes and refinements as the project evolves. This is a natural progression of a living document that improves over time.

- ❏ The Application Guide needs to be tested from time to time to ensure that all the supporting documentation is still accurate.

KEY TERMS

CSS — A simple mechanism for adding style (for example, fonts, colors, spacing) to Web documents [w3c.org].

frameworks — A set of software tools and/or code libraries that makes it easier to create applications. They typically provide functionality such as database access, templating, and session management. Frameworks provide the foundation and boundaries of how data is managed within an application.

open source — Free software created by the public.

organized chaos — A state of utter confusion in a supervised or managed environment.

SDLC documentation — A Software Development Life Cycle artifact, such as requirement documents, design diagrams, code elements, and test cases.

REVIEW QUESTIONS

1. Why is cross training developers important to a company and/or project?

2. A complete Application Guide should:

    a. list tools; explain how to integrate those tools with other tools; and document project standards, rules, and use cases

    b. list tools, explain how to design code, and document project standards and rules

    c. list project timelines, explain how to integrate tools with other tools, and document project standards and rules

    d. list tools, explain how to integrate those tools with other tools, and document project standards and rules

3. Why is it important to have all developers follow the same design patterns and frameworks? What happens to the code if they do not?

4. Who maintains and updates the Application Guide?

5. Would software development work without the use of an Application Guide? Why or why not?

6. Why is it a good idea to document coding conventions? What happens if you do not?

7. What are some key areas to look for while testing the Application Guide?

8. What happens when developers are left to follow ambiguous rules that were defined in the Application Guide?

9. What do you think should happen with nonconforming developers?

10. Why are versioning software releases important?

11. If a static variable such as a server name is used throughout most of the software programs, what should be done to it?

    a. Put it in a style sheet (CSS).

    b. Make it a CONSTANT.

    c. Put code brackets around it {}.

    d. Store it in a file.

12. Why is naming software objects (classes, program names) so important?

13. List the three key areas to which an Application Guide brings value. Provide an example of each.

14. How does the Application Guide increase the level of application security?

15. The use of an Application Guide will eliminate the need for code reviews as long as everyone on the team follows it. True or False?

16. The goal of the Application Guide is to make it easier for management to understand what the developers are doing. True or False?

17. Style sheets tell a developer where to put certain files. True or False?

18. The Application Guide can be written correctly the first time. True or False?

19. Every developer should create his or her own test data. True or False?

20. The lead developer needs to test the Application Guide for accuracy. True or False?

4

HANDS-ON PROJECTS

Project 4-1 Start Your Own Application Guide

In this project, you will start your own template Application Guide. In later chapters, you will be adding to it.

1. Open a Microsoft Word document.

2. Make up your own web project name for the Application Guide.

3. Add the categories similar to the example provided in the Chapter 4 folder of your course data (for example, software tools, coding standards).

4. Document the programming language you will want to use on this project.

5. List industry standards and coding conventions that will want to use with the programming language you have selected. For example, if you wanted to use Java, what are the coding standards for the Java language?

6. List the coding rules that you would like the development team to follow while coding (i.e. how to write if statements, how and where to write comments).

Project 4-2 Create Your Own Directory Tree

One of the goals that an Application Guide accomplishes is the creation of a standard development environment. That entails ensuring that all development machines are using the same configuration and file structures.

1. Create a directory on your hard drive with your new application name.

2. Under the application name, create all sub directories your application will need. That includes source files, requirement documentation, test plans, etc.

3. Take a snapshot of your application's directory structure and insert the image into your Application Guide.

4. Inside the Application Guide, tell the reader what type of files should go in each directory and why.

5. Hand in a copy of your guide to your instructor.

CASE PROJECT

CASE PROJECTS

Reusing Policies

Because reusing an Application Guide on other projects is a big benefit of using an Application Guide, what type of policies and rules do you think the organization would want for ownership and maintenance? Write three rules for how projects should govern their Application Guide. Do this by answering the following questions:

1. Who maintains the Application Guide and how?

2. What measures should be implemented to guarantee the authenticity and security of the Application Guide?

3. Create a policy that should be used by all team members when "other" application teams want a copy of your guidelines.

4. Add this policy or governance to your Application Guide from Project 4-1. Label the heading "Guide Maintenance."

5

Software Requirements: Hear What They Say, Know What They Mean, Protect What They Own

Upon completion of this material, you should be able to:

♦ Understand, analyze, and interpret assets

♦ Identify assets in the requirements

♦ Devise misuse cases

Software requirements describe the *what* in software applications. They are usually created and defined in Joint Application Development (JAD) sessions or by a series of meetings involving managers, customers, and analysts. These meetings produce artifacts such as high-level use cases, medium-level interaction diagrams, and detailed system requirement specifications (SRSs).

Interpreting these software requirements will be your most important job as a software developer. If you do not know what the analysts are asking you to do, you will waste hundreds of working hours writing code in iterations before you finally "get it right." This is what I call the "try now" development methodology. That is when the developer does not understand what the analyst is asking for and instead of saying "I do not know what you mean," he places a new version of the program in test. To avoid this pitfall and reputation killer, you need to become a very dynamic force during software requirements. You need to understand fully what is expected of your programs and how the user will interact with your software. If you don't, you will be that developer that businesses like to outsource. This chapter teaches you what you need to know to understand and analyze software requirements so that you can add value to the requirements process rather than just being an order taker.

What You Need to Understand, Analyze, and Interpret

Software requirements artifacts are normally conducted by business analysts (BAs). In fact, the BAs might have already documented the requirements before you (the developer) arrived on the project. All too often, though, the artifacts produced during the requirement phase are not detailed enough for developers to start coding. The reason behind this varies, but it usually comes down to this: The analyst documenting the requirements in the requirement phase cannot possibly go down to the level of detail programmers need for both quality and security. It would take too long and he or she would be bogged down with a symptom called "analysis paralysis." That is, the analyst would forever be writing and rewriting specifications.

Traditionally, BAs hand over requirements to programmers and simply say, "Let me know if you have any questions." This hands-off approach leads to programs failing to meet expectations and going over-budget because too many details have been overlooked or falsely assumed. There should be a dependent relationship between the developer and analyst that ensures that both individuals have done their jobs. BAs need to gather requirements from the end users and interpret those requirements into meaningful documentation. Software developers need to gather software requirements documentation and interpret that into code. Both groups need to gather requirements using two disciplines: functionality and security, as depicted in Figure 5-1.

Gathering software requirements is hard work. Most of it is people dependent and full of subjective statements that can very easily be misinterpreted. Requirements gathering relies on users communicating their needs to businesses, businesses relating those needs to project managers and analysts, and analysts relating those needs to developers. As you know, this approach leaves too many assumptions and unanswered questions. As a software developer, you must be able to identify those unanswered questions before sitting down to code. If you don't, you'll be "hitting brick walls" every time you sit down to code and wasting hours of your BA's time with constant guessing.

To find out what you don't know, you need to do the following:

- Understand requirements
- Analyze similar products or services
- Interpret with your peers

Understanding Requirements

When the project enters into the development phase and the requirements are ready to be handed off to the developers, the developers will need time to digest the information and get a clear understanding of what is being asked. The analyst and the programmer should have a few requirements meetings to go over the documentation and discuss the process before jumping into coding or design. The requirements come in three levels: high, medium, and detailed. Along with these levels, you must understand how to make the requirements meaningful and how to avoid scope creep.

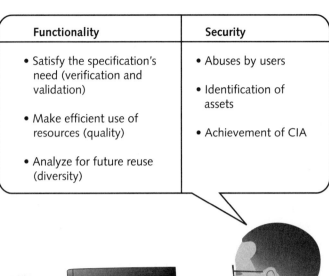

Figure 5-1   Developer's role in software requirements

High-Level Requirements

The type of documentation that should be addressed includes the high, medium, and detailed use cases. As Figure 5-2 shows, the end user logs into the application, views his account, and then makes a trade. With this high-level view, the programmer starts to see the interaction between a person and a system and the sequence of steps that needs to be coded.

Medium-Level Requirements

Each component of the high-level use case will need to be magnified to a medium level of requirements. These medium-level requirements are also referred to as interaction diagrams. Figure 5-3 provides an example of a medium-level use case.

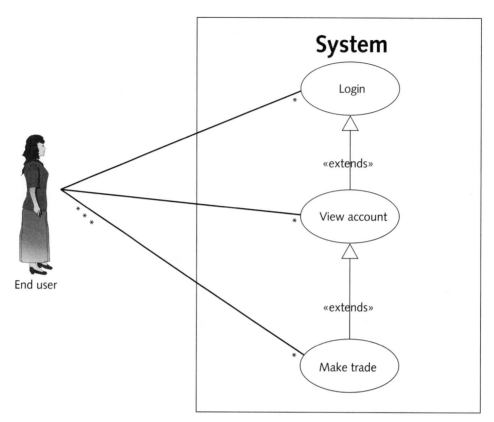

Figure 5-2   High-level use case for making a trade

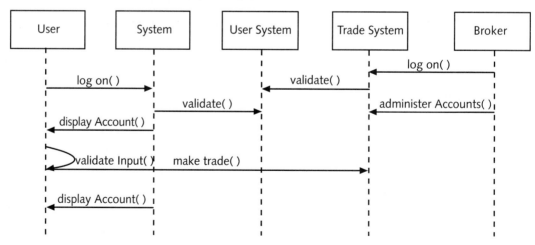

Figure 5-3   Medium-level interaction diagram

The interaction diagrams start to introduce logical data flow patterns to the programmer. They allow both the analyst and developer to visually see how the components and entities of a system talk to one another and interact with certain instructions. These diagrams start to expand on the original use case and break a high-level function up into smaller chunks of sequential instructions so that the developer can start getting a feel for the work set. After the programmer starts to get an understanding of what the system does and the types of interfaces with which he is dealing, he then needs to focus on the details.

Detail-Level Requirements

The details portion of the requirements takes the longest amount of time to define; however, if it is done correctly, the quality of the code will turn out much better than trying to work in features during the testing phase.

Detailed use case requirements can come in multiple forms: UML, Microsoft Word documents, and even e-mails. Typically, the details portion of a use case is in a Word document that explains in detail the sequence diagram.

At a minimum, you need to understand the following categories per use case:

- *Actor*: Who or what is invoking an event?
- *Role*: To what group does the actor belong?
- *Privilege*: What type of authorization belongs to the role?
- *Software module*: Is the module a stored procedure, Web service, reusable object, or GUI?
- *Software language and design*: What language will the software program be developed in and how (i.e., Java, Ajax, C++, SOAP)?
- *Input*: What parameters are coming in? How does the use case define them?
- *Output (expected result)*: What parameters need to come out?
- *Preconditions:* What conditions need to be present before the software program is executed?
- *Fail safe requirements*: What should the application do during failed attempts to call services or their programs?
- *Program name*: What is the name of the object that drives the use case? This information is useful for quick cross references for investigative purposes.
- *Program type*: Is this a Data Access Object, business object, GUI, or stored procedure?
- *System resources used*: What resources are used (table names, files, other use cases)?
- *Asset objects*: What is the asset with which the current use case interacts (i.e., a file, a database, or classified information)?
- *Asset object classification*: Is the classification high, medium, or low?

Making Requirements Meaningful

Writing detailed specifications can be a laborious, thankless job at times and it's easy to let go of the intensity after a few use cases. Accurate, up-to-date, and useful documentation will benefit the team in a lot of ways during the project. As questions arise, the documentation should be the first item that is reviewed for answers. When these questions pop up, ask the BA to look in the use case. If he still cannot find the answer, volunteer to review the code for the answer, but after finding it, ask him (BA) to update the document. If you (the developer) do not rely on documentation yourself, chances are the BA won't either.

NOTE

Software requirements are a touchy issue on most projects. If you have really good BAs who know the business and what is being asked, then you're in good shape. However, some BAs fall into this position/role (for one reason or another) and are not really business analysts but instead people who just know the business. Lack of training and understanding in requirements gathering will negatively affect the quality of the documentation itself.

Requirements are meaningful when they identify what is needed and by whom. Most of the problems with requirements occur with undefined (or unknown) data. That is, problems occur with requirements that tell the developer to go retrieve data from a database and display it in a report, but do not tell the developer what needs to be validated. So, often, when the developer writes code to extract this information and display it in a report, the data itself is wrong and the developer has to redesign the program.

TIP

Catching software requirements errors at the beginning of the development process is a lot less expensive than catching these errors at the middle or end of the process. Therefore, spend some time validating the data before you design the modules to display it.

Many times, requirements will tell the developer to display data that doesn't exist; to avoid this trap, developers need to spend some time in research and validate all database fields.

Of course, we can't forget that the developer sometimes has the information requested, but displaying it is a violation of the security policy. Remember, when BAs are writing requirements, they are just documenting the customer's needs. They are not the security experts. Thus, the developer needs to be aware of the data that he or she is exposing.

Last, the developer might find herself in a situation in which she has the data and is allowed to use it, but that data was produced with no validation process to begin with. Therefore, this can be bogus data (garbage in/garbage out). Just because the data is available doesn't make it accurate. The developer needs to take some time to research its origin and track down its creator. Is it a trusted source? How does the developer know?

Preventing Scope Creep

At the start of each project, the BAs will strive to get all the details documented as much as possible. However, after a few use cases are completed and status quo settles in, the BAs will focus their attention on other issues at hand. Requirements that were once discussed in two-way dialogue are now sent over e-mails or via voice mail. This is often referred to as **scope creep**. This is when requirements start to creep in from all angles without any due diligence or further analysis.

If you stray from a methodical process, your chance of missing something important, and thus letting in a possible vulnerability, increases. In addition to requirements creeping in from other sources, the use cases start to become less important. I have always maintained that software developers need to be the cornerstone and the driving force behind good requirements documentation. Because they are those who need to work from it, they need to make sure it is something they can use. I'm sure any stand-up, PMI-certified project manager will back you up if you request that the BA put together an actual use case for each request.

As a final comment on scope creep, remember that you are the person with the technical knowledge, and the BA and end users might not be as savvy as you are with technical information. They will not know when the latest tech wave (such as RSS feeds, podcasting, and Webcasts) truly is needed for the functionality of the use case. It is up to you to avoid adding on features that do not impact the overall functionality of the screen. You do not want to get bogged down with unnecessary, complex requirements if they're not needed.

 If you want to suggest alternative ways to handle functionality of a use case, start the conversation off with a leading sentence like "Did you know...." If your suggestions are welcome, then talk about what will be needed for implementation; if not, then let go of your suggestion and concentrate on the current use case.

Analyzing Similar Products or Services

When you interpret requirements, you need the ability to visualize the application. Try to understand what your users are going to do so that you can create software that works. If you can see yourself using an application like the one you need to code, it might help you to identify with the requirements. For example, in the "Make Trade Use Case" file from the Chapter 5 course data, can you see yourself making a stock trade from a Web site? Have you ever experienced this type of activity yourself?

Now, take another look at the "Make Trade Use Case" file from the Chapter 5 course data. How does this use case add value to the organization? What are the business goals and needs of your requirements? Some BAs might not want to give you the dollars and cents, but you can ask. If you can see how the application's requirements affect the bottom line, you will be sure to fully understand what type of features make (or save) the most money.

Visualization is powerful and it will certainly help your overall understanding of the requirements. One last thing you can do to help "see" the requirements is to get out there and look for yourself. Are there any competitors that offer similar features? Can you download trial software from another company that closely matches what you're being asked to develop? Again, you're not looking to steal another's work, but to generate some thoughts that get you in the mood for your tasks. By doing this, you not only prepare yourself for writing code, but also can uncover some answers to those unanswered questions from the original use case.

Interpreting with Your Peers

Even though we can visualize requirements and logically step through each task that needs to be fulfilled to service the request, we still might have a communication issue. Communication is defined as "the exchange of information between a sender and a receiver, and the inference (perception) of meaning between the individuals involved" (Bowditch and Buono 1985, p. 179). In a culturally diverse group of people such as software developers, that inference could be the difference between what needed to be done and what was thought to be wanted.

BAs would love it if they could just tell you what the the use case requirements are and then have you develop the application with no issues. This communication process, even though it is practiced, does not produce good software. Communication is a two-way street. You (the developer) have to be able to read and listen to instructions and put them into your own words so that the BA knows what you know. You must be willing and able to do everything you can to interpret requirements.

The ironic thing about communication is that a lot of developers go into the field of computers because they are not "people persons." Either they are introverted and prefer to keep to themselves or they are just poor communicators. Whatever the case, if you want to grow in this field and compete for good paying jobs, you need to learn how to think and how to communicate, as discussed in the following subsections.

Thinking Like the Application

When reviewing use cases for understanding, try to pretend you are the application. By this type of weird role playing, you are able to ask the BAs great questions, such as "How do I know if the user has closed his browser without logging out of the application?"

You can have fun with this exercise because it allows you to walk yourself through all the inputs, outputs, and logic to satisfy the requirement. As you get better in this trade, you will become very familiar with your technology and its limits and uses. As you gain this experience, the ability to think like an application will save you and the BAs a lot of development time and help you avoid those brick walls. It will also increase your understanding of the requirements so that it will be easier for you to design and code.

To think like an application, you have to know what comes first. What is the event(s) that triggers your whole software program? How is that event triggered? How do you validate that event? Who can do it and when? The more information you extrapolate for each event, the more detailed and refined your requirements will become so that you have a very clear understanding of them.

After you have the answers to what comes first, think about what the application needs to do next. Is there another system with which you need to interface? If so, do you know how to call it? Do you have all the inputs? Continue this sort of step-by-step analysis until you finally reach the end of your requirements. Highlight all the areas of unanswered questions and assumptions you found. Generate a list of your own questions so that you can push them back to the BA. Remember, requirements gathering is a two-step process and the BAs need to know if you have everything you need.

QUICK CHECKS

Open the "Make Trade Use Case.doc" file from the Chapter 5 course data. After reading the software requirements, answer the following questions:

1. Can you picture what the application is supposed to do?

2. How will it help the user?

3. How will it help the business?

4. What features do you think make (or save) the most money?

5. Is there enough requirements information on those money-making features? How do you know?

Now, create a storyboard or flowchart that depicts all the step-by-step executions you think the stock trade will go through before it finally gets settled. Write down a list of requirements or information that is missing from the use case. How could it have been written better? How do you know?

Paraphrasing Helps Everyone

After you have gathered your data and thoughts, sit down with the BA and start by saying, "So, what you're saying is...." Reiterate the software requirements. Tell it how you understand it. This honest, open-ended approach to communication is the best way to start the communication process. The BAs want the software to work and they want it done right the first time. They will appreciate your invitation to talk it out. If there are any "misunderstandings," they will be revealed now.

If you have to, elaborate on the use cases. Ask the BA if you can detail or add additional data to the use case. If he is protective of his work, he might volunteer to fill in the gaps on your behalf. Who does it doesn't matter; as long as you both see the glass half full, you are on the same page. Over time, you and the BA will establish a working relationship; then, this type of conversation will take place less often. Don't be afraid to speak out at first. It has nothing to do with "looking bad" or "looking dumb."

Pushing Back

Bring those unanswered questions and assumptions to the front. Hold the BA accountable for this information. He or she might never have thought about the type of information you need. Most BAs do not have a technical background like you do. A big portion of analysts come from the business side, a smaller portion of that group might not be up to speed on the latest Web designs, and an even smaller portion of that group might not even be PC literate (yes, they're still out there).

If you have a lot of unanswered questions during your analysis, push it back on BA's desk and ask him or her to fill in the blanks. The more you ask, the better his or her documentation will get (assuming the BAs get better at it). Over time, within a few use cases, a standard requirement template will start to surface and the BAs will know exactly what to tell you and how.

IDENTIFYING ASSETS IN THE REQUIREMENTS

Businesses are seeing security requirements gathering becoming just as important as functionality requirements gathering. With government policies like PCI and SOX, businesses are taking more responsibility about protecting sensitive information. C.I.A.—which stands for confidentiality, integrity, and availability—has a lot of companies realizing that if any sensitive information were exposed, stolen, or attacked, they stand to lose big money. C.I.A. gives properties that the application needs to maintain, but how? What is it that the application needs to be confidential, have integrity, and be available?

An **asset** is anything of value to the stakeholders. It could be a resource, process, or product that is assigned a value amount or that is associated with the C.I.A. of the application. When reviewing use case documentation, look not only to understand functionality but also to value assets. That is, find requirements within an application that will cause the code to interact with an asset.

As a software developer, you need to know if the assets you are coding are deemed valuable. As a developer, you will play a key role in keeping the application running safe and protecting assets because you are not only in the forefront of looking out for software vulnerabilities, but also you are the one who codes the protection. You are the one who will write the code and integrate resources that protect the assets, and you need to know what can be exposed and what cannot be.

The following sections help you learn how to search out and work with assets in the requirements.

Listing the Assets

When a project is approved with funding, there is most likely a *needs statement* that provides the main mission or purpose of the application. That main purpose might be the first asset. On the other hand, the data the application collects to provide that service or product could also be considered an asset. The whole team shares the responsibility of identifying assets.

The best place to identify assets is in the use case documentation. While reading the detailed specifications, look at nouns that are used when talking about system requirements. Often, those nouns are your assets.

Create a section in the use case documents and label it "Asset Objects." This provides an area in the use case that demands some thought as to how this requirement accesses an asset. Use case documentation is the best way to begin to identify and search for assets. By looking at interaction diagrams and reading detail specifications, both the developer and BA will come to realize where sensitive areas reside within the application.

Classifying the Assets

Asset classification is a process in which we categorize assets associated with use cases so that all pertinent assets are known to the developers and ordered from very secure (high) to important but not critical (low). For example, an asset that can negatively affect the C.I.A. of an organization would have a higher classification than one that does not. Asset classification is an important activity because it helps with quantifying extra time and money into creating misuse case and designing countermeasures.

The final artifact on asset classification is a running list of the levels of degree so that everyone on the team knows what they are. Alternatively, the preferred method is to publish the classification in the detailed use case itself. Asset classification can be carried out in many fashions, but the easiest method is to label assets with basic high/low terms.

After assets are placed within their proper classification, the developer and the project management team will start to get a feel for what they can control and what they cannot. In other words, they will learn what is a security requirement (high asset) and what is nice to have (low asset). Asset classification is a great activity to help identify which assets to protect from various threats.

NOTE By all means, make sure you know which assets are deemed high. Make sure your requirements are thorough enough that you know exactly what to do and when to do it. If you leave any unanswered questions on the table and code a piece of logic that gives away the store, you might have a short career on this project.

QUICK CHECKS

1. Review the following documents from the Chapter 5 course data:
   - "Needs Assessment.doc"
   - "Make Trade Use Case UC Diagram.doc"
   - "Trade Interaction Diagram.doc"
   - "Make Trade Detail UC1.doc"
2. Put together a list of of the use case assets.
3. From your running list of assets, classify each of them from high to low.
4. Separate all of the high category assets from the low ones.
5. Explain why you think any one of these assets is high or low.

Valuating the Assets

An asset needs to be valued from a business perspective so that the company doesn't spend $20,000.00 guarding an asset worth only $1,000.00. I've given up buying expensive sunglasses for the same reason; I know they will eventually get lost or broken, so I go with the cheap ones that look cool. Asset valuation allows you to put a sense of worth on what it is you want to protect so that appropriate countermeasures can be decided.

You can use several methods to determine the value of an asset. One method is to assign a fixed price (quantitative) to assets, and another is to determine the how and why (qualitative). In accordance with the CISSP process, three basic elements determine an information asset's value (Krutz and Vines 2003):

- How much the organization paid to develop the software.

- What the value of the asset is to the organization.

- What the value of the asset is worth in the open market (i.e., copyright).

The hardest part of asset valuation is to translate informational data into real dollars. Although assigning a value to an asset is an imprecise science, I use a method that I call "the bottom-line" price, as follows:

development costs + benefits + incremental risk = bottom line

In this formula, the first element is the cost to develop the asset (support and licensing), the second element is the benefit the asset brings into the company in terms of savings and/or revenues, and the third element is any additional costs over and above what would be lost in terms of the benefit. In other words, the third element is the cost of protecting the software. Normally, the third element would be 0 unless having the software's assets stolen would result in a loss that is greater than any benefit the software ever provided.

To help clarify this formula, consider an example in which the asset under consideration is the actual code being produced. The bottom-line cost would calculate in the following way:

1. Two people for 2000 billable hours at $100.00 per hour = $400,000.00

2. Savings that the company realized from implementing the application would bring in $1 million (this information comes from the needs statement in the Request for Proposal).

3. If someone were to gain access to the code, he or she would have access rights to secret formulas that would potentially put the company out of business. Current market price of the business is $4 million.

4. $400,000.00 + $1 million + $4 million = $5.4 million, which is the bottom-line value of the application.

QUICK CHECKS Working from the previous Quick Check, try to assign a value to three assets that you deemed as high on your list using the bottom-line formula. Don't be afraid to use some creative writing or assumptions. As with everything else, your estimates will get better as you gain experience.

Asset valuation is an activity that assigns real dollars to information. Without it, the sense of worth is not realized by the development team and, often, valuable assets are left unguarded.

5

DEVISE MISUSE CASES

For every action there is a reaction. Likewise, every function that the application's software provides is also an open opportunity for someone to misuse or abuse. **Misuse cases**, sometimes called **abuse cases**, are similar to use cases, only opposite. Misuse cases define the actor as an attacker, the means of how each attack can be executed, and the appropriate countermeasure that connects each misuse to the use case function. A misuse case is the reverse form of a use case and defines a situation that should not be desired by the application (Sindre and Opdhal 2005).

Devising misuse cases isn't as easy as developing their counterpart. For one thing, misuse case procedures and the knowledge needed to administer this exercise isn't as widespread and common as conducting functional requirements. Traditional methodologies spend little time discussing security requirements, and most users and BAs are not aware of software attack types, let alone the means of execution. Misuse case activities need to be administered by security experts who can look at a current use case and the design and determine what types of attacks are relevant to the software requirement. Those security experts can be anybody who is familiar with software attacks specific to the application's architecture and who keeps up to date with the latest tools and techniques in this field. Because you are reading this book, you are well on your way to being that person.

The following actions will guide you through devising a misuse case:

- Know your enemy
- Carry out relevant attacks
- Design countermeasures

Know Your Enemy

The first step in devising a misuse case is putting a face to your enemy. Who or what would like to attack your application and why? Brainstorm a list of threats that drive the misuse and then focus in on the threat's abilities, talents, and skills. The best method to use in defining enemies is to figure out the motivations behind an individual or entity that would like to attack you. "The attacker's motivations result from such factors as the value they place on the asset—knowledge, use, or denial—and their willingness to take the risks involved, including discovery and punishment" (Redwine, et al. 2007).

For each use case document, go through the following steps:

- Review the functionality of the application and determine if that functionality could potentially be tampered with (i.e., input values, text box on web screen).

- Is the information that the application transmits through the network confidential? If so, how can the data be secured?

- Define the software requirements of a successful execution of a misuse case. How will the application respond, assuming the defined threats are successful? This is more of a policy than a requirement but it is important to define such policies now so that the development team will react accordingly.

The great Antisthenes once said, "Observe your enemies, for they first find out your faults." Once you know who and what threatens your application, then you will know where that application's weak links are. As Figure 5-4 displays, there are three enemies identified to the right on the Login use case: the outsider, the insider, and the automated application. Because these three enemies can attack using different means, the misuse case identifies them separately (or into three separate misuse cases, one for each threat).

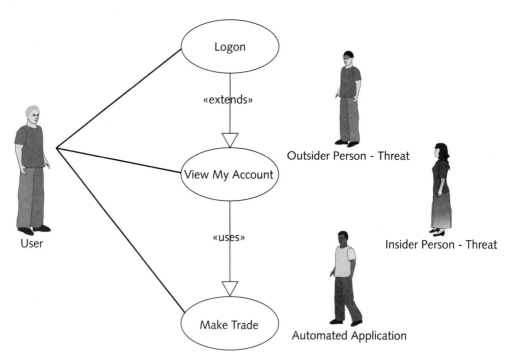

Figure 5-4   Example of misuse case actors

Carry Out Relevant Attacks

As discussed earlier in the book, it is important to know how each threat is carried out so that the appropriate attack can be documented in the misuse case. For instance, it would be hard to list SQL code injections as a threat if no one on the development team understands SQL Code Injections. Selecting the most relevant attack is done from brainstorm sessions with the development team and other security experts. These attacks, no matter how far-fetched, are used to generate ideas and thoughts that force the development team to start thinking like an attacker.

To generate a list of relevant attacks, do the following:

1. From the use case, list the types of software used in the functionality. For instance, which specific browser (i.e., Internet Explorer)? What is hosting the application (i.e., Microsoft Operating system)? What database software is used?

2. Take the list of software used and match it with any published known vulnerabilities. These vulnerabilities are published on various Web sites; the one that is most widely used is the SANS Top 20 at *http://www.sans.org/top20/*.

3. If the threat seems viable for your application, list it on the misuse case. It is easier to have the project management team tell you not to code a counter-measure for this attack than it is to never report the possibility of an attack.

QUICK CHECKS

You need to stay current with threats and how they are executed in misuse cases:

1. Go to the SANS Top 20 at *http://www.sans.org/top20/*.

2. If an application sends confidential information to its users, how could someone attack an e-mail server using Microsoft Office tools?

As Figure 5-5 shows, the list of possible attacks to the Login use case includes attacking interface, the data, and the application. The misuse case notation is documented in the same UML standard as functional use cases. The only difference is the threat is highlighted in a black background.

TIP

When listing attack types, let everyone on the team throw out options and document these options on a whiteboard in front of everyone. Have each individual explain why his or her threat is a valid option. The more experience and exposure the whole team has on secure requirements, the easier this exercise becomes for subsequent misuse cases. In fact, the listed attacks are very reusable and can be used as the starting point on the next misuse case.

So what are relevant attacks as opposed to non-relevant attacks? Consider the following scenario: A company's sales application database is backed up daily to a remote server that is

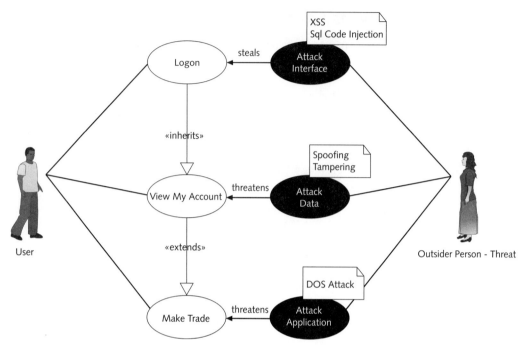

Figure 5-5   Threat types in the misuse case

located back at the company's headquarters. Even though the data is 24 hours old, it is still relevant to the business and desired by other departments within the organization. Thus, other departments write software applications to go out and get the data from the back-up server and use it in their software. The sales applications went to great lengths to analyze threats, to design and develop countermeasures, and also to implement security features such as data encryption and detailed logging within the application. Unknown to the sales application team, other department applications were using the data from the backup servers and they were not as cognitive about their security. In fact, security wasn't even a thought when those other applications were developed. As a result, those "other" applications were vulnerable to attacks and gave away all the assets that the sales team wanted to protect. No matter how much time and effort the sales development team put into analyzing and investigating secure requirements, one bad application is all it took.

The moral of this case story is that even with the most detailed and accurate misuse cases, someone somewhere can cause great harm to the application, and the development team needs to draw some boundaries to what it can control versus what it cannot.

What the application can control are the relevant attacks. To determine what is relevant, define the following:

- Preconditions needed
- Availability of attacker's tools

Preconditions Needed

What must the conditions be like for a successful attack? If sensitive data must be transmitted via HTTP, then an XSS attack might be relevant. But what if the application is hosted on the intranet only? Will the relevancy still be there? If so, then the conditions of an attack must be that the attacker has authority on the inside and must be targeting the script to a specific department or group.

Knowing the enemy preconditions will help the management team determine if the cost of developing countermeasures overrides the risk of taking a chance. As you study attacks and execution steps, you also need to know what the overall conditions need to be like for the attack to work. In Chapter 10, you will get a chance to carry out attack patterns and simulate these conditions, and the more detailed you are in this area, the more specific and accurate your testing will be.

Tools

What does the enemy need to execute the attack? If your software is written in such a way that it is heavily parameter driven and dependant on key CONSTANTS that are stored in a database, then is a simple **de-compiler** tool (which reads binary code) enough of a threat? How much time, resources, and material must an attacker have to carry out a threat and gain access?

The hardest challenge of tool selection is knowing what the options are. There are a lot of smart hackers out there that have their own homegrown tool or automated robots that attack software. Because you really don't know what they use as input, it is hard to define a specific tool that could be used to successfully attack the application.

What I have done to overcome this problem of not knowing every tool is to search the Internet for tools that could carry out the misuse case attack. For example, a lot of applications send user names and passwords to users in e-mail. A common misuse case that all applications must face is what if an attacker were to intercept a user's e-mail? How could an attacker do this and what type of tools are available to carry out such a task?

Document Relevant Misuse Cases

When the development team decides on which relevant misuse cases the application must be designed to countermeasure, those misuse cases need to turn into software requirements. Very often, when BAs gather software requirements, their focus is only on functionality and performance. As a result, secure requirements are not considered nor documented. Therefore, not only will misuse cases need to be created in this stage, but also the existing current use case (functionality) will need to be enhanced. Every countermeasure created is a new software requirement for the functionality use case.

Consider the following: In Figure 5-6, the user logs into the application and requests account activity. Upon devising misuse cases, it was determined that the attacker could try to guess the password through a series of pre-formulated calculations. In response, the decisions were made to reset the user's password after a total of four failed attempts. The application will send the user the new password and ask him or her to sign back on. The misuse case has produced an extra concept, Login Counter, for the original use case.

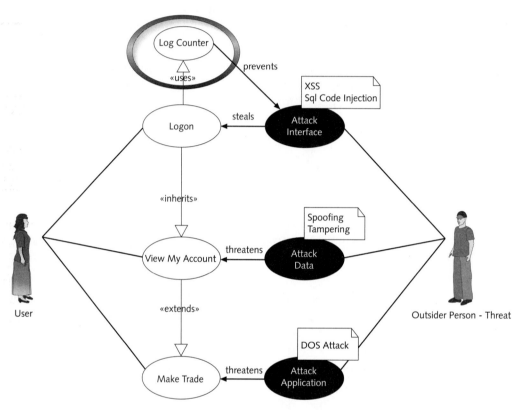

Figure 5-6   Misuse case produced more use cases

There is a dependent relationship between use case documentation and its counterpart misuse case. They depend on each other's interaction, definition, and existence as each requirement becomes even more granular in detail and prevents misuse. Together they complement each other's strengths and weaknesses and produce high-quality secure code. The relationship between the use case and misuse case can be defined through the wording of how each attack can threaten the current use case (Damodaran 2006). Descriptive words help make the misuse meaningful and specific when looking at the documentation and, most importantly, they make all requirements traceable to software need.

CHAPTER SUMMARY

❑ Software requirements can be a very challenging phase for the development team. The phase itself is very labor intensive and relies a lot on human interaction.

❑ The developer is the cornerstone for effective software documentation.

❑ The developer needs to make sure there are no unknowns when he or she sits down in front of the computer to design and code.

❑ By identifying the assets of the application and determining which ones jeopardize the C.I.A. of the application, the analysts and developers can apply proper risk analysis through use of misuse cases.

❑ Misuse cases define the attack patterns of a given attack.

❑ Misuse cases identify security requirements in the application.

KEY TERMS

abuse cases — *See* misuse cases.

asset — Anything of value to the stakeholders.

decompiler — A tool used to decompile compiled code.

misuse cases — A document that describes the attack, the pattern of execution, conditions of the surrounding environment, and available tools that must be present for an attack to occur.

scope creep — A symptom that occurs when original requirements start to spawn off into more, bigger requirements, eventually losing the functionality and focus of the originals.

visualization — An activity used for requirements understanding that allows the developer to think like an application and see the sequence of events from a systematic perspective.

REVIEW QUESTIONS

1. What is the developer's role in requirements gathering?

2. What is a software requirements document usually called?

   a. use case documentation

   b. design documentation

   c. functional information

   d. JAD artifacts

3. To help understand the overall application and the current use case, the developer can identify with the functionality by comparing similar features with other software packages. What is this type of analyzing called?

   a. use case documentation

   b. design documentation

   c. visualization

   d. functional information

4. To help understand a use case, the developer walks through each step of tasks and activities and makes sure all requirements are covered and understood. What is this type of analyzing called?

   a. step-by-step analysis

   b. thinking like the application

   c. use case interrogation

   d. defining terms

5. Why is communication so important to requirements gathering?

6. What are the two most important elements to know about a specific attack?

   a. You should know which attack type is most relevant and what tools need to be present for a successful attack.

   b. You should know what condition has to be true and what tools need to be present for a successful attack.

   c. You should know what condition has to be true and which attack is the most relevant to the use case.

   d. You should know how the attack is executed and who would want to do it.

7. What is the best way to handle communication issues?

   a. Write the program based on your understanding.

   b. Write a little code and show them how it looks before you are 100 percent complete.

   c. Say you do not understand and have the BA redo the use case.

   d. Have a meeting with the BA and paraphrase the use case in your terms.

8. Why is it important to have all the unanswered questions and assumptions defined before you design and code the use case?

9. If the requirements documentation is starting to get lax and the BA loses focus, what can the developer do to keep him or her honest?

   a. Push the work back to the BA.

   b. Fill in the detail for the BA.

   c. Have a meeting with the BA and ask him or her for the details.

   d. Tell the project manager.

10. Why is asset classification important?

11. What is the goal of misuse case documents?

12. Can you think of a weakness in doing misuse cases?

13. What is the key component of misuse cases?

    a. Use scenarios and attack patterns.

    b. Know the enemy and the attack pattern.

    c. Know the enemy and how to design countermeasures.

    d. Use scenarios and countermeasures.

14. How can a company end up spending $20,000 to protect a $1,000 asset?

15. How can you determine whether an asset should be labeled *high* versus *low*?

16. In team dynamics, what is meant by "pushing back"?

17. By using modeling, you are doing your best job to help mitigate all vulnerabilities during requirements. True or False?

18. The BA will include security requirements in the use cases. True or False?

19. Asset valuation is up to the PM. True or False?

20. Because misuse cases define a specific attack pattern to a use case, it is specific to the use case and, therefore, cannot be reused by other use case documents. True or False?

HANDS-ON PROJECTS

HANDS-ON PROJECTS

Project 5-1 Value the Asset

Read the following scenario and come up with the bottom line cost of the software asset.

My family owns an enormously successful restaurant. Ninety percent of our clientele come in to buy our famous meatloaf, which is my mom's secret recipe (and no restaurant comes close to it). Only 10% of our customers buy anything else. Until recently we only had three restaurants — all run by family members — and the secret recipe was known only to people in the family at each restaurant. We want to grow the business and we're out of family to run new restaurants so we decide to franchise. We decide to have a software system developed for our franchisees to help them run their new businesses. One of several features of this system is that it maintains the recipes for all the menu items. This feature cost $10,000 to develop and was believed to have a benefit of about $10,000 in terms of cost savings in printing, paper, shipping, etc. We have a contract with severe financial penalties for franchisees that attempt to share the meatloaf recipe, and we carefully screen each person, so we're pretty confident the secret is safe. Unfortunately, the development company screws up the security on the recipe feature and a competitor gets the recipe. Because all our company had going for it was the meatloaf, we lose $10 million and close down.

What would be the bottom line cost to this software?

HANDS-ON PROJECTS

Project 5-2 Analyze Requirements and Create a Use Case

The purpose of this assignment is to create, analyze, and understand requirements gathering.

1. Read the "Needs Assessment.doc" file from the Chapter 5 course data.

2. Create your own UML, high-level, use case diagram complete with actor, concepts, and interaction between the actor and application.

3. Create your own UML, medium-level, use case diagram complete with interaction among the user, concept, and application.

HANDS-ON PROJECTS

Project 5-3 Expanding the Use Case

The purpose of this assignment is to create, analyze, and understand misuse cases from the high-level use case created in Project 5-2.

1. Generate a list of bad actors for the misuse case. Describe whom you identified as a threat and what his or her motive might be.

2. Generate a list of threats/attacks that might be used against the current use case.

3. Provide at least one example of how a threat that you identified can be executed. You can place this description in the misuse case as a footnote below the diagram.

4. Order the list from greatest impact to least; try to guess which one of those attacks is feasible and/or relevant.

5. Has your list of threats caused the current use case to change in requirements? Does the application need to add any additional concepts to countermeasure your misuse cases?

CASE PROJECT

CASE PROJECTS

Show and Tell

Interview two or more professionals in the software development industry. Ask them how they do requirements. You might want to use questions like the following:

❏ Do you write software requirements, use cases, or misuse cases? If so, how?

❏ How do you learn how to understand software requirements, use cases, or misuse cases?

❏ Are the terms that you use different from the ones that I've learned in this book?

CHAPTER REFERENCES

Bowditch, James L. and Anthony F. Buono. 1985. *A Primer on Organizational Behavior.* New York: Wiley Publishing, Inc.

Damodaran, Meledath. 2006. Secure Software Development: Using Use Cases and Misuse Cases. http://www.iacis.org/iis/2006_iis/PDFs/Damodaran.pdf (accessed February 16, 2008).

Krutz, Ronald L. and Russell Dean Vines. 2003. *The CISSP Prep Guide.* Indianapolis, Indiana: Wiley Publishing, Inc.

Redwine, Samuel T. Jr., Rusty O. Baldwin, Mary L. Polydys, Daniel P. Shoemaker, Jeffrey A. Ingalsbe, and Larry D. Wagoner. 2007. *Software Assurance: A Guide to the Common Body of Knowledge to Produce, Acquire, and Sustain Secure Software Version 1.2.* Arlington, VA: U.S. Department of Homeland Security. https://buildsecurityin.us-cert.gov/daisy/bsi/940/version/1/part/4/data/CurriculumGuideToTheCBK.pdf (accessed February 13, 2008).

Sindre, Guttorm and Andreas L. Opdahl. 2005. Eliciting Security Requirements with Misuse Cases. *Springer-Verlag New York, Inc.* 10(1):34-44.

5

6

DESIGNING FOR QUALITY: THE BIG PICTURE

Upon completion of this material, you should be able to:

♦ Design for quality using industry frameworks

♦ Design for quality using organizational resources

♦ Design for quality in the cube

Quality and security features are no accident. These features must be carefully thought through and designed into the application early on during the development life cycle. The problem is that you cannot have secure code without first concentrating on how the code will be designed and used. This chapter is dedicated to the processes that will teach you how to create visual software design documents, which are critical for designing for security.

DESIGNING FOR QUALITY USING INDUSTRY FRAMEWORKS

Software design is the most important phase of software development. It is the last chance to uncover issues with requirements, security, and functionality. If you do not design the code for what needs to be done, the program will not work.

In the software development life cycle (SDLC), software design fits between software requirements and software construction (coding). Software design encompasses both software architectural design (sometimes called top-level design) and software detailed design activities (Dupuis, et al. 2004). Architectural design and detailed design activities flesh out software requirements and build meaningful pictures, diagrams, and charts that developers need in order to code. Furthermore, design documentation will make all requirements traceable and visual to assist the verification process.

Without conducting basic architectural and detailed design activities for the use case functionality, it is impossible to know where the code is most vulnerable to software attacks. The two activities that are conducted during design for functionality are as follows:

- Static design
- Dynamic design

Static Design

What better way is there to communicate what the software's components are and how they relate to one another than by drawing it out? The notation and style used during static design consist of images, pictures, or drawings of screens, applications, or software modules. These images are static because they do not change unless the software requirements change or become refined. In this stage, the analyst and developer need to define the big picture, that is, what is needed to satisfy the requirements.

Static design activities are used to help the analyst and the developer understand the overall application and the software requirements. It is considered to be the first step in a top-down approach to designing applications.

The most popular activities of static design include the following:

- UML
- Wireframes
- Prototypes

Unified Modeling Language (UML)

Unified Modeling Language (UML) is the industry standard software design notation for modeling systems using object-oriented concepts (Larman 1998). The UML documentation is used so that requirements and code interaction between **actors** and applications can be visual and specific. Using UML, the design artifacts are easily understood by all team members on the project.

Learning how to write and interpret UML at a high level is a must but beyond the scope of this book. Check with your team at work for the best resources to upgrade your skills.

UML plays a huge role in designing applications because the diagrams produced serve two purposes: functionality and security. At first, the UML diagrams and models become the blueprints of the application's functionality, which can be converted into code. Second, after the diagrams and models are complete, a thorough threat analysis can be conducted that will allow the security experts, developers, and analysts one more look at the overall design and a chance to look for areas of weakness. (Security design is covered in more detail in Chapter 7.)

UML has been adopted as the de facto modeling language by all the software vendors and government agencies. UML is the result of a combined effort by three leading authors: Ivar Jacobson, Jim Rumbaugh, and Grady Booch. All three authors joined the same employer, Rational, during the 1990s, and in 1997 they submitted the Unified Modeling Language to the Object Management Group (OMG) for standardization (Quatrani 2003). Since its inception, UML has been associated with object oriented design and the Rational Rose CASE tool (now part of the IBM family).

Developers use CASE (computer-assisted systems engineering) tools to produce UML artifacts. Sample tools include Rational Rose, ProVision Workbench, Microsoft Visio, Dreamweaver, Microsoft FrontPage, and any other tool that can create models, code, and diagrams. The beauty of CASE tools is that anybody can use them without needing to know the details of the programming languages. Most CASE tools are user friendly, and with a little practice, you can create meaningful visual artifacts that depict the software's design. Figure 6-1 shows an example of Microsoft's Visio CASE tool.

HTML-based CASE tools can be used to design GUIs for input and output. Modeling tools are used to design the application's architecture, software modules, and data that are housed by the application. There are even database CASE tools used to manage database design and implementation strategies.

The use of CASE tools has grown in popularity over the years, so much so that it is almost impossible not to use them in design. The result of a well-documented application design benefits not only the developers who need to understand the makeup of the application, but also the security experts who need to look for areas of weakness.

Even though UML is widely used, it is still an evolving language. Stay informed and relevant in this technology by bookmarking the following Web sites for more information: *http://www.uml.org/* and *http://www-306.ibm.com/ software/rational/uml/.*

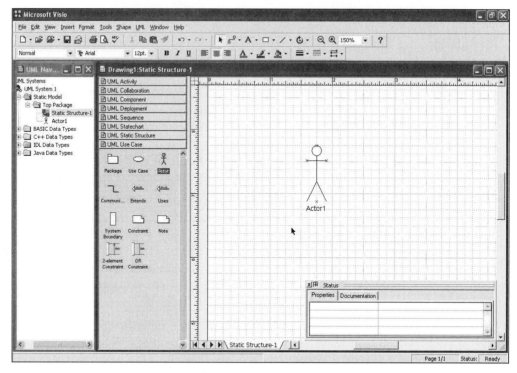

Figure 6-1 Microsoft's Visio CASE tool

Wireframes

Wireframes are simple drawings or sketches of what input modules are supposed to look like. For example, if the application needed a Web screen to collect data from the user, a wireframe would be a drawing of what that screen will look like. The purpose of wireframes is to provide a visual tool to end users, BAs, and developers so that discussions about features and requirements can be walked through easily. Figure 6-2 shows an example of what wireframes typically look like.

Using wireframes, along with the accompanying requirement use case, the developer and analyst will be able to communicate features and events of the screen. For example, if the wireframe is a visual drawing of a Web screen, the developer will need to know how the application will react to every possible event (click, button, mouseover, navigation) that the screen allows.

Prototypes

Prototypes are small programs with little to no business logic or supporting databases. Prototypes exist only to provide the end user with the look and feel of the final product. This static design activity gives all concerned an idea of the concepts, input fields, output fields, and

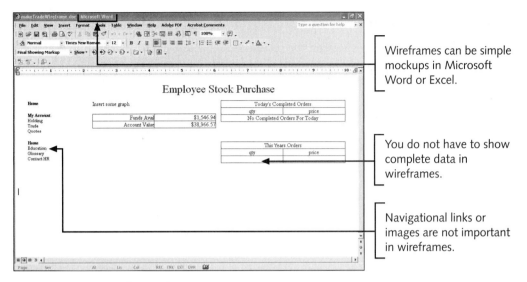

Wireframes can be simple mockups in Microsoft Word or Excel.

You do not have to show complete data in wireframes.

Navigational links or images are not important in wireframes.

Figure 6-2   A sample wireframe

navigation features available in the application. The use of prototypes provides a visual bench-mark for everyone on the team and saves hundreds of development hours from the "try now" methodology, which requires a complete product before end users get to take a look and make suggestions. Figure 6-3 shows an example of what prototypes typically look like.

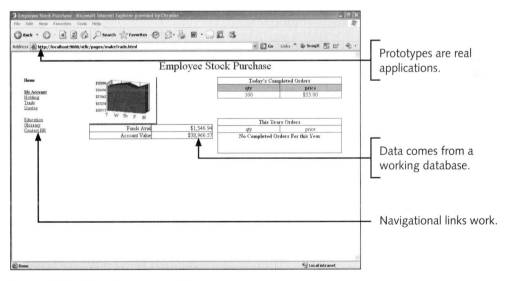

Prototypes are real applications.

Data comes from a working database.

Navigational links work.

Figure 6-3   A prototype sample

Dynamic Design

Dynamic design activities are the second step in a top-down approach in designing software. Dynamic design activities produce documentation that is used to describe the behavior and interaction of systems and components (Dupuis, et al. 2004). In these activities, the use cases, wireframes, and/or prototypes are decomposed into atomic processes that will provide the developer step-by-step instructions of how to write the program. The dynamic design process will break software requirements into smaller software modules so that the code will be easier to understand and design.

Dynamic design will clarify the following for the developer:

- Application concept
- Application interaction
- Application sequence

Application Concepts

A concept model decomposes the application into separate **domains**. A domain is a separate business entity with which software entities interact. Some domains are within the application's boundary and others are not. By defining the domains on which your application relies, the analysts and developers can point out areas of insecurity and uncertainty.

Concept models will do the following (Larman 1998):

- List the concepts (domains)
- Associate the concepts

Listing the Concepts   You need to define the concepts (domains) that make up the use case. That is, ask yourself what components are needed to complete the requirement. For example, in the "LogOnUseCase.doc" file from the Chapter 6 course data, the following domains need to be functioning for a successful visit to the Employee Stock Purchase Web screen:

- VPN token
- User
- Application server
- Database server
- LDAP

If the user were to actually purchase stock through the application and not just view the balance, two more domains would have to be present:

- Stock
- Batch programs on mainframe

As Figure 6-4 shows, concepts from the use cases are generally listed together on a whiteboard for further discussion.

Figure 6-4   Listing concepts

 Find the nouns in the use cases and prototypes. These nouns are usually concepts.

Associating the Concepts   After the concepts are listed, try to draw associations between the concepts and why one interacts with another, as shown in Figure 6-5. The resulting association diagrams will bring out the meaning of the concepts and the importance. An **association** is a relationship between concepts that tells the developer that one object interacts with another for some business reason that is not yet completely defined. These associations are not software entities like methods and arguments; instead, they are high-level models that state there is an existence of some domain that we need to use (Larman 1998).

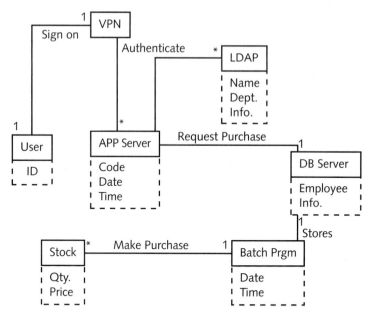

Figure 6-5   Concept association

After dependencies are out in front for all to see, you can start with the "what-if" scenarios so that you know which features are showstoppers versus which ones are nice to have. For example, what if the user logs on to the application and the database server is unavailable? What if the LDAP database is down (which is used to get username and department information)—can we still accept orders?

Once the concepts from the use case have been listed and associated, the end result is a conceptual diagram, as shown in Figure 6-6.

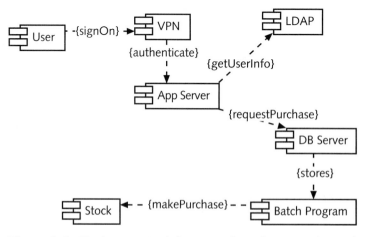

Figure 6-6   Final conceptual diagram of employee stock purchase

Read Steps 1 and 2. After you have read the background information in these steps, execute Step 3.

1. Because he listed all the concepts that are needed to order company stock, the BA just realized that no orders can be taken when the company's batch program is executing. Therefore, he mandated that the Company Stock Purchase application not take orders or display any information between the hours of 12:00 a.m. and 1:00 a.m. EST. See Figure 6-7 as an example of how the BA updated the use case.

2. After discussing the application's concepts and dependencies with the analyst, it was determined that the LDAP information was nice to have but not a necessity. Because the user has been authenticated by the VPN system and all of the user's main information is stored on the application's database, you now know that LDAP information (phone number, department number) is not required. See Figure 6-8 as an example of how the BA updated the use case.

3. To add what you have learned to the use case, open the "My Account. doc" file from the Chapter 6 course data and add the amendments shown in Figures 6-7 and 6-8.

Assumptions	User is already an active customer and has been authenticated by the company VPN system. The application will not be accessible between the hours of 12:00 a.m. and 1:00 a.m. EST.

Figure 6-7   Refining when the application needs to be accessible

---

View Holdings

1. System displays user account details
   a. The details that are returned from LDAP are not a showstopper. If the application cannot return the following, then still keep the request alive:
      - Phone
      - Dept Info
2. System waits for customer instructions
   a. If system waits more than the allotted time

Figure 6-8   Updating the current use case

Application Interaction

Application interaction diagrams show the readers how each concept (user, application, resources) interacts with the others. These diagrams should convey a general understanding of how the application fits together and works with all of the components that need to be created or used to satisfy the current use case. Figure 6-9 is an example of an application interaction diagram.

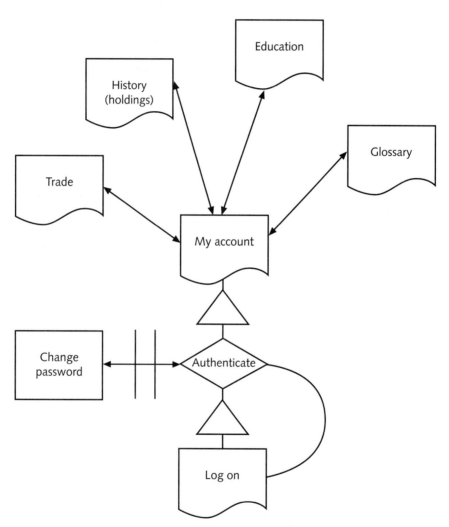

Figure 6-9   Application interaction diagram

It is important to associate the concepts that are dependent on the current use case. Very often, this information is assumed or overlooked, and it is not until you actually sit down to code that you realize you're missing something.

Application Sequence

After the concepts are integrated, communication can begin between the concepts. Application system sequence diagrams model the communication between concepts. You can use the prototype screens and interaction diagrams as the drivers for determining how many sequence diagrams need to be discussed. For example, Figure 6-10 shows the prototype screen from the "myAccountPrototype.html" file from the Chapter 6 course data. In this figure, questions that need to be asked and answered for every link, text box, button, and data elements are identified.

Figure 6-10   Sequence questions

Creating system sequence diagrams is easy. Draw the use on one side of the model and the application on the other side. Record each **system event** that is generated by the user to the application. Name each system event according to the type of operation to which the application will respond. In addition to the name of the event, document what input parameters are needed to satisfy the request. Figure 6-11 shows what a system sequence diagram should look like when documenting a customer logon event.

In the figure, the system event is logOn and the parameters passed are noted in parentheses as (userName, pwd). System sequence diagrams have a tremendous benefit for both analyst and developer. They provide diagrams that not only help define how the application will function, but also provide the starting block for object modeling (class diagrams).

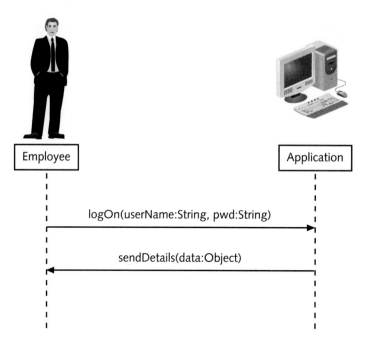

Figure 6-11   Documenting a customer logon

DESIGNING FOR QUALITY USING ORGANIZATIONAL RESOURCES

Design artifacts, such as conceptual models, interaction diagrams, and sequence diagrams, need detailed attention from the analyst and the developers. Naturally, the analysts need to ensure that these documents are complete and specific to make sure the use case requirements will be developed as specified. You (the developer) need to understand how these models work because these documents are your last chance to make sure you understand what you need to code.

Before agreeing to development timelines and promising to develop software as specified, you should review the design artifacts. To review these artifacts, you need to do the following:

- Collaborate with the analysts
- Map the data

Collaborating with the Analysts

In the design phase, you will interact with the analysts. The **analysts** are the group of people you rely on to ask business questions, clarify requirements, and interface with end users. You need to make sure that they and you are on the same page about what the programs and other interfaces look like and how the application should work.

During the boom days when any company ending with a .com was well financed, developers did not have to interact too much with analysts. There were business analysts who talked to system analysts about the requirements, and together they produced artifacts such as use cases and wireframes (screen mockups). Those artifacts then were handed over to technical writers who would make sure all documentation was completed and well noted (for example, UML, use case). All those artifacts were then handed off to technical architects and team leads for further analysis and review. By the time use cases and wireframes landed on the desks of the developers, there was nothing more that needed to be done other than to code the programs.

When the dot com era burst, businesses began to streamline the software development process a bit. Most IT shops today operate on budgets just big enough to cover the hourly rates of development. Therefore, businesses demand much more out of the software developers than any other group on the team. What was once someone else's sole responsibility (analysis and design) is now yours. You (the developer) will need to talk directly to the BA and make sure you have a clear understanding of how the application should look, feel, and operate.

The best ways to collaborate with the analysts are by:

- Hosting whiteboard meetings
- Asking the right questions
- Finalizing the drawings

Whiteboard Meetings

The purpose of whiteboard meetings is to provide an open communication between the analysts and developer(s). During this communication process, the analysts will verbally discuss the current use case and how they visualize the user interfacing with the application. Designing software is a very complex task and no one Microsoft Word document is going to be enough to explain it. The developer and analyst must collaborate on how to divide and conquer each requirement into smaller, more comprehensible units of work. Design meetings at the whiteboard are typically conducted in a conference room with the analyst and developer.

As Figure 6-12 depicts, whiteboard meetings provide a very efficient way of collaborating with the analyst. The **whiteboard** serves as a convenient tool to allow both parties to draw pictures, highlight key issues, and identify problems.

The following items are what you need to have before you walk out of the whiteboard meeting:

- Clear definition of prototypes and wireframes
- Clear definition of data access
- Clear definition of system's sequence of events
- List of requirement weaknesses that still need to be defined or thought through by the analysts

Figure 6-12   Drawing at the whiteboard

Use colored markers so that you can distinguish requirements from questions. In addition, section off a portion of the whiteboard so that questions with unknown answers can be tracked and tabled for later discussions. At the end of the meeting, copy the information from the whiteboard into a Word document and e-mail it to the meeting participants as well as to the project manager.

Asking the Right Questions

Asking the right questions when meeting with the analysts will not only make good use of time but also will keep the conversation on topic and focused. Typically, you have only an hour of the analyst's time, so you need to get to the heart of your concerns because after he or she leaves the room, you will have to wait a long time before getting another meeting.

In design, you need to know what the application will do (use cases), how the application will look (wireframes), and what needs to happen (sequence diagrams). Here is how you can ask the questions that will cover all the issues:

1. Start off by asking open-ended questions to understand the analyst's vision:

   - So, how do you envision this working?

   - How are the users going to use the application? Where will they be sitting?

2. Next, switch the focus to the GUIs and start to extract information about the interfaces:

   - What do you think it's going to look like?

- How will users navigate from screen to screen or from program to program?

3. Finally, get a handle on the type of transactions that are needed to satisfy the user's request:

- What types of options are available to the user? What should the application do when these options are used?

- What are all the interfaces, logs, and files that need to be touched per the use case?

6

These types of open-ended questions will get the analysts to open up and start discussing their requirements in terms of application executions.

Finalizing the Drawing

Design meetings will produce a lot of drawings and notations on the whiteboard. All of your diagrams, notes, and questions need to be copied and put into a formal UML drawing. Copy the sequence of events into a CASE tool, such as Microsoft Visio, or any other tool that can produce UML notations. When your UML sequence diagrams are complete, check them into a code repository tool (for example, Microsoft Source Safe or Dimensions) and e-mail them out to all the developers and PM so that they have a copy and a source of meeting minutes.

If there are any questions that need to be answered or further investigated, delegate a person on the team (analyst or developer) to be responsible for tracking down the answer. If no one is held accountable, these questions or issues will not be resolved. They will either keep coming up in future design meetings or be forgotten altogether. Don't let anything (or anyone) slip by.

Data Mapping: The Inputs and Outputs

Data mapping is the best activity you can do to ensure you have complete requirements and that any program can be called secure. The **inputs** are the data elements that are coming into the application from another source (screen, input device) and that are required to produce the desired result. The **outputs** are the data elements coming from the application or another source that were requested, updated, or created based on the input request.

Data mapping is the cornerstone to good design. It will catch major flaws in the requirements as well as set the expectations of the data. There are two activities in data mapping:

- Mapping the inputs
- Mapping the outputs

Mapping the Inputs

Using system sequence diagrams along with prototypes or wireframes, the developer and the analyst need to define every input parameter. They need to have a good handle on what types of data elements are coming into the application. The goal of input mapping is to determine the business logic needed to validate the input (authenticate and authorize) and then determine what to do with it. This can be achieved in the following steps:

1. Cleansing the input
2. Authorizing the input: pass or fail

Input cleansing is the key for secure code. Validating the data that comes into the application will prevent data tampering or other coding problems that could happen downstream.

According to the CBK (Common Body of Knowledge), input cleansing can be defined as the process of discarding input that does not conform to what is expected (Redwine, et al. 2007). That is, it involves identifying specifically what is *not* acceptable as valid input into the application. Many of the attacks on security currently employed rely on the specific formulation of input to cripple the security function. Designers/developers need to know this if they are going to combat it.

To cleanse the input, you need to define what each and every input parameter is expected to look like and then determine how to validate it. That is done by:

- *Defining business rules*: Ask the analyst what the inputs look like. How many characters or numbers? What are valid characters and numbers? How will you limit the number of options available?

- *Validating the format of input to business rule*: Validation of input is done through the use of a computer language.

Figure 6-13 provides an example of a function validating an input object by comparing the input with a listing of available characters.

```
var alphabet='abcdefghijklmnopqrstuvwxyzABCDEFGHIJKLMNOPQRSTUVWXYZ'

// This function returns a boolean indicating whether passed
// object value is alphanumeric.
function isAlphanumeric(objVal){
  if(objVal==null){
    return false
  }
  var charSet=alphabet
  for(var i=0;i<objVal.length;i++){
    if(charSet.indexOf(objVal.charAt(i))<0){
      return false
    }
  }
  return true
}
```

Figure 6-13 Validating input

After you have defined what the input looks like and how to validate it, what do you do with it? If the input validation passes, is that enough authentication for servicing the request? How about authentication? How do you know where the input came from? Will the analyst be able to provide business information about the input parameter?

If the input fails authentication or authorization, what do you do? What does the BA want you to do? What are the error messages, logs, and alerts that should be sent? These types of questions are imperative to ensure a secure application and they are easily overlooked in the requirements use case.

 After reviewing the sequence diagram for the "Log On Use Case.doc" use case, you determine that the username and password definition are undefined. Open up the "Log On Use Case.doc" use case from the Chapter 6 course data and add the revision to the username and password input parameters, as shown in Figure 6-14.

QUICK CHECKS

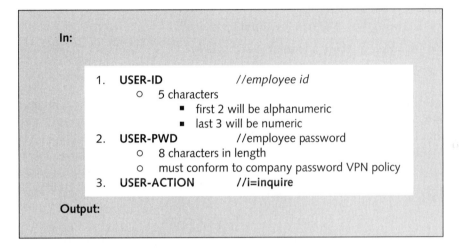

In:

1. **USER-ID**   //employee id
   - 5 characters
     - first 2 will be alphanumeric
     - last 3 will be numeric
2. **USER-PWD**   //employee password
   - 8 characters in length
   - must conform to company password VPN policy
3. **USER-ACTION**   //i=inquire

Output:

Figure 6-14   Log On use case revision

Bad Lists Versus Good Lists   **Bad lists** are data elements that are unknown; examples include a test area where a user can type just about anything or a third-party data feed that sends data transactions to your application. Creating a running list of unknown variables and where they exist in your application will help the developers design for failures for these events.

 I usually go back to the CASE tool and use a flashy color like red to indicate that this screen or system event has an unknown input. Later, when I sit down with my other developers (as discussed in Chapter 7), I will know what to be cautious of and, therefore, how to code for it.

TIP

Good lists are data elements that are known and well defined. They are input variables that can be authenticated and authorized by the application. By tracking the good data elements, the developers use certain assumptions built in to the design of the application, thereby avoiding the need for designing costly countermeasures.

Mapping the Outputs

Database design concepts and data structures are beyond the scope of this book. Proper use of storing data in tables is a whole book in itself. I would highly advise you to take a database class to learn more about database systems and DBMS (database management system) components. I am not going to teach you how to create a database. I do, however, want to walk you through the process of validating and verifying the output. Very often, users will ask for data that simply doesn't exist. Before you commit to producing the required use case, make sure you know exactly where the data comes from and if you can access it.

The output mapping activity includes the following:

- Determining if the data exists

- Designing the query

- Knowing how the query should be executed

- Justifying the cost of running each query

- Understanding database views

Determining if the Data Exists   Most databases that support applications are relational. That is, key values in one table are stored in another, related table. Those **key values** are the **primary keys** to the related table. Relational tables store information in columns about certain entities (person, place, or thing) that describe the entity's attributes and properties. The table's entities and properties can be listed and shown in a model called a **database schema**. By reviewing the database schema with the analyst, you will be able to identify which table and columns are needed to satisfy the request. As Figure 6-15 shows, all requests for data must be verified to determine if the data exists.

Most CASE tools come with data modeling features that allow analysts (or developers) to create a database schema if it isn't already defined. Database schemas can be created when the tables are defined or they can be created using reverse engineering. Reverse engineering is when you use a CASE tool to read the **database definition library (DDL)** and create the schema from the definition.

When using a wireframe or printout of the report that is to be created, check off all output data elements that are required. During this exercise, you might find yourself pushing the requirements back to the BA's desk with questions like "Where does this information come from?" or "Are you sure this is the information you need?" At the end of this mapping activity, you will know if you have the information needed or if additional software requirements are needed. As Figure 6-16 shows, the database schema will provide all the data needed to determine if the fields exist.

Figure 6-15 Mapping output

Employee		
PK	EMP_ID	CHAR(7)
	F_NAME	CHAR(20)
	L_NAME	CHAR(20)
	M_NAME	CHAR(10)
	ADDRESS	CHAR(20)
	CITY	CHAR(20)
	STATE	CHAR(2)
	H_PHONE	CHAR(10)
	C_PHONE	CHAR(10)
	EMAIL	CHAR(20)

PAYROLL		
PK,FK1	EMP_ID	CHAR(7)
	GRADE	CHAR(7)
	D_HIRE	DATETIME
	SAL	LONG

STCKPRCH		
PK PK	EMP_ID P_DATE	CHAR(7) DATETIME
	P_PRICE	LONG
	P_QTY	LONG

ACCUM		
PK PK	EMP_ID P_DATE	CHAR(7) DATETIME
	P_AMNT	LONG

Figure 6-16 Database table schema

TIP

Output mapping is more than just identifying the tables and columns. It really is the best way for developers to learn the business. By reviewing the table schemas and relationships, you will understand how the business operates and what it depends on. This information is different from software requirements such as use cases. Understanding how the business works will not only make you a better developer on the team, but also will make you an asset.

Designing the Queries   Generally speaking, writing SQL may not be an option in all environments; in fact, in situations where tools generate the actual SQL, static SQL may not even be possible. However, querying the database is the only method possible that will identify if all the tables and columns needed to satisfy the requirement are created, defined, and valid. So whether the query you create is for validation purposes or to be used in the real code, by creating the query now, you're not only saving development time, but also making sure you have the necessary inputs.

The analyst might not be interested in knowing what the actual SQL looks like, but he definitely cares what it returns. Designing and writing the SQL now will eliminate the developer running into issues when it is time to code. Write the query in a text editor or SQL command and print out the results. Hand it over to the analyst for verification. The more detailed you become in the design phase, the easier coding will become. As Figure 6-17 shows, designing queries and the results that get returned is a collaborative effort.

Figure 6-17   Verifying the output

Writing the SQL in the design phase will ensure that the developer has all the inputs (keys) necessary to produce the desired result. Leave no assumption; identify, define, and cleanse all input keys to the database. If a hacker were to attack an application, the database would be the first target. SQL code injection, trickery with HTTP data elements, and basic input manipulation will occur; code for it.

When looking at keys and other access points of your data (any data element in the WHERE clause), make sure the definition of the input is the same as the definition in the table. Don't allow for automatic truncation for variables that are too big or too small. Preventing this truncation will secure the database and improve database performance.

Next, make sure what is in your 'WHERE' clause is the same as the table index. Table indexes are used to tell the DBMS how to sort and organize the data in the table. If the query doesn't match the index, the DBMS will scan all the records on file rather than look in the exact spot where the data is stored. Imagine if you kept all of your personal data (passport, birth certificate) in a certain spot within a file cabinet and asked a friend to find it without telling him/her where to look. Your friend would have to dig through each file and folder before finding it. That search is time consuming and expensive. Your query also will be time consuming and expensive if you do not use the indexes correctly, as shown in Figure 6-18.

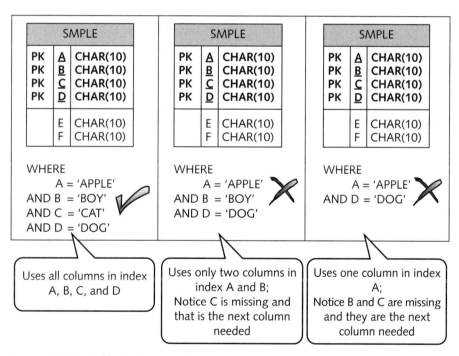

Figure 6-18   Table indexes and queries

Next, you need to check whether the final result is the expected result. Even though the SQL selected columns from a table, how do you (or the analyst) know that data is correct?

Is it sorted and grouped how the user would like to view it? Is there any additional information missing?

Last, when everyone has had a chance to validate and verify the query, add the SQL query to the use case so that the team can refer back to it when the time comes. Documenting the SQL has two advantages:

- The team is informed on where the data is coming from.
- Documentation helps the developer code when constructing the application.

How to Execute the Query   Dynamic SQL is the ability to have object-oriented programming languages such as Java write SQL that can change the columns or database tables on the fly depending on the input parameters. The flexibility of dynamic SQL provides a lot of advantages over hard-coded SQL when the inputs to a query are not known. For example, if you have a Web screen that provides a list of several drop-down parameters for search criteria, the developer has no way of knowing for sure what the inputs are. Therefore, an algorithm can be developed that creates the SQL on demand that requests only the data needed.

Figure 6-19 displays what dynamic SQL looks like. As you can see, any column, value, or table can be added when needed depending on the logic of the program.

```
public static void createSQL(String id, double salesAmount) {
    StringBuffer query = new StringBuffer();

    if (id!=null) {
        query
        .append(" SELECT COUNT(A.REGION_ID),A.NAME")
        .append(" FROM REGION A, EMPLOYEE B, SALES C")
        .append(" WHERE")
        .append(" A.REGION_ID = '"+id+"'")
        .append(" AND A.REGION_ID = B.REGION_ID")
        .append(" AND B.EMPLOYEE_ID = C.EMPLOYEE_ID");
        if (salesAmount>0) {
            query.append(" AND C.SALE_AMOUNT > "+salesAmount);
        }
        query
        .append(" GROUP BY A.NAME")
        .append(" ORDER BY 2,1 ");

    }
}
```

Dynamic SQL is created on demand.

Figure 6-19   Dynamic SQL

Table 6-1 gives the advantages and disadvantages of dynamic SQL.

Table 6-1   Advantages and disadvantages of dynamic SQL

Advantages	Disadvantages
• Easy to code and maintain • Can be managed by third-party frameworks • More object oriented • Retrieves only the data needed to satisfy the request	• Inputs are unknown • Many trips across network from data-base manager to application server

Static SQL, on the other hand, is hard-coded SQL that the program invokes all the time. This all-or-nothing approach isn't as flexible and dynamic, but it does have its advantages. With hard-coded SQL, the developers know exactly what the inputs are and the order in which they are provided. As you learn more about database tables, you will learn that efficient SQL requires appropriate use of indexes, and your inputs will dictate what indexes you use. Static SQL guarantees the developer the efficient use of **indexes** and **RUNSTATS**.

Figure 6-20 shows an example of static SQL. Unlike dynamic SQL, static SQL cannot be changed during run-time conditions.

```
EXEC SQL
   SELECT COUNT(A.REGION_ID), A.NAME
   FROM REGION A, EMPLOYEE B, SALES C
   WHERE
   A.REGION_ID = '1234'
   AND A.REGION_ID = B.REGION_ID
   AND B.EMPLOYEE_ID = C.EMPLOYEE_ID
   AND C.SALE_AMOUNT > 50.00
   GROUP BY A.NAME  ◄─────────────      Static SQL is hard-coded
   ORDER BY 2,1                         into the program.
END-EXEC
```

Figure 6-20   Static SQL

Table 6-2 gives the advantages and disadvantages of static SQL.

Table 6-2   Advantages and disadvantages of static SQL

Advantages	Disadvantages
• Can be optimized • Indexes and keys can be designed to support search criteria • Easy to debug • Promotes stored procedure usage; good use of separation of SQL and business objects that store the data	• Each SQL must be coded to match every input scenario • Promotes stored procedure usage; sometimes business logic is replicated in stored procedures and in business objects • Not flexible

TIP When to design static SQL versus dynamic SQL can be a touchy subject on most teams. Because each option has its own advantages and disadvantages, a heated debate might turn up from time to time. What you don't want is half the developers writing dynamic SQL while the other half writes static SQL in stored procedures. Remember, your ultimate goal is to have all code look the same. Therefore, try to come up with some rules as to when dynamic SQL is written versus when static SQL is written. I have always maintained the "rule of three." Meaning, if I have to cross the network more than three times to render my result, then I put the SQL queries in a stored procedure using static SQL. Otherwise, it's safe to use dynamic SQL. Of course, whatever rules the team decides on, make sure you update the new rule in the Application Guide.

The bottom line is that not all DBMSs are created equal. Static SQL is well suited for queries that are repeated frequently and run very quickly. Dynamic SQL is better suited for queries where the criteria are not known in advance and where the query won't be run frequently. For the most part, for DBMSs that support it, static SQL lets the DBMS compile the SQL and generate the plan in advance, so it saves time up front in executing the query. Dynamic SQL takes longer to get going because it has more work to do up front, but it may generate a better plan as more is known at the time it executes, so the query itself could potentially run faster.

Justify the Cost of Running Each Query Designing the queries so that they perform acceptably in the database is a developer's responsibility, regardless of whether static or dynamic SQL is used. As you work on the concept of executing queries, remember that hosting providers of database services charge applications by the transactions (usage) of the database. Therefore, the developer will need to know how the queries perform and evaluate that efficiency for both static and dynamic SQL. It is possible to get the performance on both types of queries—it just requires the developer to run multiple scenarios for the dynamic queries.

One method of tracking the queries' performance is by measuring the database CPU time or **MIPS (million instructions per second)**. As the cost in MIPS goes up in your queries, so does the cost in dollars of hosting your database. Therefore, make sure your queries are efficient; otherwise, the response time will be slow and the cost of support will be high.

Writing efficient SQL takes a lot of practice and understanding of the DBMS. Basically, it all has to do with proper use of indexing. Does your query have the necessary inputs that match the database index?

CAUTION Just because an SQL statement returns the expected result, do not assume that it is the one you will use in the program. Each query must be optimized for efficiency and performance. A lot of analysis will go into each query. Use a DBA to help you find the best query for your requirement.

Database Views   Deciding what to expose and what not to expose is a challenge in relational databases. If you have the primary key to a table, you have access to every column on that table. That is not a secure way of storing information. For example, if we needed to see if an employee were a manager grade, then I would have to look in the PAYROLL table where GRADE = 'M' for that employee. The problem here is as soon as I have access to that table, I can see that employee's salary. As cool as that sounds, I don't think that employee would appreciate it. Most data theft is caused by just browsing data to see what's out there.

A database **view** provides a way to expose table columns to certain access paths while hiding others. Unlike a physical table, a view is created by using a subset of data from the physical table to create a virtual table to be used in the application, as shown in Figure 6-21.

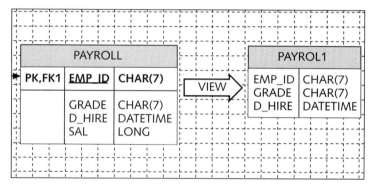

Figure 6-21   Table view

As Figure 6-21 shows, a view can be made from the PAYROLL table that does not display SAL (salary). Therefore, application developers can write SQL to go up against PAYROL1 (view) instead of the original PAYROLL table.

Views secure databases by eliminating what's displayed and then make the SQL more efficient. Because the DBMS does not have to read all columns on the table, it would be easier to index and scan a subset of the columns rather than all columns. Generally, the less data (columns) on the table, the faster the DBMS will perform.

DESIGNING FOR QUALITY IN THE CUBE

As soon as you sign off on the requirements and wireframes, your BA is going to leave you with the assumption that all is understood and he does not want to come back. He expects the application to look and act as discussed and he feels that you are well informed about the requirements and screen layouts. Before he leaves you alone in your cube, make sure you have everything you need to code the application; specifically, you will need the answers to the questions listed in Table 6-3.

Table 6-3   Last-chance questions

Review for GUI	Review for SQL
Do you know who the users are (roles/ privileges)?	Are all access paths defined (keys)?
Do you know how they navigate from one screen to the next within the application?	Do I know what the costs are in MIPS?
Is there any data that needs to be carried over from one screen to the next? Is that data sensitive?	How many times do I cross the net- work to render the results?
Is all search criteria identified in the screen along with sort orders and filters?	How can I optimize the queries?
How much data is expected to be displayed? What is the weight of the screen (bandwidth or scrolling)?	Is this data secure? If so, how do you secure it (seek advice of DBA)?

Your last call with the analysts is your last chance to make sure you have all your thoughts organized and know all the details about the application or program before you design the code. During that last call, you should do the following:

- Make sure the business logic is intact.
- Make sure there is a universal understanding of the business requirements.
- Update the system documentation when you get back to your desk.
- Print the documentation and hang it up.

Business Logic—Bridging the GUIs to the Database

In software design, you are reading through the requirements and looking for the substance of what is being asked from you. You are being asked to build an application from a certain set of requirements and specifications. As we have learned from the previous chapter, there are high-level, medium-level, and low-level specifications. All requirements are written, jotted, drawn, and scribbled on paper and whiteboards. Sometimes, too much information can be too much information. Have you ever read a letter of instruction that was more descriptive than prescriptive? That is what requirements tend to be. At first, the BAs write everything down; he or she explains the environment, the scenarios, and the users' actions and, somehow, in all this descriptive verbiage, the true business requirements are often lost.

Human factors are the primary causes of design disasters. Writing software requirements takes skill and not everyone can do it. Part of the BA's job is that he or she has to write and you have to design. Therefore, you have to make sure you understand everything about the application before you design it. Otherwise, any false assumptions or guesses could cause the project to be Over/Under (Over-budget and Under-expectation).

Universal Understanding

To work toward a universal understanding with the analysts, I like to pare down the requirements into simple, logical statements of expectation so that anybody who reads the instructions will be able to understand the requirements regardless of any literary skill he or she might have.

Figures 6-22 and 6-23 both show e-mails. However, they differ in their effectiveness. As shown in Figure 6-22, requirements are not always that clear in the first request.

6

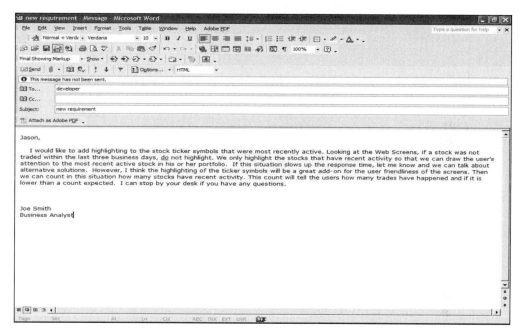

Figure 6-22   Software requirements from analyst

Fortunately, Figure 6-23 follows up with a clear restatement of what the writer thinks is expected.

The BAs might push back and tell you that they do not want to go down to that level of detail, either because it's too much like pseudocode or because that type of information is too detailed for them. If they do not want to do it, you have to. But after you have rewritten the requirement into a simple design language that everyone can understand, make sure they sign off and approve it. Leave no stone unturned and assume nothing.

Updating the System Documentation

Analysis and design collaboration bring out the best in all requirements. Areas of requirement weaknesses are exposed, new concepts are introduced, and the application will start to come to life. After walking through the prototypes, database mappings, and sequence

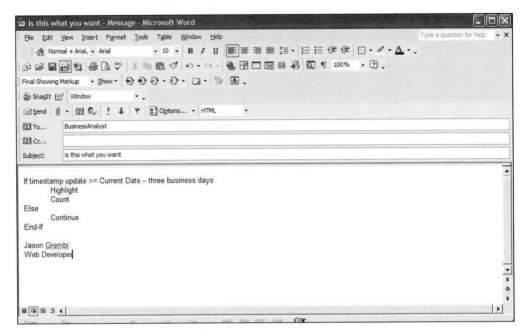

Figure 6-23   Confirmation e-mail

diagrams, make sure you (or the BA) take a moment to update the original documentation. Chances are great that this original use case information just wasn't enough and that you refined those requests tremendously. Make sure these revisions are reflected in the latest use case so that during any given time on the project, what the code does and how it does it is reflected in the SDLC artifacts.

I often include the final SQL statements that are expanded during the design in the use case documents themselves. You will be asked several times "Where are you getting this data from?" It's a lot easier looking at documentation than reading code and following logic.

Print It and Hang It Up

Congratulations, you have just finished collaborating with the analyst and you now have a complete end-to-end understanding of what you need to do. As a result, you should have some great cube decorations that you can hang on the walls. These visual diagrams will provide you with the constant focus and ultimate goal that you are going to be working toward.

Print and hang the following:

- Wireframes

- Database schemas

- The final use case

CAUTION

Of course, hang any system design documentation with caution. If any of these artifacts are deemed sensitive, make sure you pull them off the wall before going home.

The BA typically leaves the room now with a handshake and an offering of good luck. When he leaves, he doesn't care *how* you do your task, just *that* you do it.

QUICK CHECKS

1. Open the "Make Trade.doc" use case from the Chapter 6 course data. Print it out.

2. Open the "logOnPrototype.html" use case prototype from the Chapter 6 course data. Print it out.

3. Open the "myAccountPrototype.html" use case prototype from the Chapter 6 course data. Print it out.

4. Compare the use case requirements to the prototype screens.

5. Using the information covered, how would your collaboration meeting be conducted with the business analyst? What are some of the questions left that you need defined?

6. What is missing from the use case? Do the requirements provide enough information to support the prototype? Why or why not?

7. Open the "Log On Use Case.doc" use case from the Chapter 6 course data and then open the "My Account.doc" use case from the Chapter 6 course data. Print them out. Compare these two with the prototypes. In your own words, can you explain why and how a vision of a screen can flesh out problems with requirement documentation?

CHAPTER SUMMARY

❑ Software design is the most important phase of software development.

❑ Static design activities are used to help the analyst and the developer understand the overall application and the software requirements.

❑ Dynamic design activities produce documentation that is used to describe the behavior and interaction of systems and components.

❑ Design artifacts, such as conceptual models, interaction diagrams, and sequence diagrams, need detailed attention from the analyst and the developers.

❑ The analysts are the group of people you rely on to ask business questions, clarify requirements, and interface with end users.

❑ The purpose of whiteboard meetings is to provide an open communication between the analysts and developer(s).

❑ Asking the right questions when meeting with the analysts will not only make good use of time, but also will keep the conversation on topic and focused.

❏ The inputs are the data elements that are coming into the application from another source (screen, input device) that are required to produce the desired result. The outputs are the data elements coming from the application or another source that were requested, updated, or created based on the input request.

❏ Dynamic SQL is the ability to have object-oriented programming languages such as Java write SQL that can change the columns or database tables on the fly depending on the input parameters.

❏ A database view provides a way to expose table columns to certain access paths while hiding others.

❏ Human factors are the primary causes of design disasters.

❏ Analysis and design collaboration bring out the best in all requirements.

Key Terms

actor — A domain that interacts with the system.

analyst — A person who is in charge of ensuring user requirements are documented and translated to the developers.

association — A relationship between concepts that depicts some sort of meaningful interaction.

bad list — A running list of inputs that have no business requirements; these inputs cannot be trusted by the application.

database definition library (DDL) — A schema used by the DBMS to create a physical table, assign keys, and assign definitions to columns.

database schema — A model diagram representing how the database tables relate to each other.

domain — A business entity or concept with which the application code interfaces.

good list — A running list of inputs that have business requirements; these inputs can be trusted by the application.

index — Used by the DBMS to organize the data stored in a table.

inputs — Data elements that come from system events.

key value — A column in a table that must be present (populated) when the row is created.

MIPS (million instructions per second) — The CPU speed of a DBMS.

outputs — Data elements that come from the application's resources (database, file, code).

primary key — A value that must be present to get to the unique data row of a database table.

prototypes — Small, working applications that provide a user only with the look and feel of the final product.

RUNSTATS — Used by the DBMS to determine how many records and columns exist in a table.

system event — An external input event that comes from an actor (user of system).

Unified Modeling Language (UML) — The notation used for system documentation and object-oriented concepts.

view — A virtual table created by a subset of another physical table.

whiteboard — A drawing board that allows people to use dry erase markers for building visuals.

wireframes — Static HTML files or screen drawings on paper that depict what the GUIs look like.

REVIEW QUESTIONS

1. What is the main purpose of collaborating with the analysts?
   a. Go over system requirements.
   b. Refine system requirements while creating design documentation as each concept is discussed.
   c. Identify inputs and outputs.
   d. Look for weaknesses and unknowns in the requirement documentation.
   e. Design collaboration provides a discussion platform for the analyst and developer so that they can work together.

2. What is the difference between design and analysis?

3. What is the difference between a prototype and a final product?

4. Why is it important to draw out application data flow before you code?
   a. Drawing the data flow and creating diagrams reinforce understanding and clarification to the development team.
   b. Drawing pictures is legal documentation.
   c. Pictures are a great way to show upper management that work is being conducted and accomplished.
   d. Models and diagrams prove that the developers know UML.

5. What is UML?
   a. a universal language used to understand requirements
   b. a universal language used to write requirements
   c. a universal language used to interpret requirements
   d. all of the above

6. In conceptual modeling, with what do the software entities interact?
   a. applications
   b. requirements
   c. business entities
   d. domains
   e. both c and d

7. Why is it important to associate the concepts to one another during conceptual modeling?

    a. so that the BA knows what the concept does

    b. so that the developer knows the concept exists

    c. so that the meaning and importance of the concept can be documented

    d. so that the concept can be later reviewed for security

8. What activity can be used to ensure that the software requirements are complete?

    a. conceptual modeling

    b. sequence diagrams

    c. data mapping

    d. UML

    e. all of the above

9. What is the fundamental key for secure programming?

    a. writing SQL

    b. writing in UML

    c. looking for areas of weakness

    d. input cleansing

10. Why would you write SQL code during the design phase?

11. _____ is a running list of all input data that has not been identified.

12. Why is it important to put requirements in terms of conditional statements instead of verbose text?

13. Making requirements _____ is a way of visually seeing that software requirements are identified in the design documentation.

14. Why is it important to compare the SQL query to the table index?

    a. to ensure efficiency and performance from the DBMS

    b. so that the SQL will work

    c. so that the DBA will approve the query

    d. so that the user will see the result

15. When the design meetings are finally done, what is the best thing to do with all the design documentation?

    a. e-mail it to everyone on the team as meeting minutes

    b. hand it over to the project manager for approval

    c. formalize the documentation and hang it up

    d. hang it up for review

16. For what are database schemas used?

    a. to accommodate conceptual models

    b. to finalize system sequence diagrams

    c. to relate databases

    d. to provide a visual representation of how database tables are related

17. What are the benefits of writing the SQL in the design phase?

    a. verify that tables, code, and users exist

    b. verify that inputs, indexes, and outputs are correct

    c. verify that inputs, keys, and outputs are correct

    d. verify that inputs, outputs, and tables exist

18. A database view is a good way to secure sensitive information on a database table and yet still be able to share other data on the same table with the public. True or False?

19. Application interaction depicts how the application works with other applications. True or False?

20. Sequence diagrams document all user activity with the application. True or False?

HANDS-ON PROJECTS

Project 6-1 HTML Editor

1. Open up your favorite HTML editor (for example, FrontPage or Dreamweaver) and try to re-create the GUI shown in the "logOn.html" file from the Chapter 6 course data.

2. Save your mock-up as "MockUp6.html."

3. View the source and see what type of extra HTML code the tool created versus what the HTML looks like in the "logOn_Stripped_HTML.html" file that is located in the Chapter 6 course data.

4. Identify which HTML tags you need to produce the screen and which ones are extra that the tool provided.

Project 6-2 Create Wireframe for Trades

1. Open up the use case "HOP_Execute_Trade_Use_Case.doc" from the Chapter 6 course data.

2. Read the requirements and try to visualize how the Trade screen will interact with the "My Account Screen.doc" file from the Chapter 6 course data.

3. Create a wireframe for this GUI by providing areas for input, labels, and buttons.

4. Now list the concepts (domains) for this screen.

5. Model those concepts and associate them with each other.

Project 6-3 System Sequence Diagrams for Trades

1. Using the wireframe from Project 6-2 and the accompanying use case, list the sequences between the user and application.

2. What is each message doing (passing)?

3. What is the sequence of events the application must do to satisfy the request?

CASE PROJECT

Database Check

Mapping requirements to the database fields is an important step for validating software requirements. Using the database schema in "Database of Employee Stock Purchase Program.doc" (from the Chapter 6 course data) for the Employee Stock Purchase Program, do the following:

1. If a third-party application provided the employee's ID to your application, can you code a cleansing algorithm in a program language of your choice that will validate the input data?

2. Can you write a SELECT statement that uses the employee's ID that will return the first and last name as well as the date of hire (F_NAME, L_NAME, and D_HIRE, respectively)?

CHAPTER REFERENCES

Dupuis, Robert, Pierre Bourque, Alain Abran, James W. Moore, Leonard L. Tripp, IEEE Society. 2004. Guide to the Software Engineering Body of Knowledge. Version 2004. http://www.swebok.org. (accessed February 14, 2008).

Larman, Craig. 1998. *Applying UML and Patterns: An Introduction to Object-Oriented Analysis and Design*. Upper Saddle River, New Jersey: Prentice Hall PTR.

Quatrani, Terry. 2003. Introduction to the Unified Modeling Language. http://www-128. ibm.com/developerworks/rational/library/998.html (accessed February 16, 2008).

Redwine, Samuel T. Jr., Rusty O. Baldwin, Mary L. Polydys, Daniel P. Shoemaker, Jeffrey A. Ingalsbe, and Larry D. Wagoner. 2007. *Software Assurance: A Guide to the Common Body of Knowledge to Produce, Acquire, and Sustain Secure Software Version 1.2*. Arlington, VA: U.S. Department of Homeland Security. https://buildsecurityin.us-cert.gov/daisy/bsi/940/version/1/part/4/data/CurriculumGuideToTheCBK.pdf (accessed February 13, 2008).

7

DESIGNING FOR SECURITY

Upon completion of this material, you should be able to:

◆ Design for security using industry patterns

◆ Understand organizational security resources

◆ Understand autonomous team decisions

◆ Work with intra-team decisions

Designing for security involves creating detailed design artifacts that will be used to build each software component needed to satisfy the use case requirements. Then, you take each software artifact and conduct a thorough analysis for every feature, property, and service that exists in every component for possible vulnerabilities. By analyzing each software component for use case and misuse case scenarios, the developers will be able to design the appropriate countermeasure up front and publicly for the whole team to see how software security is being handled in the application. In the previous chapter, you learned how to design for functionality by collaborating with the analysts about the software requirements. In this chapter, you will learn how to bring those concepts to life by creating more detailed design artifacts that will be used to create the code.

DESIGNING FOR SECURITY USING INDUSTRY PATTERNS

To design for secure software, you first have to define what it is you are securing. You can do so by asking the following questions:

- What software modules need to be created to satisfy the use case?

- What other programs will use those modules, and how?

- What types of properties go into those modules?

All of these questions need to be answered before applying any security principles. The only way to find the answers to the listed questions is by converting the software concepts to industry standard diagrams so that those diagrams can be reviewed during threat analysis. During this design analysis stage, every use case will need to be separated by unit of work (function) to effectively start on object modeling.

UML diagrams provide a visual representation of the software so that each use case/misuse case can be broken down and analyzed for common secure design patterns and reusable components. Secure requirements include the use of SSL and/or digital certificates, where applicable, while others include the securing of CONSTANTS and other feeding files. All of these design factors need to be considered in order to secure the application. As Figure 7-1 shows, you must consider many external resources when building the overall design of the application.

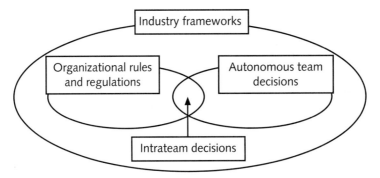

Figure 7-1   Design factors within the application

The industry standard UML design activities that this part of the chapter addresses include the following:

- Object modeling

- Interaction diagrams

- Class diagrams in UML

- The printing of the final design

This chapter is meant to teach how to design security into a use case. It is not meant as a fully formed OOP (Object Oriented Programming) design tutorial. OOP is a much broader concept that includes inheritance and polymorphism, which are not touched on in this book, and it has profound implications to the design of the application. This chapter assumes that the reader already has a general idea of the broader concepts of OOP.

Object Modeling

Object modeling is a way to visually create the UML models of the software components that are needed to satisfy the use case requirements. These models can be created by using the conceptual models and system sequence diagrams created with the analysts in the "Log On Use Case.doc" file from the Chapter 7 course data, as shown in Figure 7-2.

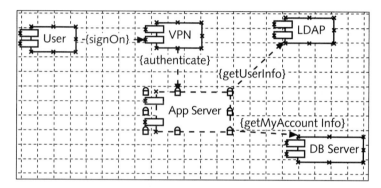

Figure 7-2   Use case conceptual model

The concepts from Figure 7-2 clearly show that there is a user, a VPN connection, and an application server that has to do more authentication and authorization from LDAP and a database. The activity that defines how those concepts carry out the requirement is the starting object. For example, the user is defined as a concept, but in object terms, it really is a browser. Furthermore, the VPN system is a third-party **black box** application that we can assume authenticates the user. The application server concept can also be broken down into smaller objects.

When decoupling concepts, think in terms of what the software must do first to satisfy the requirement. In the manner that you broke down the concepts with the analysts, you need to break down and identify each object in the use case; that is, the application server must take in a business model as input and validate those parameters. The application will then transmit that request to an LDAP object, a database object, and then, finally, back to the client. The object model for the use case is defined in Figure 7-3.

As Figure 7-3 shows, object modeling defines how many objects are needed by labeling the object names on top of the diagram.

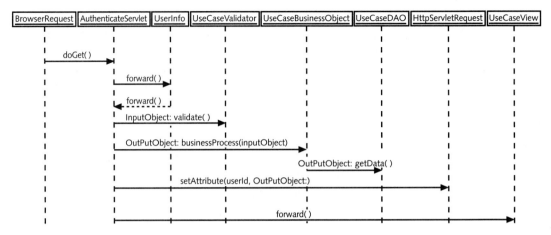

Figure 7-3   Object modeling the use case

TIP

Object naming is one of those conventions that we discussed when you learned about the Application Guide. Be sure to document the object-naming rules your team develops in the Application Guide.

NOTE

Make sure your Application Guide is updated with design rules such as naming conventions. Review the Application Guide you created in Chapter 4 and be sure to add design rules for naming conventions. Following standard object naming conventions is an important part of any project because it increases the maintainability and readability of the code. Note the following:

1. Object names should be nouns in mixed case with the first letter of each word capitalized. For example, the "Log On" use case requires a logon servlet, so the object name will be LogOnServlet.

2. Methods should be verbs, in mixed case, with the first letter lowercase, and the first letter of each second word capitalized. For example, you would look up the user's data using the userInfo( ) method.

3. Variables should be declared in class constants. They are spelled in all upper-case with words separated by underscores ("_"). For example, a constant in the "Log On" use case would be DEBUG or TEST_SERVER.

Interaction Diagrams

Interaction diagrams focus more on how the software objects interact with themselves and other objects. An interaction diagram looks more like a very detailed system sequence diagram, only instead of listing "user input," it lists the **messages** between each object. As you can see in Figure 7-4, interaction diagrams start to separate the objects into logical units of work.

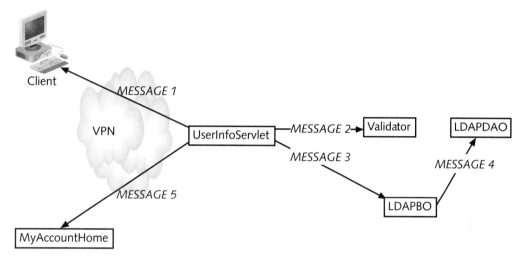

Figure 7-4   Interaction diagram

Interaction diagrams are the most important artifacts in design because they essentially are the specifications to class diagrams. The next step in interaction diagrams is to assign the objects messages by documenting what is being communicated back and forth between objects. Messages are the links between objects that show what object is being called, who the caller is, what is being communicated, and what is being returned.

As Figure 7-5 shows, planning the attack includes these steps:

1. Add a sequence number to every message in the execution order of the thread, from the first step of execution to the last.

2. Illustrate each message, giving the argument (which is shown inside the parentheses) and the return value (which is shown on the left side of the colon).

3. If messages exist within the scope of a current thread, assign sequence numbers as Steps 1.1, 1.2, and 1.3.

TIP

It is very important to define every message with each object; you should assume nothing. The more detailed and specific the interaction diagram is, the easier it is to create class diagrams and code.

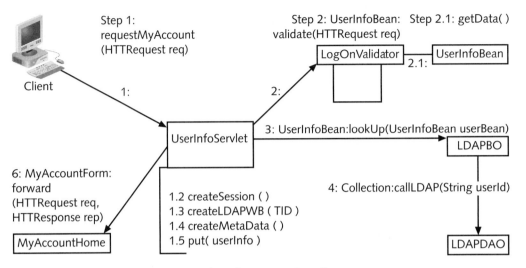

Figure 7-5   Assigning messages within the interaction diagram

Class Diagrams

With the detailed object interaction diagrams done, you are ready to convert those objects into real software class specifications for code. **Class diagrams** are the software requirements specifications for each module in an application. The information pieces that are documented in these diagrams are as follows:

- Properties
- Methods

NOTE The only difference between a class and an object is through instantiation. An object is nothing more than a live class. If you were to create a bridge, you would first draw a blueprint, complete with specifications and measurements. You would then give that blueprint to developers, who would create a real bridge (instantiated object). Classes are blueprints of objects, and objects are living (instantiated) classes.

To create class diagrams, do the following:

1. Identify all classes from the interaction diagrams and draw them on a whiteboard.

2. Using the UML class diagram notation, add the methods to each class from the interaction diagram.

3. Add the attributes and any other method that the class will need.

As Figure 7-6 shows, class diagrams tell the developer what method and attribute goes in each class. As long as the interaction diagram is thoroughly detailed, class diagrams should be an easy exercise to perform.

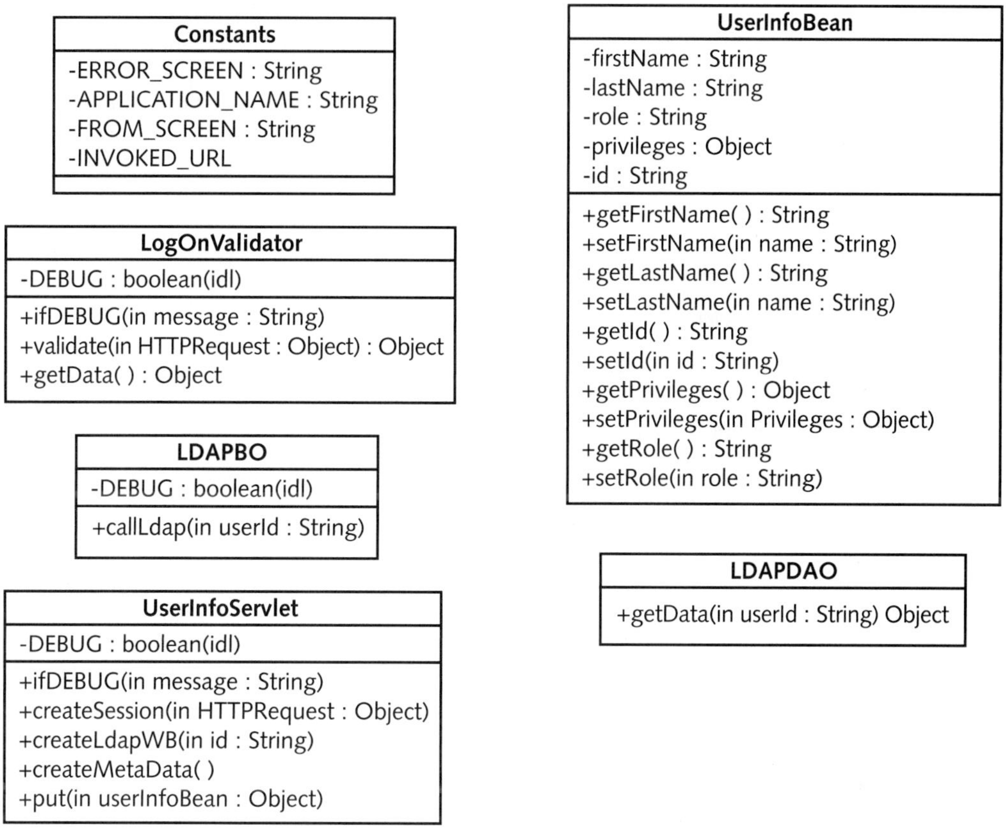

Constants
-ERROR_SCREEN : String
-APPLICATION_NAME : String
-FROM_SCREEN : String
-INVOKED_URL

LogOnValidator
-DEBUG : boolean(idl)
+ifDEBUG(in message : String)
+validate(in HTTPRequest : Object) : Object
+getData( ) : Object

LDAPBO
-DEBUG : boolean(idl)
+callLdap(in userId : String)

UserInfoServlet
-DEBUG : boolean(idl)
+ifDEBUG(in message : String)
+createSession(in HTTPRequest : Object)
+createLdapWB(in id : String)
+createMetaData( )
+put(in userInfoBean : Object)

UserInfoBean
-firstName : String
-lastName : String
-role : String
-privileges : Object
-id : String
+getFirstName( ) : String
+setFirstName(in name : String)
+getLastName( ) : String
+setLastName(in name : String)
+getId( ) : String
+setId(in id : String)
+getPrivileges( ) : Object
+setPrivileges(in Privileges : Object)
+getRole( ) : String
+setRole(in role : String)

LDAPDAO
+getData(in userId : String) Object

Figure 7-6   Class diagram of the "Log On" use case

Assigning Properties

To determine which class has the property and which one does not, use a normalization method of association. That is, the properties of the class should describe the class itself and that placeholders should be used when the property itself may have properties of its own. In the example from Figure 7-6, we assigned a role in the UserInfoBean class. In reality, a role does not describe a user; rather a user has a role. Therefore, we need to create a new Role class and associate that class to the UserInfoBean. Figure 7-7 demonstrates how this is done.

Assigning the right properties to each class will not only eliminate duplicate data in the design but also make each software component more modular. Modular design is more reusable and easier to understand and maintain over the course of the SDLC.

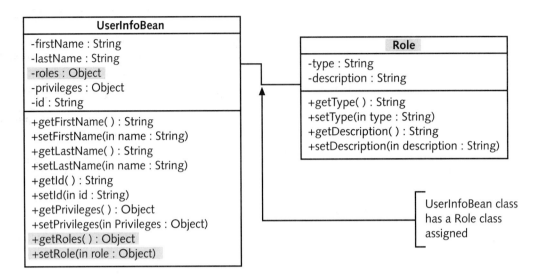

Figure 7-7   Property assigning

Assigning Methods

Methods are functions on objects that perform specific logic. When modeling methods in class diagrams, the developer needs to document the signature of each method.

A **signature** contains the following:

- The name of the method
- The arguments that it takes as input
- What the method returns

The way to document methods in class diagrams is to assign a method name with a parentheses notation after the name, as was the case with getLastName( ) in Figure 7-7.

Print It Out and Hang It Up!

By following the standard modeling activities, the developers will have a complete end-to-end understanding of the design of the use case. Make sure all the whiteboard drawings, notes, and any e-mails regarding these artifacts are finalized into UML documentation using a CASE tool, and check the application's source code repository. The design documentation can even be appended to the use case so that all the specifications are packaged together.

As Figure 7-8 depicts, it is a lot easier to have the UML artifacts in front of you while reviewing the data flow of security weaknesses and possible attacks.

Figure 7-8   Reviewing the data flow

ORGANIZATIONAL SECURITY RESOURCES: RULES AND REGULATIONS

Designing security into the application costs organizations time and money. It costs money to analyze threats (misuse cases), develop and implement countermeasures, and test for security features in each use case and misuse case. Most organizations have specific rules and regulations regarding how security features are built in to software applications. For example, some organizations will have strict, generic rules such as "all sign-on activity must go through company VPN," and other organizations let the individual project teams make their own design decisions.

Organizational resources are entities that are beyond the realm of the developer's control, yet they must be known by the development team so that the developers can make informed decisions. The rules and regulations to organizational resources will vary from company to company, but they include how teams are to secure the following:

- The data transmitted
- The network
- The host
- The application

These elements are discussed in the following subsections. In addition, information about how the users must be trained on all pieces of the application with which they interact is included as a wrap-up to the discussion.

Securing the Data Transmitted

The process in which your application picks up data for further processing needs to ensure that the data is quarantined, sanitized, and double-checked before being trusted. Because most applications today need to be Web enabled, the main protocol you will work with is HTTP. HTTP uses the internet TCP/IP protocol for the information you read and write on the Web. Most software attacks come from manipulating the HTTP protocol to work in favor of the attacker and to go for vulnerable points of entry in the application (Grossman 2005).

The following security models are an organization's way to secure data in transit:

- Secure Sockets Layer (SSL)
- Code signing
- Personal digital certificates
- Two-factor authentication

Secure Sockets Layer (SSL)

Secure Sockets Layer (SSL) is a cryptographic protocol that uses two keys, known as certificates, to encrypt data in transit to a specific port on the Web server, as shown in Figure 7-9. SSL uses a public key to encrypt the data being transferred from the client, and the private key is used to decipher it on the server. Before any data is sent, the server sends the client its public key. The client then generates a random key, encrypts it with the public key from the server, and sends it to the server. Then, the client and the server generate a master key that will be used in the rest of the session. That master key is used to encrypt messages before sending data across the network.

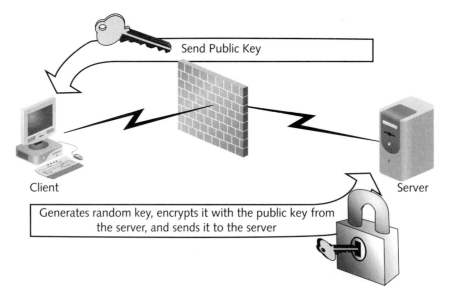

Figure 7-9   SSL secures the transportation of the data

The certificate is created for a particular server in a specific domain for a verified business entity and is issued only by a certificate authority (CA). When the SSL handshake occurs, the browser requires authentication from the server. If the information does not match or the certificate has expired, the browser displays an error message or warning (VeriSign 2007).

You should know the following two important items about SSL:

- SSL does not guarantee secure data.
- SSL can prevent phishing scams.

SSL Does Not Guarantee Security   SSL guarantees only that a client is communicating with the intended server and that the communication is encrypted and secure. It does nothing to ensure that the data itself is protected from malicious attacks. It only makes it very hard for hackers to eavesdrop. If the data that is being transmitted is sensitive, use an SSL CERT and accept only data that has the public key.

SSL Does Prevent Phishing   SSL can be used to help fight **phishing** scams, where links within e-mails lead consumers to counterfeit Web sites. Hijacked Web pages use real company logos, Web designs, and text to make the user think that he or she is at the real site.

In spite of the SSL protection, you still need to educate your users on verifying their SSL certificate before typing in their data. As Figure 7-10 shows, train your users to verify that the certificate belongs to the appropriate server by clicking on the lock icon located at the bottom right of the browser.

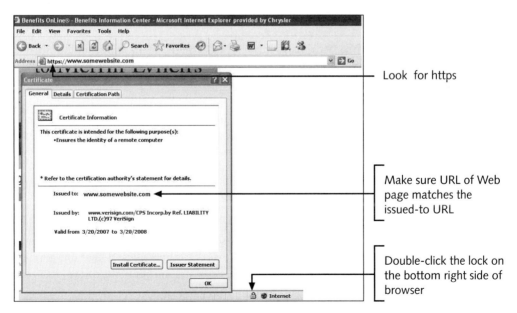

Figure 7-10   Browser using SSL

Code Signing

Code signing secures the machines involved with data transportation. Like SSL, code signing relies on public and private keys to send and receive data. The difference with code signing is that the sender must install software on the machine that wants to send data to the receiver.

Code signing is used when a software developer wants to create software that will run on a user's machine and will be trusted to perform activities not typically allowed inside the **sandbox**. A code signing certificate generated by a trusted CA assures the user that the software comes from where it claims to come from. As Figure 7-11 shows, both the client and the server need to be secure to send and receive data.

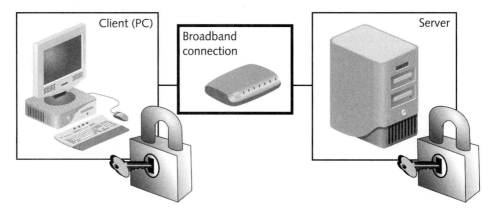

Figure 7-11 Code-signing machines

Code signing can work with many more types of applications and protocols than just HTTP. The certificate is created for a machine(s) for a verified business entity and issued only by a CA.

 It is also important to note that while the signing certificate can guarantee the source of the software, it does not go further than that. CAs follow a process to ensure they have accurate information about each company for which they provide certificates, but they don't stop malicious attacks (and in fact they probably make them easier to carry out), so you have to consider the source as well.

Personal Digital Certificates

Digital certificates are a very general term used to describe an authenticated message between two parties. The SSL certificates used to secure SSL web sites are, in fact, a type of digital certificate. There are, however, personal digital certificates that are generally used to either verify the identity of the user or to verify the authenticity of the data the user sent.

For the identity part, web servers can be configured such that you must have an acceptable digital certificate installed in your web browser to establish an HTTPS connection with the server. Certificates can also be used for encryption (as mentioned in the Secure Sockets

Layer (SSL) section using the public/private keys). Finally, certificates can be used for signing. Signing does not encrypt the message itself, but authenticates the sender.

Consider the following example:

1. You create an e-mail and want to sign that e-mail with a certificate.

2. A hash function is run on the full e-mail and it generates a **digest**. The hash functions are designed to make the digests as unique as possible based on the content, but they are of course limited by the number of bits in the digest (i.e., an 8-bit digest would have only 256 possible values, but it goes up exponentially with the number of bits).

3. The digest then is encrypted with the private key and appended to the e-mail to form the signature.

4. At the receiving end, the public key is used to decrypt the digest. The same hash is used on the content of the message and then this is compared to the unencrypted digest.

5. If they don't match, someone has changed the content of the e-mail since it was created. If it does match, it proves the identity of the creator and that the content was not changed.

Figure 7-12 displays the steps of how digital certificates are added to a browser.

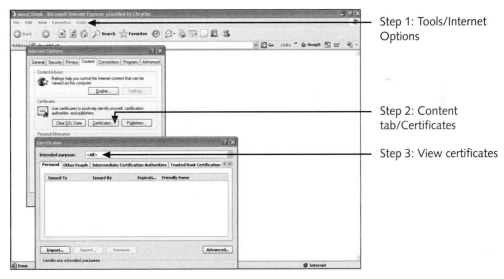

Step 1: Tools/Internet Options

Step 2: Content tab/Certificates

Step 3: View certificates

Figure 7-12   How digital certificates are added to a browser

Two-Factor Authentication

The two-factor authentication model requires the user's password along with another physical device for authentication. For example, for a person to get money out of an ATM machine, a physical device (an ATM card) and a person to enter a password must be present. In the Web model, an authentication device such as a VPN token is used for authentication. A VPN token concatenates a system-generated password (fed via satellite) with the user password and passes the encrypted data through a virtual private network.

Two-factor authentication makes it difficult for hackers to guess (or steal) a person's password. This model can be used as yet another layer of defense when designing applications that protect sensitive information or company assets.

Securing the Network

Historically, network topology such as firewalls, routers, and host machines were out of the realm of the application developer. However, because today's application is only as secure as the weakest link, the developer should know what the application runs on and how it is hosted.

When a corporate network firewall is set up, a thorough understanding of all the available ports and access must be understood (Graff and Van Wyk 2003). A **firewall** is software that most often runs on dedicated hardware that acts as a filter between a private network and a public one. The firewall's responsibility is to allow certain traffic through based on a **security policy**. Knowing where the application sits in relation to the firewall limits the exposure of the application and lets the development team know what other applications are on the same network.

Most companies divide two separate perimeters between networks to help manage security between different computers, operating systems, and application hosts. This division is known as the **perimeter defense** method (Gong 1999). The perimeter defense method divided computers into two camps: "Us" and "Them." "Us" includes those computers that can be trusted, whereas "Them" includes all other computers.

As a developer, you need to know how the network topology is set up on the network that runs the application. At a minimum, create a network diagram of where and how the application is hosted. Figure 7-13 shows an example of a network diagram.

TIP

Because inside threats are more likely than outside threats, assume "Them" is every application on the network outside yours.

Securing the Host

Web servers and application servers are another big target for hackers. It makes sense to model the application's host server and know what software components (and versions) support it. The US-CERT Vulnerability Notes Database publishes information on a wide

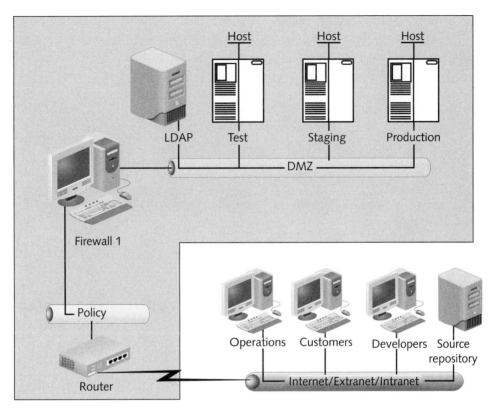

Figure 7-13 Network diagram

variety of vulnerabilities (US–CERT 2008). While developing software on an application, search this database for the tools, servers, and languages you are using. This Web site is a great way to stay on top of security issues and keep informed.

While modeling the application architecture, you might have to contact other parties such as operations (usually separate from application development in big companies). If you are the one who configures the servers and installs applications, you will definitely need to model the hosts and stay on top of vulnerabilities. To create a model, figure out how the servers are set up, and then document the versions. Most server configurations follow the standard three-tier model.

Securing the Application

Securing the application is yet another way to look at the supporting architecture and find out what the weakest link is in the network design. Where could your application be compromised or stolen? It's very common for companies to spend thousands of dollars per year on digital certificates and SSL(s) and yet not even consider restricting privileges of file directories on servers. In Figure 7-14, the areas of the network in which a copy of the application code exists are circled. Who has access rights to the file directories on the development machines? Who maintains the privileges on the file directory? How are those privileges tested or updated?

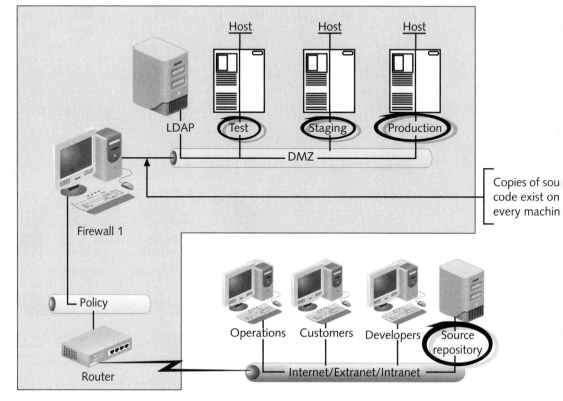

Figure 7-14   Areas of the network where the application exists

Also, binary code is not secure code. There are many code decompilers on the market and hackers will spend hours researching, analyzing, and tinkering with the code and trying to put the software back together looking for a way in. Don't make it easy.

Train the Users

Security is everyone's business. Software developers, architects, and business owners are not the only ones responsible for protecting user information. If the application deals with sensitive information (for example, credit card numbers and SSNs), there is also some ownership on the users' part to ensure they follow secure policies. Work in some gimmick or advertising campaign in the development process that warns your users of what to do and where to look.

Awareness is a two-way street and both parties are responsible. Have Web training podcasts, Webcasts, and newsletters that advertise how to use the software securely.

TIP

AUTONOMOUS TEAM DECISIONS

Designing code is a lot like organizing a baseball team. In baseball, a coach will rely on special coordinators to design plays that will win games. The coach then chooses players who are best suited for those plays, and the players fulfill their roles by hitting and throwing a baseball to the correct postion as directed.

In software, the project managers rely on special analysts and developers to design software to accomplish similar goals. The software that needs to be written will have to compete against malicious attacks but instead of throwing and catching baseballs, the software will be handling sensitive data. As with all successful teams, each player needs to play out his or her own role and responsibility to complete the overall picture, as shown in Figure 7-15.

Figure 7-15   Software program modules are like a team

The autonomous decisions that a team must make are how to incorporate the organizational rules for data transportation into the application (SSL and digital certificates) and what to do when the data arrives. In the process, the team needs to decide on the steps for the following:

- Cleansing the input data
- Choosing the right countermeasure for the misuse case

Cleansing the Input Data

In baseball, players throw and catch a baseball; in software, players (classes) throw and catch data holders (beans). These data holders are passed in and out of many objects, fiber optics, and WiFi before finally reaching their destination. Security measures need to be taken to make sure no one else catches or copies that ball while it's moving. As Figure 7-16 shows, a software application will take input data from all types of origins. The first step in data collection is to run the data fields through a validation process and clean the data.

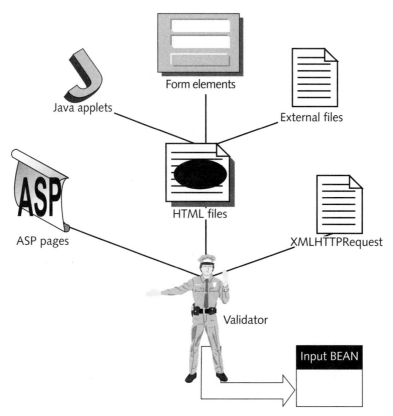

Figure 7-16 Turning external data into cleansed input beans

If a person is going to hack into an application, the data objects will be the first target. A hacker will sit in front of Web screens for hours entering faulty data in text boxes, text areas, and input parameters. He will also view a Web page's source code to figure out how the application is coded, what JavaScript objects are being used, and how data is being sent to the server. Even worse, a hacker might create an automated tool to scan for common exploits for him. Hackers tinker with software in every imaginable way looking for a chance to break the system or steal data.

Securing input parameters is the first priority in any application. The tasks of collecting data from external sources, validating the data, and creating input objects (beans) need to be designed into the application from the start so that there is a validation layer between the external data coming in and the application's resources. As data comes into the application, you need to ensure that the values entered are valid before processing the request. Validation is done at the point of entry (client side), at the point of origin (server side), or on the fly. There are advantages and disadvantages to each, as discussed in the following subsections for web applications but the concepts can be applied in client server settings as well.

Client-Side Validation

Client-side validation happens when the browser (or other GUI) executes code on the fly before sending data to the server. In most Web applications, FORM validation is typically done using client-side JavaScript. JavaScript commands can be developed in stand-alone files that end with a .js file extension or embedded right into the HTML GUIs.

The advantages of this method include the following:

- Data can be validated before being sent to the server, thus avoiding unnecessary trips across the network.
- It works well with DHTML.
- It is free to use.

The disadvantages of this method include the following:

- There is no control over the user's browser settings.
- Most handheld devices (such as a BlackBerry) do not run JavaScript.
- It is hard to maintain and debug.
- It allows all users to view the validation logic by looking at the page's source.

Server-Side Validation

Server-side validation happens when a Web browser (or other GUI) transmits data via HTTP to the Web server so that a server-side language, such as Java or PHP, can validate the data. Server-side validation is the preferred method because server-side languages have more powerful features and are more secure than JavaScript.

The advantages of this method include the following:

- Logic is stored on the server, not the client.
- Input data can be validated using database, session, or other server attributes.
- Server-side languages are easier to maintain using IDEs (integrated development environments) with debug capabilities.

The disadvantages of this method include the following:

- It requires page requests for form submittal.
- It allows unnecessary trips to the server.

Choosing the Right Countermeasure for the Misuse Case

Choosing the right design principle to code is the best defensive countermeasure a developer can take to secure the code. As Table 7-1 shows, a developer should be able to link the misuse case requirement to a design countermeasure as well as to a sound design principle for rationale.

Table 7-1   Mapping a misuse case to design countermeasures

Misuse case	Design countermeasure	Principles
Man in the middle	• Secure Sockets Layer (SSL) • Personal digital certificates	• Practice defense in depth • Promote privacy • Be reluctant to trust
Tamper with input fields	• POST methods • Web browser security • Secure Sockets Layer (SSL) • Personal digital certificates	• Promote privacy • Practice defense in depth • Be reluctant to trust
Code tampering	• Validating the input • Choosing a framework • Design patterns • Logging user navigation/requests	• Fail securely • Follow the principle of least privilege • Compartmentalize • Keep it simple • Remember that hiding secrets is hard • Be reluctant to trust • Use your community resources
Steal username/password	• Two-factor authentication (VPN)	• Secure the weakest link (users)

NOTE

If a design countermeasure requires the software requirement use case to be updated, now is the time to do so. For example, the misuse case for the "Log On" use case required the developers to log user navigation. This new request must be added to the use case.

INTRATEAM DECISIONS

Designing for security is a collaborative effort among developers, security experts, analysts, and other members of the project management team. These design meetings are best held in a conference room using a whiteboard. The purpose of these meetings is to plan the best approach to develop the current use case while evaluating the system design, architecture, and environment. Collaborating with other developers about the design of each software module provides time to go over each software specification and security feature.

These "open-design" discussions will show everyone on the team what the software components look like, how they interact, and what you need to use it. As object modeling and class diagrams begin to define the code, design flaws will become more obvious for both quality and security features. Collaborating on design details reinforces the "open-design" principle taught by Saltzer and Schroeder (Saltzer and Schroeder 1975). The more people who analyze the design for security weaknesses and quality issues, the more durable and reusable the code becomes. Designing for these details cannot be done by individuals working in isolated areas. Designing secure code takes teamwork and collaboration from all peers to ensure that the application's C.I.A. is met.

Essentially, what we need to do during code design is to take the conceptual models and system sequence diagrams that were created with the analysts and convert them into objects that developers can use for software specifications. When you get ready for such a meeting, bring the following with you:

- *Application Guide*: For review or updates. During design, a lot of new common components are created. Make sure to mandate that all developers use these modules and note the rationale behind the design.

- *Color markers*: One color for code design, one color for secure design, and one color for unanswered questions.

Here's what to remember when the meeting starts:

- Design meetings should last no longer than two hours. With anything more, people tend to burn out and lose focus.

- Try to limit the amount of meeting attendees to just relevant decision makers. Too many people offer too much advice.

- Encourage participation. One developer will explain his use case, what he expects from other screens, and what data they need to take and give. The other developers are there to offer advice, look for areas of weakness (security awareness), and gain overall understanding of the software module.

Choosing a Framework

Frameworks provide application design out of the box. Frameworks are existing bodies of code that are used to lay the foundation of how your application will be organized and designed. By using frameworks, application developers can spend more time on meeting software requirements rather than dealing with system architecture. Development teams have to consider their framework fairly carefully because it has a big impact on the project. There is a pretty good chance the framework you pick today will be the one you are using several years down the road.

You need to look at the capabilities of the framework, the skills of the development team, the platform, etc. Even before that, you need to look at the standards in the organization that you are working for (there may not be a choice). For example, Apache Struts provides Web application navigation controls between pages by mapping HTTP requests to the correct controllers (servlets).

 Frameworks offer many features and reusable code to applications. There are many frameworks from which to choose, and they are very requirement-specific.

NOTE

On any given project, it is very common to use five to ten different types of frameworks for various reasons. Make sure they come from reputable sources (for example, Apache) and make sure all other developers on the team use whichever one is chosen.

Choosing a Design Pattern

While analyzing object modeling and class diagrams, certain repeatable processes and methods will keep popping up. For example, each use case will need input validating, objects will need to call other objects for the same reason (i.e., database connections), and each use case will need logging capabilities. These common, repeatable software modules can be handled by certain design patterns.

To some extent, the use of frameworks enforces design patterns by their nature of reusability. Other times, design patterns will have to be selectively chosen or created as each use case is analyzed and modeled. The most common design pattern used in a Web application is the MVC (Model-View-Controller) framework, which is a design pattern created for web applications largely due to the use of the Apache Struts framework. In an MVC design pattern, the presentation (View) is separate from the business logic (Model) and each use case is assigned a dispatcher (Controller) that is in charge of making sure the request is satisfied. Figure 7-17 is a diagram of the MVC controller.

Notice in Figure 7-17 that the View, Controller, and Model have their own roles and responsibilities. The best thing about design patterns is that design patterns force software components to play out their part by nature.

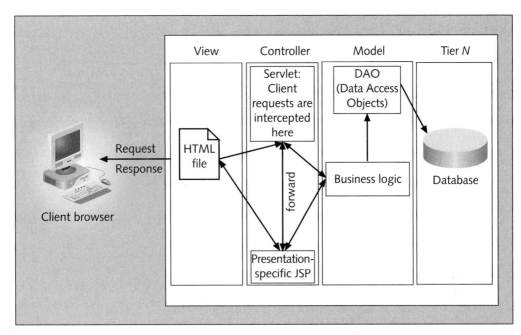

Figure 7-17   MVC design pattern

Note that MVC design patterns not only help organize code libraries, but also assign roles and responsibilities to the code instances themselves. For example, if you needed to code an SQL query, you wouldn't put that code into a view object; rather, you would put it in a database access object commonly known as DAO.

Separating display data from business data also enforces security and access rights. Web services are a great example of this. In a Web service, the business logic is hidden from all views and requires authentication before usage.

CHAPTER SUMMARY

- ❏ Designing for the details is an all–encompassing task that converts the use case concepts to actual software requirement specifications.

- ❏ Designing for the details also provides the developer a chance to go over the application's architecture, design, and network infrastructure.

- ❏ The network, architecture, and supporting software should also be reviewed for vulnerabilities.

- ❏ By keeping up to date with the latest vulnerabilities and translating that knowledge to how it affects your application, you will be prepared for disasters when and if they strike.

- ❏ If a threat is identified as a potential risk, a countermeasure must be designed into the application.

- ❏ Hold design meetings with other team members and other intracompany resources.

KEY TERMS

black box — A term used to describe a process where everything about the process is unknown except for the inputs and outputs.

class diagrams — Software module blueprints that serve as the software specification for a specific module/component.

firewall — Security software stored in a device, such as a router, that is configured to permit or deny data requests to and from machines connected to a network.

interaction diagrams — Diagrams that display interaction activity between the objects within a model.

messages — Communication links between objects that define input parameters and return parameters.

object modeling — The process of creating a visualization (using a standard notation) of a software system, design, or component.

perimeter defense — Drawing a perimeter between two classes of networks, those trusted and those that are not.

phishing — A fraudulent activity in which an attacker hosts a Web site posing as another business or sends an e-mail with links to the fraudulent Web site. The intent is to trick the user into entering his or her username, password, account numbers, and so on.

sandbox — A tightly controlled area for resources to be used by visiting applications. Sandboxes allow for self-contained programs, such as Java applets, to run within browsers.

security policy — Constraints on access to machines for external systems and people. These policies are created by the company, application, or department and are enforced through administrative rights and configuration (software installation).

signature — The method name, number and type of parameters, and return type of a specific method.

REVIEW QUESTIONS

1. What is the main purpose of collaborating with the developer?
   a. to go over use case requirements
   b. to translate use case requirements and conceptual modeling into object interaction diagrams and class diagrams so that code specifications can be planned
   c. to identify inputs and outputs
   d. to look for weaknesses and unknowns in the use case documentation
   e. to provide a discussion platform for the developers so that they can work together

2. What is the main purpose of object modeling?
   a. to convert the concepts into objects
   b. to refine conceptual modeling
   c. to identify what software objects are needed for the current use case
   d. to test the knowledge of other developers for their modeling skills
   e. to help educate the team on the software requirements

3. Why are interaction diagrams important?

   a. They list the messages between objects.

   b. They ensure object modeling is complete.

   c. They force the developer to step through each function and list what message is used in each step.

   d. They become the code specification for the class diagrams.

   e. all of the above

4. A _____ is when a hash function is run to generate a unique number to be used as part of the communication key or authentication.

5. A _____ is software that most often runs on dedicated hardware that acts as a filter between a private network and a public one.

7

6. Why is choosing a development framework considered to be very important to a team?

7. Explain the difference between a class and an object.

8. What are class diagrams?

   a. software requirements specifications

   b. diagrams that explain the communication between objects

   c. diagrams that depict user input

   d. diagrams that depict input validation

9. When assigning properties to class diagrams, what is the rule for determining if a property belongs to one class over another?

10. What is the signature of a method?

   a. class name, method, property

   b. method name, return value, argument

   c. method name, return value, class name

   d. method name, argument, class name

11. Which of the following is not a security model for HTTP?

   a. SSL

   b. digital certificates

   c. POST transactions

   d. input validation

   e. user training

12. If an application required a physical device for a user to sign on, what security model should be followed?

    a. SSL

    b. personal digital certificates

    c. code signing

    d. two-factor authentication

13. If a piece of software needed a public key to locate files on a remote hard-drive to install hidden files, what security model should be followed?

    a. SSL

    b. personal digital certificates

    c. code signing

    d. two-factor authentication

14. _____ states that one Web page can access data on another Web page if the two pages do not exist within the same domain.

15. _____ is an existing body of code that is used to lay the foundation of how an application is organized and designed.

16. What is the "perimeter defense" approach to security?

17. Network security is not the job of the application developer. True or False?

18. When ordering messages in interaction diagrams, you should order the sequence from the most important method to the least important method. True or False?

19. If a Web site uses SSL, the encrypted data is secure. True or False?

20. An MVC is a framework. True or False?

HANDS-ON PROJECTS

HANDS-ON PROJECTS

Project 7-1 Working with an Interaction Diagram

1. Read the CONCEPTS of a use case at the end of this project and become familiar with each name and its role within the application.

2. Open the "HOP 7-1 Interaction Diagram.doc" file from the Chapter 7 course data.

3. Place the appropriate concept name in the matching interaction model diagram from the Chapter 7 course data.

4. Place the appropriate method name and signature in the matching sequence number in the interaction diagram from the Chapter 7 course data. Illustrate each method by giving the argument (which is shown inside the parentheses) and the return value (which is shown on the left side of the colon).

The following CONCEPTS are provided for you: WEB CLIENT, CONTOLLER, VALI-DATOR, USERINFO, USERBEAN.

WEB CLIENT

From the WEB CLIENT, the user will enter a user id and password as input parameters. Those input parameters will be passed to the application's CONTROLLER, which will handle the request.

CONTROLLER

The CONTROLLER will send the request to a VALIDATOR to validate the input parameters.

Method: processRequest

Input: HTTPRequest

Input: userId

Input: password

Output: HTTPResponse

Logic

If VALIDATOR Successful

 Log the user

 Send the request to USERINFO

 Send the request to WEB CLIENT

Else

 Log the user

 Send the Request back to the WEB CLIENT

VALIDATOR

Method: validate

Input: userId

Input: password

Output: boolean

USERINFO

Method: getUserInfo

Input: userId

Output: USERBEAN

7

Project 7-2 Securing the Data

1. Open the "HOP 7-2 Securing Data.doc" file from the Chapter 7 course data.

2. Using the security models listed below, place each model into the appropriate lock box in the diagram. Note: Each lock represents data in transit, and you have to choose which security model best protects the data during the time of transaction.

   - Secure Sockets Layer (SSL)

   - Personal digital certificates

   - Two-factor authentication

CASE PROJECT

Evaluate the Networks

1. Using UML notation, draw a network diagram of your office, home, or school.

2. List all the applications that are used on that network; these applications include e-mail software, databases, Internet.

3. What would you do, if anything, if you were in charge of securing these applications?

4. Present your findings to the class.

CHAPTER REFERENCES

Gong, Li. 1999. *Inside Java 2 Platform Security: Architecture, API Design, and Implementation.* Boston: Addison-Wesley.

Grossman, Jeremiah. 2005. Phishing with Super Bait: White Hat Security. http://www.whitehatsec.com/home/resources/presentations/files/phishing_superbait.pdf (accessed February 20, 2008).

Saltzer, Jerome H. and Michael D. Schroeder. 1975. The Protection of Information in Computer Systems. http://web.mit.edu/Saltzer/www/publications/protection/index.html (accessed February 20, 2008).

US-CERT. 2008. Welcome to the US-CERT Vulnerability Notes Database. http://www.kb.cert.org/vuls/ (accessed February 20, 2008).

Graff, Mark and Kenneth R. Van Wyk. 2003. *Secure Coding: Principles and Practices.* California: O'Reilly.

VeriSign. 2007. Secure Sockets Layer (SSL): How It Works. http://www.verisign.com/ssl/ssl-information-center/how-ssl-security-works/index.html (accessed February 20, 2008).

8

DEVELOPMENT TOOLS: CHOOSE WISELY

Upon completion of this material, you should be able to:

♦ Understand the use of development tools in the industry

♦ Understand the use of development tools in the organization

♦ Understand the use of development tools in the cube

♦ Know how to maintain your toolbox

Without tools, developing code, building security features, and testing your work will become much harder. The use of tools in today's development process has taken over so much of the small, behind-the-scenes activities in coding that most developers would not be productive without them. In fact, tools are taking over the development landscape with smart integrated program language compilers by software vendors. The goal of this chapter is to explain why tools are of the utmost importance in software development and which tools you will need in your development process.

THE USE OF DEVELOPMENT TOOLS IN THE INDUSTRY

A development tool is any hardware or software device that is used to create a software program. Development tools are used to assist the programmer in completing a function, unit of work, or task within the software creation. Several years ago, programming activities consisted of a programmer typing cryptic commands in an MS-DOS prompt or Telnet session. In today's modern environment, software vendors are creating intuitive GUIs with integrated click-and-drag options, source-code assistants, and built-in syntax checkers that do all the ugly, MS-DOS command prompting for the developer.

The industry is responding to the needs of business consumers by creating integrated tools that can seamlessly cross over multi-language programs, allowing the developer to compile, debug, and run any project anywhere. This technological breakthrough will have an immense impact on the developer. First, tools will allow the developer to do more with less because of the built-in capabilities and ease of use that tools provide. However, as more and more developers are trained to use tools instead of native languages, they could lose the total understanding of how technology works and, thus, would never see potential security vulnerabilities.

Overall, the goals of the industry in issuing tools are as follows:

- Providing total automation
- Making the development process dependable and trustworthy
- Keeping development costs down

Total Automation

Automation produces consistency. If you can create quality, secure code through the use of automated tools, you can build a development process that relies on automation. This means taking a repetitive task that a developer has to perform and automating that task with the precision and speed of another piece of software (tool). Total automation helps ensure that all tasks are complete, accurate, and efficient while at the same time eliminating human error, such as syntax or forgetting that certain tasks need to be executed in a logical order.

Using construction tools for automation reinforces the working relationship between humans and computers. Computers are left to carry out the methodical tedious work with precision while the human codes software with instructions based on creative designs (Dupuis, et al. 2004). Therefore, the more complicated the tasks that developers have to perform, the more that tools are needed. No matter how many tools are used in the development process, it is important to note that automation is no substitute for human creativity and design. Humans have the unique ability to break down complicated problems into smaller, easier-to-understand segments. Typically, tool automation has a nominal effect on logical issues. The tools cannot know the intent of the coder, so it is hard for them to follow with logical issues in coding.

Table 8-1 illustrates common tasks a developer performs while writing software. Along with each task is a brief description of the type of work performed. As this table illustrates, for every activity a developer has to do, a tool can be used to help ensure the activity is conducted as thoroughly and accurately as possible. The tools listed in Table 8-1 are just some examples of the many tools available to assist in the automated world of software development. Chances are that you will work with most of them, if not all of them, during your career.

NOTE   One thing to point out is that software tools continue to evolve. The amount of tasks that are possible with a single tool has increased substantially. Not that long ago, development involved using an editor, a compiler, a debugger, version control, etc., whereas today all of that functionality often can be found in a single tool. This is really where Integrated Development Environments have come into the picture.

8

Table 8-1   Automated development tasks

Task	Activities involved	Tools that can provide related automation
Design code	• Perform object modeling • Build use cases • Sketch algorithms • Write pseudocode	• Frameworks • CASE • RAD • Visio
Secure design	• Perform risk analysis • Create misuse cases	• @Risk • UML
Develop code	• Write precise instructions using a linguistic computer language	• Some CASE tools can create the stubs, but manual techniques do apply. • IDEs
Secure code	• Run static code analyzers • Run packet sniffers	• Fortify Secure Code Analysis • FindBugs
Test code	• Perform unit test • Perform stress test • Perform regression test	• IDE • Load testers • Networking monitors • Third-party plug-ins
Debug code	• Walk through errors	• IDE • Debugging tools
Compile code	• Compile modules from the linguistic software language to computer machine language.	• IDE
Build code	• Use WAR and EAR components • Create EXE files	• ANT • IDE • OpenMake • .NET

Table 8-1 Automate development tasks (continued)

Task	Activities involved	Tools that can provide related automation
Deploy code	• FTP files (binary or ASCII mode) from server to server • Turn off debug statements	• FTP software • ANT

Dependable Process

The software development process becomes more dependable when developers' tasks move toward tested automation. Absolute dependability and trustworthiness, while desirable in theory, often are impossible to obtain in reality. Instead, developers must strive for increasing dependability and trustworthiness as much as is practically possible. Fortunately, automation increases repeatability, which allows each task to be carried out consistently, over and over. If the automation is well tested for accuracy and security, it will be dependable.

As an example of dependability, suppose you have an application that needs to be deployed from the testing environment to a staging environment every day. You can either manually FTP all files to the staging machines or you can use an automated tool that does this work for you. An automated tool can be set up to get a specific version of code from a repository (tool) and FTP (tool) that code to the staging environment. Once there, the same tool can then execute a SHELL script (tool) that would restart the server. Here, you have several tools and software programs interacting with one another in a very precise and efficient way, leaving the developer free to concentrate on his or her next requirement.

Keeping Development Costs Down

Many developers shy away from learning how to use new tools. They are afraid that the time invested on the front end will not pay off on the back end. They are not convinced that the tools, after being integrated into the development process, will pay dividends. In this part of the chapter, you will learn why the use of common tools often *does* save money—consistently so—due to the achievement of the following:

- Sharing of similar designs and tasks
- Dispersing of knowledge
- Sharing of the talent pool

Sharing Similar Designs and Tasks

One big cost savings that stems from relying on tools for total automation is the reusability it offers to a company as a whole. Typically, developers on one project do not interact with developers on another. For whatever reason, the tools and configuration used are hidden from other teams (partially because it is what makes developers successful), and each project's team members are left to reinvent the wheel themselves. Even assuming that individual teams have their own talent and ability to automate tasks (most teams do not have these talents and abilities, by the way), the teams will spend hundreds of billable hours evaluating, downloading, and configuring the same tools as their colleagues.

Large companies often have hundreds of projects and separate applications being worked on by different teams and it is possible to share similar designs and tasks throughout multiple projects. In other words, what works for one application often will work equally well for other applications.

TIP   Although cost savings aren't a concern for the individual application developer, knowing about this benefit could help you earn bonus points with project management. By showing a desire to save costs, you are justifying your existence as well as displaying your teamwork approach to development.

8

Dispersing Knowledge

A development process that relies on tool automation for code development and deployment isn't jeopardized because of the loss of key individuals. Using tools instead of the heroics of talented individuals enables other developers to strengthen their skills and knowledge of the system as well, making the team strong as a whole. This dispersing of system knowledge allows for a very productive and efficient development process.

Consider two development teams, A and B:

Team A has five developers in all, and one of the five is the official team lead. The team lead is responsible for deploying the code to the production servers, but to do this activity, the source code must be prepared. CONSTANT values must be changed, XML file locations have to be altered, and all logging to the system file needs to be stopped. The leader of Team A has been doing these activities for two years and knows all of these requirements like the back of his hand. What do you think could happen to the deployment process if that team lead were to quit his job today?

Team B has five developers in all, and one of the five is the official team lead. The team lead is responsible for deploying the code to the production servers, but to do this activity, the source code must be prepared. The team lead has automated all the deployment activities with tools and has documented the tool set along with the instructions in the Application Guide. What do you think could happen to the deployment process if that team lead were to quit his job today?

Sharing the Talent Pool

In addition to applications sharing the same tools and tasks, they can also share the same human resources. For example, if the development tools are the same and all the applications in the company are coded and designed in a similar fashion, the developers can go from one project to another with no problem. This alone saves a small fortune because an individual project need not incur the cost of training new team members on the system.

THE USE OF DEVELOPMENT TOOLS IN THE ORGANIZATION

Choosing tools for software development cannot be done by the development team alone. Most development tools cost a lot of money, and project managers must obtain approvals from purchasing departments before any decision can be made. Organizations use tools that can be supported, that work within supporting IT infrastructures, and that correspond with long-term IT goals, such as versions, operating systems, and vendors.

Organizations are always on the lookout for newer techniques and tools that make their current processes more efficient. Because software developers are on the front line of writing code, they typically see new tools or different versions before the organization's managers. Therefore, developers will, from time to time, need to explain what types of development tools they need and why.

TIP

Company policies and/or project managers ultimately choose which tools to use; developers can only recommend them.

Tool recommendations by the developers and tool selections by the overall development team are based on certain criteria and rationales gathered from an evaluation process. Your team can narrow its choices by doing the following:

- Understanding the company's infrastructure and constraints
- Evaluating only industry-standard tools

Company Infrastructure and Constraints

What software and/or licenses are available to the development team is largely determined by the types of servers, operating systems, and support the company has. For example, if a company's IT infrastructure uses Microsoft as its primary software vendor and its servers run IIS Web servers, the .NET Framework along with VB and ASP will be the tools of choice because that is what the company has already paid for.

Platforms

Every company has an application platform that it chose to support and its policies will mandate that the tools that are chosen work with that platform. Two common application platforms are as follows:

- **J2EE**: The Java 2 Enterprise Edition platform provides the specifications and the tools for developing and deploying enterprise-scale, multi-tier applications. Based on the popular Java language created by Sun Microsystems, J2EE builds on the Java 2 Standard Edition (J2SE) by providing server-side components with built-in capabilities, such as JDBC and EJB.

- *.NET*: The Microsoft .NET Framework is a common environment for building smart client applications, XML Web services, and mobile and Web-based applications with common class libraries, such as ASP.NET, ADO.NET, and Windows Forms.

As Figure 8-1 shows, the IT infrastructure, current licensing agreements from approved vendors, and the platforms on which the applications need to run all determine the viable options for the team.

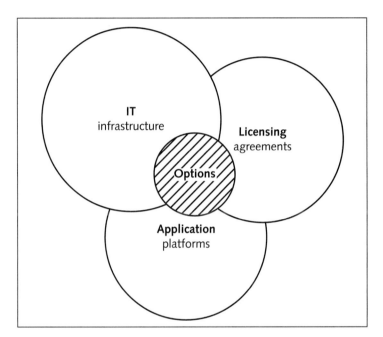

Figure 8-1   Knowing the options

Working Within and Outside of Comfort Zones

Because of the complexity of modern applications, it is extremely important that each developer on the same project use the exact same tool as his or her colleagues. Most programmers tend to favor one construction tool over another, because that's all they know. Whatever the case might be, the developers need to decide on a standard set of construction tools before coding. This decision among the programmers will help standardize the construction process so that code integration and software development will be less of an issue.

TIP   Getting out of your comfort zone is about using tools that the team wants to use and not using just your own individual preference. Choose tools that are good for the project and the company, not what is good for your personal résumé.

Code that is developed by one tool does not necessarily integrate well with other tools. As Figures 8-2 and 8-3 show, each tool has its own way of displaying data. Because of the differences in tools, the code will not export easily from one IDE to another. That is, different tools will not align code statements the same or display code in the same readable format.

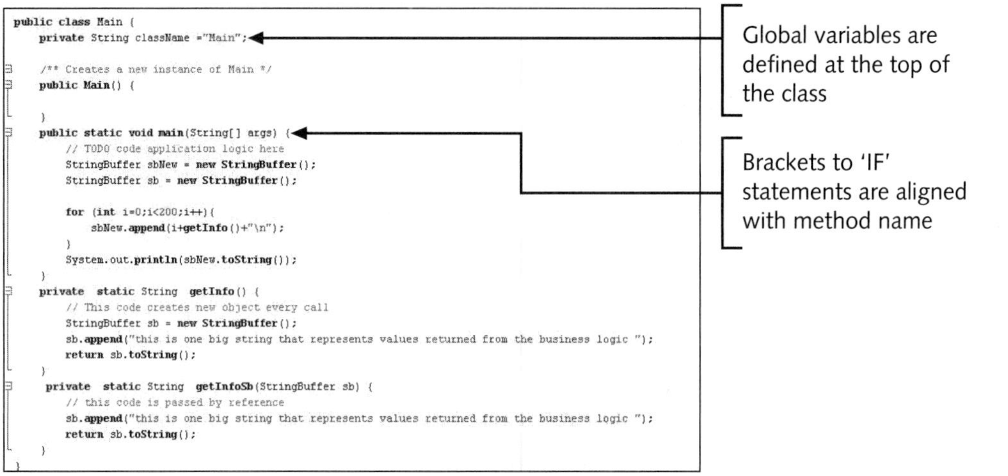

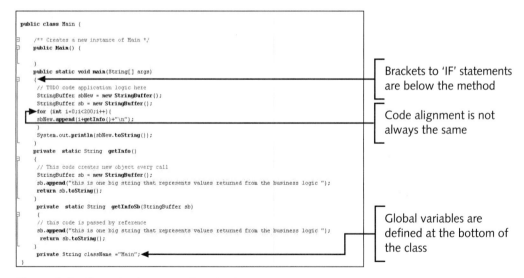

Figure 8-2   Code in one tool

Figure 8-3   Same code on another tool

Having all developers on the team use the same tool is important for the following reasons:

- *Help factor:* If one person has a problem trying to get a tool to automate a feature, such as turning off debugs, it can be hard for the other programmers to help because they might not be familiar with that tool or because that tool doesn't have the automated capability that the other tools do.

■ *Integration factor*. Developers do not have that much time to read through one another's code statements. The code needs to read the same so that their eyes can be trained to look in the same areas for certain specifics, such as variable declarations, error handling, and code imports.

■ *Configuration factor*. All tools need to be configured to work with one another. If the tool set is different, configurations might or might not work.

■ *Code maintenance*: Code becomes easier to maintain because of the common look and feel.

■ *Same code translation*: Code is compiled from the same version of compilers.

Open Source Versus Proprietary

Proprietary tools charge a fee for license(s), either per seat or per server, and they are owned by the company that issues the tools. The fees can be charged as a one-time flat rate or annually by the vendor providing the tools. Proprietary tools typically come loaded with extensive features, full-time support, and well-documented help and assistance.

Open source tools are free to use in accordance with the open source license agreement, typically the General Public License, and are owned by the originating author. Typical open source tools allow developers and other practitioners from all over the world to apply fixes to bugs or add more features to the current baseline. Some companies, like Red Hat and Novell, offer full-time support on a contract basis for such open source tools because the success of these tools helps their other products and services grow.

TIP

How does your team choose the tools? It depends on prior licensing agreements and restrictions and how well each type of tool fits into the overall vision of the project.

QUICK CHECKS

To appreciate the depth of what GNU has to offer, do the following:

1. Log in to the GNU Web site *www.gnu.org*.
2. What is the official logo for GNU?
3. What does GPL stand for?
4. Can you write software using tools from GPL and sell that program at a profit?

If you decide to use proprietary tools, make sure you understand the licensing agreement and that you read the fine print. I once used a tool within an application that required one license per application per server. Because my application was the first one to be hosted on the company's server, my project paid for only one license. Several months later, the vendor checked their audit logs and found out that 50 other applications had been installed on that server since. Needless to say, all current development stopped until a solution was worked out to replace the proprietary tool. To prevent costly lawsuits, make sure you monitor licensed software closely.

Avoid having licensed tools issued to the names of individuals on the team. This can create problems with company policies and license renewals. Further, you should ensure that:

- The company owns the license.
- Those who request the license actually use the tools.
- Those who use the tools actually requested the license.

Evaluating and Using Industry Standard Tools

Evaluate only those development tools that are industry accepted and widely used in various software projects. These tools are usually very well documented and tested; furthermore, it will be easier to get support or to find working examples on how to do something. In addition, when the need arises to hire additional team members, finding programmers with industry-standard tool experience is easier than finding programmers who want to learn your homegrown solution.

TIP

Industry-standard tools usually come with additional bells and whistles and they are made to work with other standard tools. If you find the tool you're evaluating does not match your needs, evaluate another one. As an application developer, you do not have the time to try to make your own tool. Don't waste project time competing with industry-leading tools.

Tools should be evaluated on the following criteria:

- Does the tool satisfy the need?
- Does the tool help find security vulnerabilities?
- Is the tool readily available?
- Is the tool easy to use?
- Does the tool integrate with other technologies and tools that are currently used on the project?
- Does the tool have visibility and reporting features?

The following sections discuss each of these criteria in turn.

Satisfying the Need

First and foremost, the tool selected needs to satisfy the need. As the project evolves, the need for specific tools might change. It would be a shame to spend any amount of money for a tool only to find out that you really did not need it. Make sure your needs are defined and that the tool can actually fulfill that need. To avoid making this costly mistake, try before you buy! All tools will come with a trial version; take the time to download, configure, and use it. When possible, call the tool's technical support and explain your needs to them. The support should be able to give you the instructions you need, and with today's PC remote connection, the support team could even help you with setup and configuration.

Helping Find Security Vulnerabilities

Security tools scan binary code for common vulnerability traits found in modern software. Security tools act a lot like antivirus software tools that scan computer files for known viruses. Instead of the latest definitions of common viruses, security tools scan for definitions of software attacks. For example, a security tool will look at the source for variables and methods that have vulnerable logic, monitor the expected behavior in memory, and check whether the code is networked for port or socket vulnerabilities. It then will highlight the sensitive areas and create a report that tells the developer what needs to be done before the code is used in production.

The human eye and brain cannot compete against the accuracy and precision of these types of tools. Security tools should be selected based on their ability to look for weak or vulnerable areas of the application. You check for this ability by looking at how the tool finds common vulnerabilities (where does it get its internal definitions) and how the tool works for your programming language. There are also security tool "bake-offs" that are conducted by practitioners and software vendors who are in this market segment. These bake-offs consist of several leading security code scanners that parse through sample programs that have vulnerable code hidden in them. At the end of the contest, the reports that get generated from the tools are displayed and sometimes published for the industry to see.

Readily Available

From time to time, the need to reinstall all of your tools and reconfigure the developer's box appears. This is true when you need to install the next version of an operating system, such as Windows, or because of a nasty virus that can't be cured. Whatever the reason, you're going to need your tools to be readily available when your PC gets blown away. Make sure the source to your tools, whether on CD or Web site link, is readily available.

Software vendors can go out of business or merge with their competitors and sometimes their tools don't always make their expected shelf life. In addition to products from vendors, you might choose to use an open source tool from an unknown author whose Web site can no longer be found. Remember how you obtained the tool and make sure you can still install it at anytime.

Ease of Use

Deadlines are tight on software projects, and it is hard to find the time for learning how to use the newest tools. The tools you select should be user friendly and simple to figure out. Some things to look for include working examples, trial versions, APIs, and how-to documents. Obviously, we all learn differently and what seems complicated to one might seem easy to another. Experience, exposure, and familiarity play a key role when determining whether a tool is easy to use. For example, if you grew up creating images with GIMP, Adobe Photoshop might seem like a walk in the park. However, if you had never been exposed to a graphic generator before, even Adobe Photoshop might seem like an intimidating tool.

TIP

Ease of use is relative to the team's makeup and background. If you have a chance to evaluate a tool and within a few hours you are up and running with it, chances are that others will pick it up easily too.

Integration with Other Tools

Software applications require an army of tools to help keep things running smoothly. Therefore, tools need to be able to automatically work with other tools and help run tasks that the other tools cannot run. When you're selecting a tool, make sure it runs with your current software configuration (Windows versus Macintosh) and check to see if it allows for third-party plug-ins for easy integration.

Open source tools have been moving in this area for quite some time. It is very common to have open source tools plug in to other open source tools for easier development. Proprietary tools, on the other hand, tend to integrate well only with other tools in their family. For example, Microsoft tools integrate very well with other Microsoft tools, and IBM tools integrate very well with other IBM tools.

NOTE

There is a current push in the industry that aims to help bridge the gap between open source tools and proprietary tools.

As Figure 8-4 shows, Sun Microsystems' Java IDE NetBeans comes preloaded out of the box to integrate with other tools (frameworks), such as JavaServer Faces and Apache Struts.

Visibility and Reporting

It's easy to see why a development team can spend thousands of dollars on tools they think they need. What's hard, especially for management, is to quantify the spending versus improvements. Therefore, tools that you select should come with a "workbench" feature so that developers can take before and after shots of their software. Management likes to see

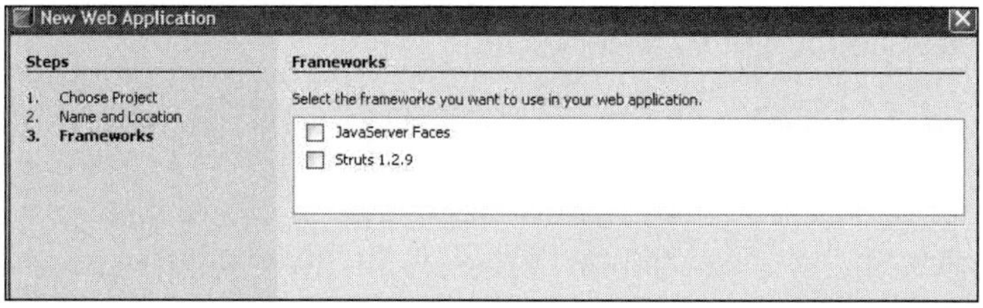

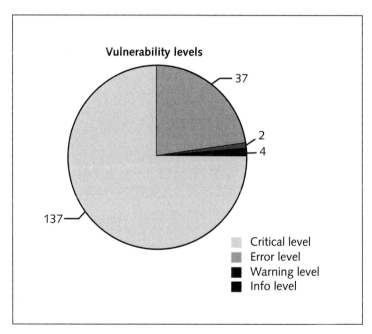

Figure 8-4   Sun NetBeans IDE

improvements in the form of graphs, charts, or percentages; thus, the tools you select should come with some sort of reporting feature.

Tools should report progress and information to the development team. For example, everyone understands pie charts, so make your work visible by showing the progress. Reports such as source code scanning results, heap size reports, or number of bugs found can be captioned in reports by today's tools and shared with the team. As Figure 8-5 shows, results from a source scanner can help everyone gauge success.

8

Figure 8-5   Reporting progress

The Use of Development Tools in the Cube

The right tool for the right job makes all the difference in the world. Highly skilled developers are the ones who know how to use their tools well. If you want to grow within the ranks of software development, you need to know how to master your tool types. To become a master developer, you need to master tools in the following categories:

- Tools that assist in writing code
- Tools that enhance quality
- Tools that enhance security
- Tools that assist with deployment

Tools That Assist in Writing Code

Tools that assist with the development of code are much easier to use than the old Notepad or VI editors. Today's code assistants are faster and much more accurate. In the newer code assistants, the code statements are evaluated and tested while the developer types. Built-in code intelligence watches the syntax entered and tries to assist the developer by catching typos or broken If statements up front before the compile process takes place.

The most popular tools for code assistance are called integrated development environments (IDEs). IDEs are tools packaged together as one application program to assist developers in writing code. Typical tool packages include the following:

- *Code editors*: These are code assistants built in to the GUI that autofill method signatures, brackets, and key words.
- *Compilers*: These tools turn programming languages into machine code (binary) that the CPU can use.
- *GUIs*: These are sophisticated screens that allow click and drag, text box fill-ins, and other user-friendly features while building the code, XML files, or configuration files behind the scenes.
- *Global search tools*: These tools allow developers to search for all instances of key words, object names, or methods.
- *Automated refactoring tools*: These tools refactor code for the developers so that logic is broken up into smaller modules.
- *Automated debuggers*: These packaged debug tools step through the code while executing. This tool allows developers to see how the code executes and what the values of each parameter and variable are during run time.
- *Integrated test servers*: These tools execute code either as stand-alone programs or on built-in application servers. The server tools emulate production servers so what happened on the developer's machine (execution steps) will also happen on production machines.

Using an IDE is easier than writing code in the old command-line format. Because of the vast features and ease of use, IDEs should be encouraged on all projects. IDEs are still mainly program language–specific, so whatever language you code in, choose an IDE that fits your needs.

TIP   There are all types of IDEs on the market today, from proprietary to open source. Proprietary IDEs tend to come with a lot of bells and whistles out of the box, but open source IDEs offer the same features as long as the development team members don't mind getting their hands dirty with configurations. The ones I use for the Java languages are Sun's NetBeans or IBM's Eclipse.

Tools That Enhance Quality

Quality tools not only analyze application code for quality issues but also the resources the code uses. It was once possible for a programmer to work his entire career without having to run external tools on the code, but now that so many applications share the same resources, you, as the developer, have to consider whether your own actions will cause problems for everyone else. Tools that will help you do that include the following:

- Heap management tools
- Profiling tools

Heap Management

Nothing diminishes application performance like inefficient code that takes up all of the available memory. Unlike **memory leaks**, which occur when the application loses the ability to release memory resources when they are no longer needed, heap size can also eat away at the application's memory if the code is not properly developed. Heap size is not really a memory leak in the sense that if you had enough memory and performance, the code would resolve itself.

You have to work a lot harder to get memory leaks in modern environments like Java or .NET because you really only have to manage the allocation side of the equation whereas in the old days of C and C++, you had to manage both allocation and deallocation of resources. The management of deallocation is what causes a lot of memory leaks. Java and .NET just require you not to hold references to objects when they are no longer needed; thus, the only concern to a modern developer is to code efficiently.

There are two areas of heap size you need to look for in the application:

- Does the application free up memory efficiently? This is a type of memory leak that could easily be solved by running a memory debugging tool against the code and viewing the memory CPU monitor. When the memory exceeds the allotted usage (100%), look at the code that is being executed.
- Is there any code within the application that carries a lot of overhead?

Figure 8-6 shows an example of a code snippet with two methods. One method, getInfo(), creates a new StringBuffer object every time it is called. The second method, which is getInfo(StringBuffer sb), takes a StringBuffer as an argument and uses a reference to an existing object. Naturally, the first method that creates a new StringBuffer inside the method will cause a substantial increase in the application's memory bank.

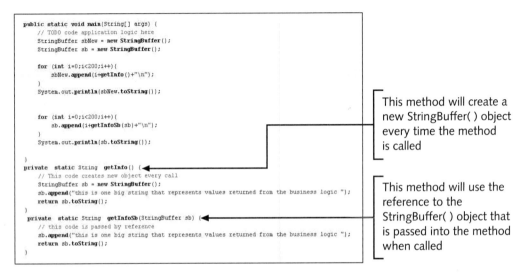

This method will create a new StringBuffer( ) object every time the method is called

This method will use the reference to the StringBuffer( ) object that is passed into the method when called

Figure 8-6   Memory test

When the code from Figure 8-6 runs using the first method, getInfo(), a steady increase in memory will keep rising until the space allocated for the application's heap size is maxed out, which will cause the server to crash, as shown in Figure 8-7.

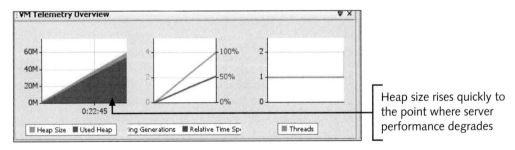

Heap size rises quickly to the point where server performance degrades

Figure 8-7   Spike in heap size

When the code from Figure 8-6 runs using the second method, getInfo(StringBuffer sb), a steady increase in memory will rise enough to complete the method, but the heap size will not exceed any more than what is needed. As Figure 8-8 shows, the heap size raises to a manageable size in heap.

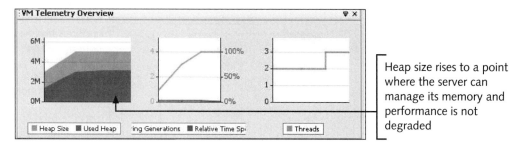

Figure 8-8   Manageable size in heap

Obviously, if the method creates an object every time it is run (and it doesn't need to), then that is not efficient. In Java, if that object is created and referenced only in a method variable, however, then as soon as the method completes, the variable goes out of scope and the object becomes eligible for garbage collection.

Profiling

Sometimes, the way developers *think* they coded the application isn't always reflected in how the application runs. This discrepancy between intent and outcome often is the result of hours of evaluating code statements and following lines of logic trying to figure out what the application is doing (or not doing). If the developer isn't sure which objects are getting called in the program and the order in which those objects are called, profiling the code will help. Profiling is a way to identify the performance bottlenecks in an executing path. **Profiling** can provide the following information:

- Time of execution
- Number of objects created

It can also:

- Help security analysis by auditing applications
- Provide software documentation

This information is very valuable when response time is slow and the developer needs to figure out what is taking the longest time to execute. As Figure 8-9 shows, a profiler tool will inform the developer which methods or hot spots are being called, how long that method is taking in the total use case, and how many times the methods and objects are being called and invoked.

Tools That Enhance Security

Today's generation of security tools "can only tell you if you're in deep trouble, not how secure the application is" (McGraw 2006, p. 23). However, knowing you're in deep trouble is always a good thing because it gives you, as the developer, a starting point from which to work.

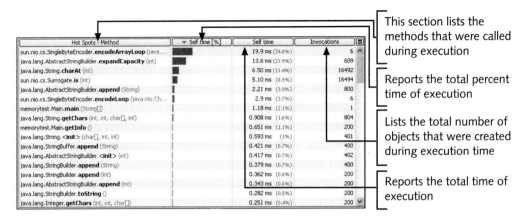

Figure 8-9   Profiler tools

The use of security tools within the development process comes with a twofold benefit. First, it allows the programmers to eliminate all the susceptible code that the tools found. In addition, and more important, it raises the *awareness* of potential security vulnerabilities across the board. These tools challenge the programmers to think about the "what-ifs" of software security. That in itself is a huge step for secure code.

A code analyzer tool is a software program that parses through binary code syntax and finds areas of weak code. While scanning code, the analyzers automatically trace the data flow from one object to the next, highlighting vulnerable areas in the application where an attack can take place. After scanning, the tool will report a list of possible code flaws and/or weaknesses so that the programmer can go back and properly correct the logic.

Popular code analyzers on the market today include the following:

- ■ *Fortify Source Code Analysis (SCA)*: Advanced features enable security professionals to review more code and prioritize issues in less time, while helping development teams identify and fix issues early and with less effort. Fortify SCA supports a wide variety of languages, frameworks, and operating systems and delivers depth and accuracy in its results (Fortify Software 2007).

- ■ *FindBugs*: FindBugs is free software, available under the terms of the Lesser GNU Public License. It is written in Java and can be run with any virtual machine compatible with Sun's JDK 1.4. It can analyze programs written for any version of Java. FindBugs was originally developed by Bill Pugh and David Hovemeyer (FindBugs 2007).

Security tools are new to the market and have yet to mature. I expect a lot of growth and adaptability in the coming versions, but as of now, there are a lot of **false positives** and **false negatives**. False positives are code warnings that just indicate to the developer that something might be wrong and that the callout should be checked. False negatives are real security vulnerabilities that are not reported in the code analyzers.

Tools That Assist with Deployments

Deployment tools assist with the building and deploying of application code. They are essential to a secure development process because they automatically off-load the work of file transfers and the building of executables or jar files without being tainted by non-tested software. They also can invoke other programs via SHELL scripts.

Deployment tools include the following:

- Code repositories
- Code transportation

Code Repositories

A code repository is used for code storage. On any given project, code is developed on the developer's workstation. Code repositories allow that programmer to check in the code from the workstation and into a centralized data house. Having a centralized code repository offers an opportunity to centralize the backups of source code and ensure that current backups of the entire repository are available for recovery in case of a failure.

Code repositories are very important to a development team for the following reasons:

- *Code sharing*: All other programmers have access to the latest and greatest without stepping on one another's code.

- *Versioning/baseline*: Developers can manage which features go out in the next version. As mentioned in the Application Guide discussion from Chapter 4, versioning needs to be addressed by the development team, and the rules need to be documented in the Application Guide.

- *Centralizing storage*: This allows the code to be deployed from one centralized place rather than relying on an individual developer to have the latest code base on his or her local machine.

Build Management

ANT (Another Neat Tool), located at *http://ant.apache.org/*, is an XML-based tool that calls out targets (or specific tasks) in a treelike structure in which various tasks are executed sequentially. Each target is run by an object that implements a particular task interface.

Developers use ANT version control tools when doing code deployments from one environment to another. (These deployments include test, development, and production.) The tool should be able to pull code versions (baselines) and move the selected files to a specific destination automatically.

ANT replaces all the manual tasks that developers do before deploying code. Common targets of repetition include (Apache 2007):

- *FTP (File Transfer Protocol) code*: Automatically FTPs code files (class or ASCII) from one machine to another.

- *Get code*: Automatically interfaces with version control software and extracts baseline code.

- *Move code*: Takes files or directories and moves them anywhere desirable. Typically used when code being deployed can be moved to a directory that is not under development.

- *Message code*: Changes parameters automatically before deploying into production. For example, you might want to turn off all debug statements before going into production so that an automated script can be used to turn DEBUG = true to DEBUG = false.

- *Compile code*: Turns ASCII files into class files (binary), jar, WAR, EAR, EXE, or DLL files.

KNOWING HOW TO MAINTAIN YOUR TOOLBOX

After the construction tools have been selected, configured, and programmed to carry out tasks, they will become almost permanently embedded within the overall construction process for that project. The developers will establish such reliance on these tools that if they were to break or not work one day, the whole process of developing, testing, and deploying code might be jeopardized. Fortunately, productivity is ensured when toolbox maintenance is done on a regular basis, as discussed in the following sections.

The following are two ways to maintain your tools selection:

- Reevaluating what you have
- Testing the Application Guide

Reevaluating the Tools in Your Toolbox

Reevaluating and ultimately replacing existing tools isn't as easy as it sounds. All too often when existing tools have to undergo such scrutiny, features that were included in the old tools are not found in the replacement tools. The tool selection process becomes a lot harder in this case because of the diligent research and testing that needs to be conducted before placing a new tool into the current development toolbox.

Tool reevaluation requires diligent impact analysis and coordinated efforts. The whole point of using tools is so that certain methodical tasks can be automated and reused across many applications. If more than one application used the same tool configuration, then pulling that tool out of the current mix can stop those applications from running.

When New Is Better

When new tools or upgraded versions hit the market, it usually means that there is a solution available that is better than the one you have now. Hopefully, all the bugs have been worked out and the software behind those new tools is much faster and more efficient than the old ones. Based on this premise, a lot of developers on the cutting edge like to play around with the new tools and features.

New tools allow the developers to expand their horizons and take on different challenges. For example, as IDEs become more integrated with multiple programming languages and code assistants, developers will have the ability to code in multiple languages without ever switching the editor. That is not only powerful, but also very efficient.

Generally, you will replace tools when:

- Increased security is required. Security is probably one of the main reasons companies upgrade. Say, for example, that support goes away for WebSphere 4, so IBM is no longer releasing security patches for it. Many people will want to upgrade to the secure version. As a result, tool upgrades are necessary.

- Support runs out. The vendor was bought out, went out of business, or just no longer supports that tool.

- New requirements exist. The new tool offers features that do not exist in the old tool.

- Compatibility is required. When new tools are required, they must remain compatible with upgrades to other parts of the infrastructure.

When New Is Not Better

Every year, new tools and versions enter the market and older ones become obsolete or hard to find. But be careful: New tools can also introduce new problems. For example, **deprecated** methods that the code relied on before can no longer be used, leaving the developers to design and figure out a new method. As you are now aware, every new alternative design could lead to a new window of opportunity for attackers.

In your company, a great amount of time and money has been invested in securing the requirements, analyzing the design for threats, building security principles into the code, and thoroughly testing the outcomes of the program. One simple decision to switch from a deployment tool like ANT to a process that has not been as thoroughly analyzed and tested could put the application at risk.

Generally, you will *not* replace tools when:

- You are simply enamored by the latest and greatest version of a selected tool on the market.

- Your existing tool isn't broken. Replacing tools and updating the Application Guide can be very time consuming.

- There is no plan to analyze and test the new tool for threats and or risks.

The Application Guide Is Part of the Toolbox

As we have learned in previous chapters, the Application Guide is the one document that holds the process together. A big portion of the guide has to do with tools: which ones to use, how they are configured, and where they exist. Any time you choose to use a tool in the development process, that tool must be included in the Application Guide. That includes tool replacements, upgrades, or add-ons.

The Application Guide is the configuration management document for the toolbox. Which tools are used on the project? Where are the tools located? Why did you choose those tools over others? All of these questions that you learned how to answer in Chapter 4 are key to a successful toolbox. Make sure the Application Guide is up to date and test it from time to time by having either a new guy on the team build his PC or by having a PC on the team reloaded with the current operating system. There is no better way to test the guide than to rebuild a development machine from ground zero based on the content of that guide.

CHAPTER SUMMARY

- ❏ Tools make the development process dependable and trustworthy through the use of automation, after the tools are tested.

- ❏ Industry tools and their usage keep costs down because they enforce similar design patterns across the board, which enables developers to assist in developing multiple projects within the same company.

- ❏ All organizations have specific policies and procedures on which tools are available. Because IT architecture is an important part of availability, the developers need to know what policies exist before they investigate which tools to use.

- ❏ Proprietary and open source tools both have advantages and disadvantages. It is important to realize that proprietary tools come with loads of options and full-time support.

- ❏ Developers need tools that deal with quality and security. For code to be secure, it must first be of high quality and vice versa. Therefore, there should be many tools in the developer's toolbox that will assist in the development and deployment of code.

❏ When tools make it into the product mix of the development process, they become part of the rules and methods of that project. Every developer on the team should be using the same tools for the same reasons. Enforce this use in the Application Guide.

❏ Replace or upgrade tools only when necessary. Don't use the latest and greatest just because it's the latest release. You should replace or upgrade only when the existing tool no longer serves your purposes.

KEY TERMS

.NET — The Microsoft .NET Framework and the tools that access the framework.

ANT — A tool that automates common repetitive tasks that developers do every day.

code editors — Editors that have built-in error handlers that highlight coding errors while the code is being typed in.

compilers — Small programs that convert ASCII characters into binary code.

debugger — A small program that steps through the execution of code inside a GUI so that the developer can visually see how the code is being executed and what the current values of each variable are at run time.

deprecated — A term that describes a software function that was previously available but whose use is now discouraged.

false negatives — When a system reports code as good when it is really susceptible.

false positives — When a system reports code as susceptible when it really is a good piece of code.

FindBugs — A code analyzer that is used to check binary code (Java) for common software vulnerabilities such as unchecked input parameters and SQL Code injections.

Fortify Source Code Analysis (SCA) — A static code analyzer that is used to check binary code (C++ and Java) for common software vulnerabilities such as unchecked input parameters and arrays for buffer overflows.

GNU — A project that encourages the use and sharing of software programs that are nonproprietary.

GUI — A screen through which users interact with an application.

J2EE — A specification created by Sun Microsystems.

memory leaks — A situation when an application or operating system runs out of allocated memory.

open source tools — Tools that are free to use in accordance with the open source license agreement, typically the General Public License, and that are owned by the originating authors.

profiling — The process of defining steps of execution, time of each execution, and memory usage of each step.

proprietary tools — Tools that charge a fee for license(s), either per seat or per server, and that are owned by the company that issues them.

8

Refactoring tools — Automated features that can break down large methods or bodies of code into smaller methods or objects.

REVIEW QUESTIONS

1. What are the goals to using software construction tools?
   a. automate tasks, replace developers, secure the development process
   b. automate to keep costs down, build a dependable and trustworthy development process
   c. automate tasks, replace manual tasks, keep costs down
   d. automate tasks, keep costs down, create reports for management

2. Memory debugging tools that monitor heap size are best used for finding what?
   a. Memory leaks
   b. Inefficient code
   c. Logic errors
   d. Speed of CPU execution

3. Development costs can be kept down by:
   a. reusing the same tools in multiple projects
   b. using all open source tools
   c. using only the tools that the company has already paid for
   d. all of the above

4. _____ tools cost a certain amount of money per seat and typically come with full-time support.

5. Tool evaluation should be based on answers to all of the following questions, except:
   a. Does it satisfy the need?
   b. Is the tool readily available?
   c. Is the tool easy to use?
   d. Does the tool come with a warranty?

6. Which tool will help analyze the following situation?
   The application seems to take longer to reply after the code executes the database calls.
   a. IDE
   b. debugger
   c. profiler
   d. memory monitor

7. Which tool will help in the following situation?
   While typing code in Notepad is easy and free, the developers make a lot of mistakes and typos.

   a. IDE

   b. debugger

   c. profiler

   d. memory monitor

8. Which tool will help in the following situation?
   The application freezes up or sometimes just dies and the developer doesn't know why.

   a. IDE

   b. debugger

   c. profiler

   d. memory monitor

9. Which tool will help in the following situation?
   The program was coded to call a subroutine only if the user is an internal customer. For some reason, the developer does not know why that subroutine is not being called.

   a. IDE

   b. debugger

   c. profiler

   d. memory monitor

10. Which tool will help in the following situation?
    There are five developers on the team and they have trouble synchronizing their code. Currently, they are e-mailing each other files and merging them ad hoc.

    a. IDE

    b. version control

    c. ANT

    d. Merger tool

11. Which tool will help in the following situation?
    The development team currently has an automated development process. When the code is written, it is automatically checked into a version control tool, then gets pushed out across the network to the testing server where the users play with the latest change requests. The only problem is that it takes seven individual tools to install and then configure them to work together. Unfortunately, no team member knows how to build the code.

    a. IDE

    b. version control

    c. ANT

    d. Application Guide

8

12. Which tool will help in the following situation?
    The development team uses ANT to do production deployments. Even though the IDE comes equipped with deployment tools itself, the developers want to use a separate deployment process that doesn't involve the code on their machines. The problem is there is nothing to enforce this decision.

    a. IDE

    b. version control

    c. ANT

    d. Application Guide

13. _____ is a tool that can be used to automate a lot of manual activity when it comes to automatically transporting files and other manual tasks.

14. _____ is a tool that can be used to back up every software module that exists within the application.

15. Developers can typically choose any tool they want as long as the rest of the development team agrees. True or False?

16. Security tools help with the quality of the software product. True or False?

17. You should replace tools when support runs out. True or False?

18. It is easier to evaluate new tools than to reevaluate existing tools. True or False?

19. Software developers are more like tool masters than program language masters. True or False?

20. A code scanner is a security tool that will tell the programmer that the code is secure. True or False?

Hands-On Projects

HANDS-ON PROJECTS

Project 8-1 Working with ANT

The purpose of this project is to download, install, and configure ANT.

1. Follow the directions in the "ant/ANT Installation Notes.doc" file in the Chapter 8 course data.

2. Using the print screen option on your computer, take a snapshot of what your C: drive looks like. This picture will be used for Project 8-3.

3. Run the scripts and prove that ANT is working by printing the report from the log directory that ANT created.

4. Using the ANT documentation (API), choose any task from the list of options and incorporate this new task into the example provided.

5. Run the scripts and prove that ANT ran your new task by printing the report from the log directory that ANT created.

6. Write a summary report on your experience using ANT.

7. If you were a developer, what else might you want to use this tool for? Note: You might want to look at the API for ideas.

8. Hand in your scripts in working order. In addition, hand in your reports from the log directory and your ANT summary report.

Project 8-2 Tool Configuration

Developers work with tools that work with tools. It's amazing how complex and intertwined our work processes become with our tool configurations. In this project, you will learn a bit about making two tools work together.

1. Download Sun's JDK and NetBeans IDE latest version (version 5+ at the time of this writing).

2. Download a trial version of JPROBE latest version (version 7+ at the time of this writing).

3. Read the configuration notes on JPROBE and learn how to integrate JPROBE with NetBeans.

4. Import or copy the Java file "Main.java" from the Chapter 8 course data into NetBeans and run it to make sure you have it working.

5. Run Main.java with JPROBE turned on and hand in a screen shot of the reports.

Project 8-3 Updating the Application Guide

In this project, you will document the tool selection and configuration from Project 8-1 into your Application Guide from Chapter 4.

1. Building on the Application Guide from Chapter 4, document all the installation steps you completed in Project 8-1. Include steps of execution, pictures of installation processes, and how you would walk the reader through the process of installing ANT.

2. Hand in your Application Guide.

CASE PROJECT

Reporting on a Software Construction Tool

Because developers are on the front line of software development, they tend to know what they need more than the project managers do. Thus, needs analysis and proposals might be required from the developers to let management know what they need and why.

The purpose of this case is to evaluate a tool and report on its usage and functionality to the class. Choose a software construction tool of your choice and write a technical report on your findings. This report should be in your own words. Write about your experience with the Web site or software. Tell the reader about the installation process. Was it easy to understand or hard to configure? Topics to report on include the following:

❑ What is the tool used for?

❑ What type of environment is the user in (Web, client, server, and so on)?

❑ What are the costs?

❑ What are the system requirements?

❑ Is it easy to use?

❑ Is there a trial version?

❑ Are there tutorials or examples in the tool or on the Web? Did you do them?

❑ What language is it for? Does it matter?

❑ Does it integrate with other tools?

CHAPTER REFERENCES

Apache. 2007. ANT. http://ant.apache.org/ (accessed February 23, 2008).

Dupuis, Robert, Pierre Bourque, Alain Abran, James W. Moore, Leonard L. Tripp, and IEEE Society. 2004. Guide to the Software Engineering Body of Knowledge, Version 2004. http://www.swebok.org (accessed February 14, 2008).

FindBugs. 2007. FindBugs Fact Sheet. http://findbugs.sourceforge.net/factSheet.html (accessed February 23, 2008).

Fortify Software Inc. 2007. Fortify Source Code Analysis (SCA). http://www.fortifysoftware.com/products/sca/ (accessed February 23, 2008).

McGraw, Gary. 2006. *Software Security: Building Security In*. Boston: Addison-Wesley.

CHAPTER

9

CODING IN THE CUBE: DEVELOPING GOOD HABITS

Upon completion of this material, you should be able to:

♦ Code for security

♦ Code for quality

♦ Code to facilitate debugging

♦ Develop social skills in the cube

The objective of this chapter is to display coding styles and techniques that will make the software secure, resilient, and diverse. The first thing you must do before you can write secure code is become a good developer. Only after certain principles and styles for creating code are learned can you concentrate on securing the application. This chapter presents two distinct styles of code that need to be incorporated into the way you (as the developer) write software: security styles and quality. The examples shown in this chapter can be applied to any language and any platform.

Coding for Secure Code

Secure coding styles are developed and honed by understanding what software attacks are, how they are administered, and how you can code defensively for them. It also takes a good understanding of the programming languages you are using, their vulnerabilities, and their weaknesses. Secure coding means building the application to defend itself against the misuse cases by monitoring all user activity and tracking the users' requests. If a request does not have the necessary keys from the sender, the code must be able to kick the user out of the application and either shut down features or inform the right people. The activities to secure coding are defined as follows:

- Validate the request.

- Handle exceptions.

- Create self-monitoring code.

- Secure the code base.

- Know the programming languages.

Validating the Request

Every request that comes into the application should be treated as a potential attack. If the information is coming from the Web, assume that all input has malicious code such as **SQL code injection** or **XSS (Cross-Site Scripting)**. It's up to you to prove that the data is clean by rejecting all tampered requests and allowing only valid data to pass. During the requirements and design stage, you learned about defining the business rules on all input variables and locating all points of entry in the application. Validating the request is accomplished in three steps:

1. Authorizing the sender.

2. Cleansing the request.

3. Encapsulating the data.

Authorizing the Sender

Before wasting any more valuable CPU time on a request or taking the risk of allowing corrupted data into the application, make sure the user has the authority to use the services requested. Users need to be assigned to roles and those roles will be assigned to capabilities (add, update, delete, search only). User roles and capabilities should have been identified and fleshed out in the requirements and design phase. For example, in the Employee Stock Trade use case, the requirements stated that all employees can log in to the application and view their accounts.

Figure 9-1 shows a method named isAuthorized() that takes an object, ValidatorForm, as an argument (input parameter). In Step 1, the request is authorized by making sure the request came from a specific application by calling the getApplicationName() method. In Step 2, the logic then continues to evaluate the user's group to make sure the user is assigned to the right role for the information he or she needs. User roles are yet an extra layer of defensive code that prevents random attacks by unauthorized users. Finally, in Step 3 of this validation process, the logic checks to see from what interface the request came (Web screen, in this case).

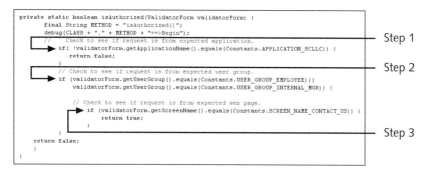

Figure 9-1 Steps to authorize

Authorizing users' requests eliminates the bad requests that do not meet the minimum criteria. Data authorization is a two-way street: first, the user's ID must be validated before the application responds to the user so that it knows what features to make available. Second, the user's request needs to be authorized again to make sure that data (the user's privileges) has not been changed or tampered with since it originally displayed on the screen.

Cleansing the Request

Input cleansing is critical for securing the application. Hackers will type in all sorts of data, SQL, comments, and so on just to see how the application responds. If holes are found, the hackers have free reign to modify your application. Input validation takes place up front in the application design and away from other application resources so that the holes can be fixed. Keeping input data clean and intact between point of entry and final destination is the single best style a developer can adopt to ensure security.

Whitelist values are predefined values that are acceptable for input. Take the **whitelist** values that were identified from the use case requirements and place them into a CONSTANTS or, better yet, into a database. Then code some utilities that reject HTML tags or **blacklist** values.

Figure 9-2 shows a method that strips out HTML from an input string. Some software attacks, such as XSS, like to insert JavaScript or HTML tags into the variables so that when the data is displayed back to the browser, the data could be corrupted with active links or other HTML data. A very common routine for validating data in Web development is stripping any unwanted tags from the input variable. As Step 1 in Figure 9-2 shows, one of the first items of logic is to get the length of the input String. In Step 2, the logic then iterates through each value of the String looking for HTML or JavaScript tags starting with <. If it finds a tag, the logic strips it out.

```
public static String stripHtml(String inStr) {
    boolean inTag = false; // Are we inside an html tag
    char c;
    int tagPos = 0;
    StringBuffer outStr = new StringBuffer();
    int len = inStr.length();                                    ◄──────── Step 1
    for (int i = 0; i < len; i++) {
        c = inStr.charAt(i);
        if (c == '<') {
            outStr.append(" ");                                  ◄──────── Step 2
            tagPos = 0;
            inTag = true;
        }
        if (!inTag) {
            outStr.append(c);
        }
        if (c == '>') {
            inTag = false;
            if (tagPos == 1) {
                outStr.append(" <> ");
                tagPos = 0;
            }
        }
        tagPos +=1;
    }
    return outStr.toString();
}
```

Figure 9-2   Utility that strips out HTML tags

Another common method of validation is verifying the input values against a whitelist. This validation step is critical as a countermeasure to a misuse case, such as SQL code injections where users will enter real SQL query language as input. Here, the goal of the attacker is to either extract information from the database or delete the database all together. Figure 9-3 shows an example of how input values can be compared with whitelist values.

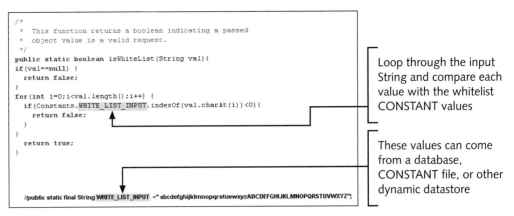

Figure 9-3   Utility method that will accept only whitelist values

Encapsulating the Data

Encapsulation is the grouping and storing of data inside a single object; encapsulation makes data available only through the use of code, most commonly referred to as **getters and setters**. Data encapsulation hides all internal code, variables, and logic from the outside world, thus restricting access to any outside callers. Basically, when you create data-encapsulated objects, you have created a black box with only one entry/exit point for everyone to use.

An example of data encapsulation was provided in Figure 9-3. The logic that determines that a value is whitelisted is protected within an object and can be accessed only through the isWhiteList() method. Data encapsulation involves creating objects for all use case parameters (the parameters needed to render a request). The encapsulated object provides yet another defensive layer in the application and hides its values within.

Handling Exceptions

"Motivated attackers like to see error messages and look for information that may give clues as to what types of attacks they can unleash on the application" (OWASP 2006, para. 2). Application errors expose a lot of information about the code and its environment. If not handled properly, errors can tell attackers database information such as table names and columns, names of objects used, code location, Web server information, and even IP addresses.

There are only two types of errors in application development: compile-time errors and run-time errors. Compile-time errors occur when the developer misspells a keyword, or does not pass the appropriate argument to a method's signature. **Compile-time** errors are found at compile-time and the code will not execute until they are fixed. IDE development tools have done a great job in eliminating (almost) compile-time errors; they do this through their built-in intelligence. **Run-time errors** are harder to find. Run-time errors occur when a data flow does not flow as expected. These types of errors are the ones that give away a lot of secure information about the application if not dealt with up front.

To deal with run-time errors, all code should be wrapped around a try{} catch{} code block. What the program does in the catch{} statement can mean the difference between a secure application and one that isn't secure. The following are the steps that need to be performed while handling errors:

1. Code your own routine.
2. Create application-specific exceptions.
3. Manage the views.

Coding Your Own Routine

Control the logic by writing an error-handling routine that catches specific run-time errors. In an error-handling routine, every code statement has to be surrounded by traditional try{} catch{} blocks so that the appropriate exception can be caught and handled. Figure 9-4 shows an example of the try{} catch{} block.

```
try {
    // put business logic here


} catch (Exception e) {
    // do something with the error
}
```

Developer needs to log the Exception (error) and then decide what the application should do with the Exception (i.e., stop the request or continue processing)

Figure 9-4   The try{} catch{} block

There is no such thing as error-free code; all languages throw errors and all applications have errors. Therefore, all errors need to be caught and dealt with so that the application can determine what to do. I will demonstrate how to handle common application errors using the Java API; you might not use the Java API as your programming language, but the example is the same for all languages when it comes to dealing with errors.

Programming languages, such as Java, allow you to nest the try{} catch{} blocks inside try{} catch{} blocks so that the developer can catch specific errors when they happen; thus, the application can reset itself to default values and reexecute the same logic. The outer try{} catch{} blocks will catch other run-time errors that the application developer never would have thought about. Figure 9-5 shows an example of nested try{} catch{} blocks.

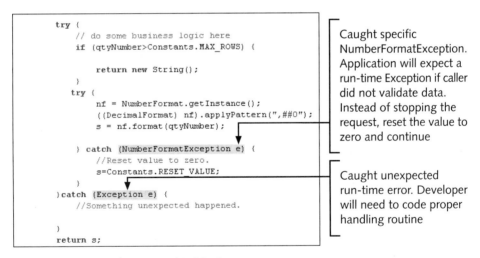

```
try {
    // do some business logic here
    if (qtyNumber>Constants.MAX_ROWS) {

        return new String();
    }
    try {
        nf = NumberFormat.getInstance();
        ((DecimalFormat) nf).applyPattern(",##0");
        s = nf.format(qtyNumber);

    } catch (NumberFormatException e) {
        //Reset value to zero.
        s=Constants.RESET_VALUE;
    }
} catch (Exception e) {
    //Something unexpected happened.

}
return s;
```

Caught specific NumberFormatException. Application will expect a run-time Exception if caller did not validate data. Instead of stopping the request, reset the value to zero and continue

Caught unexpected run-time error. Developer will need to code proper handling routine

Figure 9-5   Nested try{} catch{} block

NOTE Many programming languages also allow you to propagate errors up the call stack (in Java this means using the throws clause in the method signature). All exceptions should be caught at some point in the call stack, but it doesn't always make sense to catch them in the same method where the call occurs. For example, if you write a generic logging class that logs to a file and uses the Java File class to access the file, in some cases, an IOException may be generated by the file. It may make sense to pass that IOException on to the calling class for handling.

Creating Application-Specific Exceptions

When catching exceptions, the application needs to determine what to do when the exception occurs. Does it abort the execution all together and tell the user to come back later or does it reset a variable to some default value and continue executing? To help make this decision, an encapsulated error class can be created to handle events for all use cases/misuse cases within the application. By creating a class that extends the Java Exception class, you can create your own type of application exception; this exception will deal with the complexity of continuing the user request and logging each error message for the developers to see in a separate log file. Figure 9-6 shows an application-specific error class, ApplicationError, that extends Exception. This class can now be used throughout the application.

Figure 9-6   ApplicationError class

After the ApplicationError class is created, it can be embedded within the code in the catch blocks. Figure 9-7 shows an example of how the ApplicationError class can be used within the try{} catch{} code block.

```
try {
    userBean = new UserBean();
    // you could go to a database and get more information on user
      debug("==>getUserId =="+requestForm.getUserId());
    userBean.setUserName(requestForm.getUserId());
    requestForm.setUserBean(userBean);

} catch (Exception e){
    logger.writeMsgLog("\n error occured"+CLASS + "." + METHOD +e.getMessage());
    ApplicationError ae = new ApplicationError();
    ae.setException(e);
    ae.setUserViewMessage("An error occurred while processing your request."+
        "Please try resubmitting your request.  "+
        "If the problem continues, call the technical support team "+
        "for further assistance.  Thank You! ");
    ae.setErrorMessage(e.getMessage());
    throw ae;
}
```

Create an instance of the ApplicationError class and set its properties

Figure 9-7   Application error object within the try{} catch{} code block

Exception handling is the cornerstone for all secure code. If properly done and thoroughly tested, the application will be able to monitor itself for any errors that will provide outside intruders or curious onlookers the ability to see the properties and attributes of the application in error messages or system log files.

CAUTION   I have seen a lot of applications that just wrap every exception that occurs in one generic application exception class (that just gets logged in the end and shows an error message to the user). This really adds no value as it obscures the real problem by burying it one level deeper. You could just as easily put throw clauses in all your methods and have one top-level catch that catches the exception and logs it. Your application-specific exceptions should represent real exceptions that actually occur in the application code; they shouldn't just be generic wrappers for exceptions that occur elsewhere.

Managing the Views

What you choose to tell the user in error messages is up to you, but it should specifically benefit them. For instance, the error message "A section 43 error has occurred because you do not have authority and you have been logged out" is better than simply giving the user a message that says, "An error has occurred." It is okay to log and keep errors for the user so that when the user contacts the help desk for support, he or she has specific information; the more specific an error message, the better the response the support team can provide. The error messages the users see, however, should not be the error messages the developers see.

The developers need to see the raw error codes, the invalid SQL statements, or the object names of the defective code. The users, on the other hand, should see only friendly messages that gracefully tell them only what they need to know. For instance, you could give the users some direction as to what they should do next or perhaps a phone number to call to get the problem fixed.

NOTE

Whether the messages are friendly or not, any variation in the error messages may serve as a hint to potential attackers that they have made progress. Most users really only care if the function worked or not. Hopefully all errors are unexpected, so I don't think you need to use "unexpected" in your message, and you probably would want to avoid specific references (such as "application error," "database error," and so on).

Even subtle differences in the messages indicate that something is different from the prior request. The only types of messages that I think are acceptable variations are things such as maintenance messages (for example, "This function will be unavailable from XX to YY time due to system maintenance."). The application should log the exceptions in such a way that they can be tied back to the user so that the people supporting the application can see what went wrong for the user without needing the user to e-mail them a message generated by the application.

An exception handler can be created that not only logs error messages for developers, but also displays appropriate messages to users. As Figure 9-8 shows, using the methods from the ApplicationError class, it is possible to have a handler object do both tasks for you: log the messages the developers *need* to see as well as the messages the end users *want* to see.

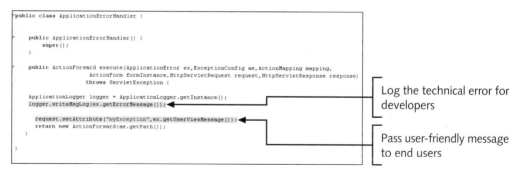

Figure 9-8   Application error handler with two types of messages

TIP

Document how to handle errors in the Application Guide, including the types of errors to be handled. For each type of error, document how that information is going to be shown to the users and what information is going to be logged.

Creating Self-Monitoring Code

Self-monitoring code watches the user's activity and looks for unusual events. Examples of unusual events include the number of times a single user has tried to log on, submit values, or request sensitive information that exceeds "normal" conditions. Self-monitoring applications add credibility to the company because they show that the application is developed to protect the company's assets and has been designed to react to misuses. Some examples of self-monitoring code include the following:

- Canceling user passwords
- Requiring physical requests for data
- Alerting stakeholders of invasion

Canceling User Passwords

If a program touches an application's assets, as specified in the use case/misuse case, a countermeasure must be developed to protect that asset. For example, one countermeasure might be a code algorithm that counts the number of times errors occur and locks that user out by canceling his or her password after the number of attempts exceeds a specified threshold. SQL code injections and data manipulations can sometimes take a lot of failed attempts before a hacker creates a successful path. The application should not provide users with an unlimited amount of failed attempts or false data submissions. If the user cannot successfully fill out form data more than three times, send them to FAQs or a help/support number. You should cancel a user's ID or password when the following events occur:

- Login times exceed a specified threshold.
- Errors during program execution exceed a specified threshold.
- The application detects a malicious attack, such as SQL code injections, XSS, or any of the misuses identified during security requirements.

Requiring Physical Requests for Data

Requesting the application to provide sensitive information over the public network can sometimes be too risky. The Web certainly makes it convenient to view as much information as possible about a given subject, but personal information, such as Social Security numbers, passwords, and account numbers, should be shared only with a person and never with an automated request. This rule is more of a security policy than a coding style, but enforcing security policies helps tell the developer what not to code. If you have an application that allows users to read reports, claims, or other sensitive information, code the application to display just headings and some light introductory text to the subject; then have the users place a personal phone call or provide other channels of distribution for follow-up.

Alerting Stakeholders of Invasion

Self-monitoring applications should also have the intelligence to send out alerts during critical events. If the application deals with valuable information, you're going to want to send out alerts immediately when the application detects foul play. Alerts should have a service-level agreement (SLA) for the support group so that support group members know that a text message requires immediate response over an error log. **SLAs** are contract agreements between the application owners (sponsors) and the support group. SLAs are important to the development teams because they contractually bind the team to responding to issues such as bugs, downtime, and other undesired results. Alerts are important to SLAs and the development team because the developers need to be able to respond accordingly when problems occur.

TIP

Of course, as you plan your SLA, don't forget about the little boy who cried wolf. That is, don't overdo alerts to a point where they lose their meaning.

The types of alerts that can be built in to the application include the following:

- Publishing attacks in a log file
- Text messages, e-mails, and pages

Publish Attacks   Logging user traffic, events, and data flow is one of the best analysis techniques you can do for an application. Information in log files can tell you who is (was) on the system and for how long, what they did, and what they tried to do. This information can be used for further analysis and to determine whether the application was attacked. However, the application can only provide this information if the developers coded the programs to write to the log file.

When logging tailored messages for an application, use a file separate from the server logs and secure the privileges on that file. How much information you choose to log depends on application performance and the importance of the information. Constant file I/O will degrade the response time, so make sure the data logged is relevant. Numerous open source loggers are available into which applications can easily plug. Log4j is one that I use and it has a built-in severity level that controls what is important and what is not. Log4j can be found at *http://logging.apache.org/log4j/*.

The best strategy is to log as much as possible, because if you log only those attacks for which you planned, you will miss the ones you never would have thought of. Additionally, logging does not always have to be to a text file. You also can log to a database or other repository sources. It may also be possible to use message queuing (MQ series) to handle unprocessed log messages to manage the performance impact of logging.

Text Messaging, E-mails, Paging   Application software can be coded to send out **SMS (Short Message Service)** text messages to cell phones, pagers, and e-mail. If the application sends these types of alerts to the appropriate people, those people can respond to attacks very efficiently. Information is key during these critical times, and you want to code the program to do whatever it takes to inform the appropriate people ASAP.

Securing the Code Base

Open source code is great to use and highly encouraged within the software development community. However, it does have its own vulnerabilities when it comes to security. For instance, you probably know that JAR files are bundled Java classes that can be stored in a server's classpath instead of as individual classes. However, don't assume that a **JAR file** that comes from a friend that is stored on a server somewhere is the same JAR file that is downloaded from a trusted source like Apache or SourceForge.

NOTE

A lot of open source software that is available for download on the Internet is hosted on mirrors that provide local servers and bandwidth for the hosting of the downloads. This introduces some risk that the files could be altered in some way even before you get them from the source. Many sites offering such downloads also offer a PGP signature or a checksum (usually MD5 or SHA1) hosted at the "main" site that you can use to verify the authenticity of your download. You should always check these (and the sites almost always offer instructions on how to do so). That way you know that you at least started with a good file.

Wherever the JAR files (or EXEs and DLLs) are stored, make sure no one else had access rights to that directory. Anyone with access to certain directories can un-JAR a file, tamper with a class, then re-JAR that file and put it back in the classpath. It would take even very smart developers weeks or months before figuring out a JAR file had been tampered with. JAR files almost never get reviewed and most people do not know what *should* be in there anyway. If logic bombs or Trojan horses were to be snuck in, JAR files would be the most likely target because JAR files are the last place developers themselves double-check or evaluate for vulnerabilities.

TIP

After you have selected the necessary external files (JAR) needed from a trusted source, store those files into a code repository like CVS. CVS will allow developers to look at changes in the code base through tracking reports. Document where the external files came from in the Application Guide and log the date that files were retrieved in case you have to update them over time.

Knowing the Programming Languages

All software programs will have security vulnerabilities inside the logic if the programmers don't know how to use the programming language correctly. Each language offers advantages and disadvantages with respect to security, and some languages are considered more secure than others. You need to know the ins and outs of the security features and other API freebies in the programming language you are using so that you can leverage what has been given to you. Leveraging code versus writing your own features, such as bubble sorts or encryption, not only saves time and effort, but also mitigates writing software bugs.

Security in programming languages can be found in the APIs or just by doing some Internet research. Some popular programming languages that deal with security include the following:

- Java
- PHP
- C/C++

Java

Java's J2EE (1.2 or higher) platform has a very robust security model. Sun Microsystems' Java technology offers security objects that provide data encryption, authentication, and exception handling already built in. Java is the most popular server-side language in Web development and continues to evolve as the market leader in application security. Java's security goals are to provide authentication (JSSE) and encryption (JCE) services to the developers so that the code base used for security is well audited and verified by the Java community (Oaks 2001).

Java's strict API implementation, security model features, and automatic garbage collection have sheltered programmers from many common software vulnerabilities. Java's API protects developers from complex issues such as multiple inheritances and cleaning up old pointers, but developers can still make programming mistakes, which could also lead to software vulnerability. The two most common security mistakes programmers make when developing are as follows:

- Not reducing the scope of methods
- Not reducing the scope of variables

Reducing the Scope of Methods   J2EE Web applications operate in a server's memory (RAM). All objects are instantiated by a Classloader and stored in a Java Virtual Machine's (JVM's) memory. Typically, software attacks to Java applications occur during run time so that the methods and properties are loaded and ready to take requests. Therefore, you need to know the types of access Java allows to methods. The access types include the following (Sun Microsystems 2007):

- *Private*: This modifier makes the method accessible to code that is within the same class.
- *Default*: This modifier makes the method accessible to code that is within the same class and within the same package.
- *Protected*: This default modifier makes the method accessible to code that is within the same class, same package, and code that is a subclass (extends).
- *Public*: This modifier makes the method accessible to all code.

CAUTION When you code methods, make sure you open access just enough so that the calling programs have enough rights to that method but not more than they need.

Reducing the Scope of Variables   Reduce the scope of variables used in a program so that the values cannot be tampered with or exploited. For example, an application server creates a thread per request that executes code sequentially. If multiple requests come into the same code base, it is possible for two threads to change the value of a variable simultaneously, producing the wrong result for each thread.

Consider the code snippet in Figure 9-9. A user tries to log into an application, and a method called CountLogAttempt() is called. The method first logs the user in an application log file and then increases a counter variable that is stored at the class level, which is outside the scope of this method. Say a client logs in and thread A is created and executed. At the same time, another user logs in, which causes the JVM to create thread B and execute the same method. With thread A, the counter starts at zero and attempts to get the logger; thread B comes in before A is done and now both A and B are equal to zero. As a result, the counter value is equal to 1 instead of 2 after two threads have successfully executed.

```
protected int CountLogAttemp(ReferFriendForm myForm) {

    Calendar now= Calendar.getInstance();
    logCounter++;
    ApplicationLogger logger = ApplicationLogger.getInstance();
    logger.writeMsgLog("user "+myForm.getUserId()+
            " has log in =" + logCounter + "number of times"
            + now.getTime());
    return logCounter;
}
```
Get Logger and log user activity

Figure 9-9   Scope problems with variables

Make global variables final so that the values cannot be changed. If global variables cannot be final, as in the sample code in Figure 9-9, consider local variables (declared within the method) or synchronizing the code. Code synchronizing is when the JVM ensures that only one thread can execute the method at a time.

PHP

PHP is a server-side language that runs on Web servers, not application servers like J2EE applications. PHP has become a popular choice among Web developers because of the popularity and cost of Web servers like Apache's HTTP Server that supports PHP. "PHP is designed specifically to be a more secure language for writing CGI programs than Perl or C, and with correct selection of compile-time and run-time configuration options, and proper coding practices, it can give you exactly the combination of freedom and security you need" (Olson 2007, Chapter 15, p.1).

The PHP Security Consortium (PHPSC) is an international group of PHP experts that ensure education materials, tools, and standards exist for PHP developers (PHP Security Consortium 2007). PHPSC has focused a lot of efforts on application security for Web development and publishes articles and white papers on its Web site. Articles on PHP security, code snippets, and other configuration necessities can be found in the PHP Security Guide at *http://phpsec.org/projects/guide/1.html#1.1*.

C/C++

C/C++ has been around since the early 1980s, and a lot of software out on the market today has been built on it. Like a lot of other languages, C/C++ offers a lot of features that deal with security and, if developed and tested, can be a safe programming language to use. The most notable security flaw with this language, however, is the ever popular buffer overflow attack.

A **buffer overflow** occurs when a variable such as an input field is written to another variable of smaller length in the program's memory. A **buffer overflow attack** occurs when an attacker takes advantage of buffer overflows and attempts to purposely overwrite data that controls the program execution path and takes control of the program by executing the attacker's code instead of the process code.

Whatever language you are coding in, the bottom line is this: Know what security features or flaws come with that language. And remember, new ones come up everyday, so stay informed.

9

CODING STYLES FOR QUALITY CODE

Quality code is maintenance free, easy to change, and extremely reusable. After you learn how to write quality code, the act itself will seem natural and you won't want to code any other way. No matter what language you program in, there are common coding styles that need to be inherent in the code. These styles are learned after years of experience with coding applications. You will not learn how to apply these styles by taking a Java course or by reading a C++ book. You learn quality coding styles by looking at examples of great programs and understanding what makes a piece of code better than another.

To determine if someone's work is of the utmost quality, you should look for the following:

- Organized code
- Well-designed code
- Refactored code
- Diverse code

Organized Code

Good code organization eliminates clutter, duplication, and high maintenance costs in the long run. Just like when you were growing up and your mother wanted all your socks in one drawer and shirts in another, your code needs to be organized as well. Grouping like objects in one package helps keep code organized and makes it easier to work with. Organized code is also aesthetically pleasing. When other developers or reviewers read the code, the statements and instructions should be well written and very formal.

To organize code, do the following:

- Use only what is needed.
- Declare variables at the top.
- Avoid spaghetti code.

Using Only What Is Needed

OOP features such as file-includes, import statements, and the calling of other programs and services are all benefits of OOP, but they can hurt the program if one of the external references has some malicious code. As an example of malicious third-party code, consider that in Java, the import statement calls classes from one package and makes them available for use in another. There are two ways a developer can import classes: by wildcard (*) or by single call-out reference. Figure 9-10 shows a very common but also very bad way of importing code by using wildcards. The problem with Figure 9-10 is that wildcards do not tell other developers or code reviewers which classes are used in the program. This provides a window of opportunity for other developers to sneak other code classes in.

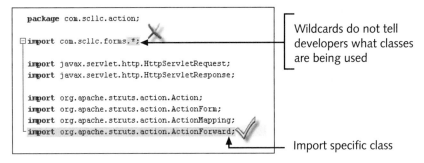

Figure 9-10 Import by wildcard

Declaring Variables at the Top

For code to be maintenance free and reusable, developers need formality. They want to look in one spot for variables used rather than to read the entire method to determine how to use it or how the code works. Declaring the variable in one spot, such as at the beginning of the code, as shown in Figure 9-11, standardizes how the code is set up and designed. During code reviews or maintenance enhancements, your time will be spent in more productive ways than trying to determine how the code is put together.

```
public static String addCommasToWholeNumber(int qtyNumber)
    throws Exception {

    final String METHOD = "addCommasToWholeNumber()";
    debug(CLASS + "." + METHOD + "==>Begin");
    NumberFormat nf = null;
    String s = null;

    try {

        nf = NumberFormat.getInstance();
        ((DecimalFormat) nf).applyPattern(",##0");
        s = nf.format(qtyNumber);

    } catch (NumberFormatException e) {

    }

    return s;
}
```

Define all local variables at the beginning of each method to give the code a standard look and so that other developers can see exactly what objects are being used with that method

Figure 9-11   Declaring variables at the top

Avoiding Spaghetti Code

Spaghetti code occurs when a method is executed and a daisy chain of objects is called. For example, an object gets created and calls another object to do something. Then, that object calls another and that one calls another, and so on. Spaghetti code is expensive to maintain because of the arduous tasks of endless investigation and analysis. The code itself is impossible to test and, thus, produces buggy upgrades and unreliable services. To avoid spaghetti code, have one "main" object as your controller and program that main object to call one method at a time. After each method is done executing, the control needs to go back to the main object for further direction.

In Figure 9-12, the processRequest method is the main method for the LogInForm business class. The order of execution is more step-by-step, executing one unit of work at a time and maintaining the point of control. This style of programming will save hundreds of hours in maintenance while making each object more reusable and granular. Break down OOP into simple statements. It doesn't have to be as step-by-step and procedural, but it does have to be read, maintained, and debugged by human eyes.

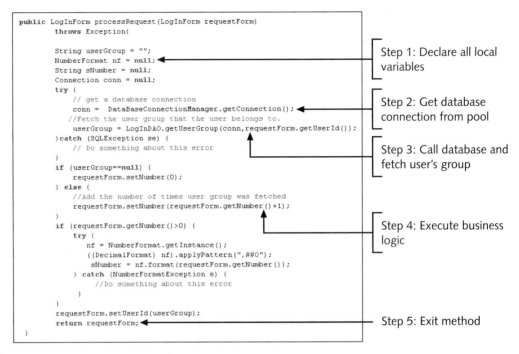

```
public LogInForm processRequest(LogInForm requestForm)
       throws Exception{

    String userGroup = "";
    NumberFormat nf = null;
    String sNumber = null;
    Connection conn = null;
    try {
        // get a database connection
        conn = DataBaseConnectionManager.getConnection();
        //Fetch the user group that the user belongs to.
        userGroup = LogInDAO.getUserGroup(conn,requestForm.getUserId());
    }catch (SQLException se) {
        // Do something about this error
    }
    if (userGroup==null) {
        requestForm.setNumber(0);
    } else {
        //Add the number of times user group was fetched
        requestForm.setNumber(requestForm.getNumber()+1);
    }
    if (requestForm.getNumber()>0) {
        try {
            nf = NumberFormat.getInstance();
            ((DecimalFormat) nf).applyPattern(",##0");
            sNumber = nf.format(requestForm.getNumber());
        } catch (NumberFormatException e) {
            //Do something about this error
        }
    }
    requestForm.setUserId(userGroup);
    return requestForm;
}
```

Step 1: Declare all local variables

Step 2: Get database connection from pool

Step 3: Call database and fetch user's group

Step 4: Execute business logic

Step 5: Exit method

Figure 9-12 Process one object at a time

Well-Designed Code

One of the best patterns to model from is the **singleton design pattern**, which ensures that only one instance of an object is created at the time of execution (Gamma, et al. 1995). This design pattern forces the server to create only one object in its heap, thus making the server run very efficiently while using minimum RAM. A singleton object also provides only one access method to its services so there is only one way in and out for the whole program.

Use singleton objects when a common object or task will be used across multiple use cases for the same reason. A great example of this is a database connection manager class. Because all use cases will need a connection, the database connection manager should be a singleton object so that only a single instance of the object will be created. As Figure 9-13 shows, a singleton object will reflect its own property to see if a reference has been created. If an object exists, it returns that one; if not, it creates only one.

Refactored Code

Code **refactoring** occurs when existing bodies of logic are broken up and moved into many smaller bodies of code. It's amazing how much good code could be reused if only

```
public class BusinessUtil {
    /** A constant that controls messge output */
    private final static boolean DEBUG = true;

    /** A constant that contains the name of this Class */
    private final static String CLASS = "BusinessUtil";

    /** A variable for maintaining a single reference to an instance of this object */
    private static BusinessUtil instance = new BusinessUtil();
    /**
     * This method ensures that only one instance of this object is created.
     * @returns BusinessUtil A reference to the singleton instance of this class.
     */
    public static BusinessUtil getInstance() {
        return instance;
    }
}
```

You are guaranteed that the class variable will be initialized when the class is loaded before any of its methods run

Caller uses this method to return a reference to the BusinessUtil class

Figure 9-13   Singleton objects

refactoring were practiced more by developers. Developers focus so much of their attention on how to solve specific problems or complex formulas that maintaining stringent coding styles is not always top on the to-do list. During these stressful situations, when solving the issue at hand seems to be the only important thing, algorithms and other reusable logic get written within other surrounding bodies of logic.

When reusable code gets buried into other code, the logic cannot be reused by other use cases. As a result, developers code the same algorithm within many software modules—making code duplication costly to maintain. Consider the code snippet in Figure 9-14. If the number in the requestForm is greater than 0 (zero), it applies a number pattern that adds commas to any number greater than 1000.

```
String userGroup = "";
NumberFormat nf = null;
String sNumber = null;
Connection conn = null;
try {
    // get a database connection
    conn = DataBaseConnectionManager.getConnection();
    //Fetch the user group that the user belongs to.
    userGroup = LogInDAO.getUserGroup(conn,requestForm.getUserId());
} catch (SQLException se) {
    // Do something about this error
}
if (userGroup==null) {
    requestForm.setNumber(0);
} else {
    //Add the number of times user group was fetched
    requestForm.setNumber(requestForm.getNumber()+1);
}
if (requestForm.getNumber()>0) {
    try {
        nf = NumberFormat.getInstance();
        ((DecimalFormat) nf).applyPattern(",##0");
        sNumber = nf.format(requestForm.getNumber());
    } catch (NumberFormatException e) {
        //Do something about this error
    }
}
```

Reusable logic that can be refactored

Figure 9-14   Before refactoring code

Although the code inside the If statement is good code and works, I'd bet that it isn't the only use case that can use code like this. When you have a piece of logic that can be reused by other use cases, break it out into its own method or class and then call it. As Figure 9-15 shows, when the reusable code is removed from the original object and moved into its own method, it can be called by a variety of other objects.

```java
        }
        /**
         * This method will reformat an int number into a whole number with commas.
         * @return String A String object that contains the formatted number.
         * @param qtyNumber A quantity number in the primitive whole format.
         */
        public String addCommasToWholeNumber(int qtyNumber)
            throws Exception {                                    ◄──────  Create a new method

            final String METHOD = "addCommasToWholeNumber()";
            debug(CLASS + "." + METHOD + "==>Begin");
            NumberFormat nf = null;                               ◄──────  Declare local variables
            String s = null;

            try {

                nf = NumberFormat.getInstance();
                ((DecimalFormat) nf).applyPattern(",##0");
                s = nf.format(qtyNumber);             ◄──────  Code has been refactored
                                                              so that this logic can be
            } catch (NumberFormatException e) {               called by any other method

            }

            return s;
        }
    }
```

Figure 9-15   After refactoring code

 TIP   Code refactoring not only makes great code reusable, but also helps keep to a manageable size the logic needed to code. If you find your logic to be more than what your monitor can display without having to scroll down, refactor the code.

Diverse Code

Coding for software diversity is what is going to make you a great developer and the software even better. **Software diversity** is that ability to anticipate change (Dupuis, et al. 2004). The software should be developed on the premise that specifications, data, and environments will change. Unfortunately, no one knows what the requirements are going to be in the future. However, there are some coding customs that support diversity and that will make your code stand the test of time:

- Code parameter-driven applications
- Don't limit your code

Coding Parameter-Driven Applications

When a programmer can change an application's meaning, its look and feel, and its business logic by checking the settings on a few switches and parameter fields, life is good. **Parameter-driven software** is software that looks up values stored in a database and determines what to display, allow, or execute based on those values. We've all used Web screens that offer drop-down data, Submit buttons, and menu options. Did you ever wonder where those values came from or how the application knew what to display?

Any time applications depend on specific data, time, or events to execute logic, make sure the data/information comes from a database table or external property file. Drop-down options change over time and so do formulas to business problems. Give the customers administration screens so that they can manage the application themselves and not have to rely on a team of programmers to make the changes.

Don't Limit Your Code

Writing a piece of software for a specific purpose creates **limited code**. A simple example of this can be something as easy as a method's signature. For example, passing a single object, such as String userName, to a method limits the method's ability to do anything else but deal with userName. On the other hand, if the method's signature required an input object bean called User and on that bean was a property called name, then the method could access all other data that deals with the user and not just the name.

You do not want to create limited code because when a method is coded, it usually gets called from tens or hundreds of other objects across the board. What if your signature had to change? Or what if the logic used within that method needed the userName and userPhone values? The changes to the method's signature would affect a lot more code than your one method. If you coded the method to use a bean as an input, the code could be changed one time and in one place to use the userPhone value if available.

Overall, when you code for "too" detailed specifics, the code becomes limited and is not reusable. You should develop a coding style that creates a middle ground, somewhere between ambiguous and specific, as described in Table 9-1.

Table 9-1   Samples of limiting code

Method name	Type	Rationale
doSomeThing(String name)	Limited	One field just limited the use of the method
doSomeThing(String name, String phone, String email, String address)	Limited	Not only do long signatures look bad, but they also limit the code and force anyone who wants to use it to supply all values
doSomeThing(UserBean userBean)	Dynamic	By creating an input bean object, all properties of the user can be assigned to one class and used throughout all code

CODING STYLES FOR DEBUGGING CODE

Software is created in sequential steps:

1. Write code statements.

2. Compile code.

3. Execute code.

4. Evaluate results.

If the end result was not what was expected, the developer will loop back to Step 1 and redo the logic until the code produces the correct outcome. A lot of times, this continuous looping of steps can take days before the answer is found. Ideally, the software should have built-in debugging mechanisms to assist the developer.

Code **debugs** statements in the software so that you (the developer) can trace the execution of the logic during the software run time. These debug statements are not part of the testing process; rather they are part of the coding process. There will be complex loops, null pointers, or just plain "don't knows" that you will come across, and the ability to look at values or properties during a live run will be handy.

 Know where to code for debug statements and when to turn off debug statements.

TIP

Where to Debug

Make debug statements part of your coding style and build the debug logic into the code before you need it. If you wait to add debugging techniques to the code when the code is broken, chances are that you will be adding more code statements into an already complex problem—making the code hard to read and error prone. Instead, make debugging techniques part of a reusable template or a parent class of all other objects. For example, you can add debug statements after every method's signature so that your debug statements are always reporting activity while coding. Figure 9-16 shows how such a method can be created and built into a program.

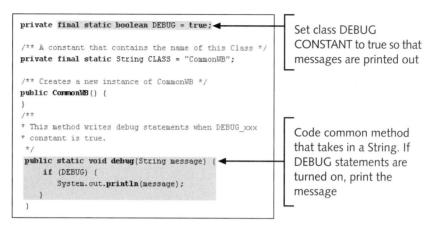

```
private final static boolean DEBUG = true;

/** A constant that contains the name of this Class */
private final static String CLASS = "CommonWB";

/** Creates a new instance of CommonWB */
public CommonWB() {
}
/**
* This method writes debug statements when DEBUG_xxx
* constant is true.
*/
public static void debug(String message) {
    if (DEBUG) {
        System.out.println(message);
    }
}
```

Set class DEBUG CONSTANT to true so that messages are printed out

Code common method that takes in a String. If DEBUG statements are turned on, print the message

Figure 9-16 Adding debug methods

After the debug methods are built into the program, they can be called anywhere at anytime within the program you need to test. For example, in Figure 9-17, the debug method is called upon entry of another method called processRequest. After debugs are built into the code base, the developers will have an easier time following the logic and identifying bottlenecks as they occur.

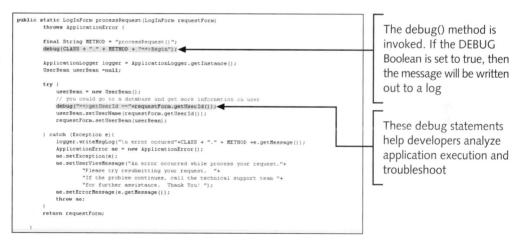

```
public static LogInForm processRequest(LogInForm requestForm)
        throws ApplicationError {

    final String METHOD = "processRequest()";
    debug(CLASS + "." + METHOD + "==>Begin");

    ApplicationLogger logger = ApplicationLogger.getInstance();
    UserBean userBean =null;

    try {
        userBean = new UserBean();
        // you could go to a database and get more information on user
        debug("==>getUserId =="+requestForm.getUserId());
        userBean.setUserName(requestForm.getUserId());
        requestForm.setUserBean(userBean);

    } catch (Exception e){
        logger.writeMsgLog("\n error occured"+CLASS + "." + METHOD +e.getMessage());
        ApplicationError ae = new ApplicationError();
        ae.setException(e);
        ae.setUserViewMessage("An error occurred while process your request."+
            "Please try resubmitting your request. "+
            "If the problem continues, call the technical support team "+
            "for further assistance.  Thank You! ");
        ae.setErrorMessage(e.getMessage());
        throw ae;
    }
    return requestForm;

}
```

The debug() method is invoked. If the DEBUG Boolean is set to true, then the message will be written out to a log

These debug statements help developers analyze application execution and troubleshoot

Figure 9-17 Call debug methods in every class

For the purposes of this book, I did not want to go too deep into logging libraries. In the figures provided throughout this text, I have been using simple DEBUG statements for the ease of understanding the concept of logging messages. One advantage of a more professional logger, such as log4j, is that developers typically put a lot of time and energy in its design; the work focuses on minimizing the number of processor cycles used in determining whether the message will actually be output. You can save yourself a lot of effort and potentially save a lot of CPU resources by using one of these professional logging libraries over my simple DEBUG examples.

NOTE

Having professional loggers provides levels as opposed to just an on/off like a DEBUG CONSTANT. Using levels of debug statements (i.e. WARNING, ERROR, and DEBUG) allows the development team to use the same logger classes for local debugging as they do for production troubleshooting. Also, turning off DEBUGS requires a change to the code and a redeployment of the application. Wouldn't it be more diverse to set levels in the external properties file without touching the code and debug right in the production environment?

Turning Off Debug

The best way to turn off these statements is to automate a script (similar to the ANT script from Chapter 8) that scans the code base and turns off all debug statements. The debug statements are turned off by changing the Boolean switch from Figure 9-16 from true to false. After the code has been changed, a recompile is issued and the new code is sent to the servers for production use. Debug statements are very helpful and the developer will come to rely on them. Hence, you can leave them in the code for production use because as long as the Boolean switch is turned off, they can do no harm.

DEVELOP SOCIAL SKILLS IN THE CUBE

Software development is not just a job; it's a lifestyle. Because of the constant change in technology, software attacks, and language upgrades, the only way you're going to evolve in this field is if you treat this field as a hobby and passion, not just a day job. Coding styles, algorithms, or solutions to complicated problems do not come and go when you check in and out of the office. They will stay with you and on your mind throughout the day and night. Your mind will be working overtime, thinking about better ways to write the same logic or wondering what can happen to the logic you've written. All of these mind games are just part of the territory, and just like developing styles in your code, you have to develop styles in your daily life. In the meantime, however, make sure you do the following periodically to stay fresh and relevant:

- Take breaks.
- Find your thinking time.
- Learn something new.
- Learn diplomacy.

Taking a Break

When you sit down to start your day, talk to your fellow developers. Ask them what they have on their daily agenda. What are they working on? Do they need any help? You are not trying to question their workload; rather, you are just letting them know that you care and you are available to help if needed. Sometimes, by just getting other developers to talk about their workload, you might be able to help them by offering advice or other solutions.

Take a break and go for a walk every five hours or so. Step away from the PC and get your mind off the current task. Invite fellow developers to walk with you and share your work-related problems with them. They might be able to help you or know someone who can.

Finding Your Thinking Time

Solutions for current problems don't come easy. They often need time to sink in so that you can logically move through each scenario step-by-step. My best ideas come to me while jogging. That is when my mind is at ease and I have nothing but time to think about solutions to complex problems. Find your thinking time and table major decisions until you can get there. Whether it's a shower, a walk, or a long car drive, everyone needs a place to think.

9

Learning Something New

At night or on the weekends, pick up books and tutorials on different languages, frameworks, or tools. Stay on top of the technology and keep abreast of what is going on in the market next to you and worldwide. Nothing can regenerate your interest in this field more than the gratification of learning something new and then having the ability to use that knowledge in your current job.

Learning Diplomacy

The days of the geeky programmers are over. Developers now need to be collaborators, problem solvers (both proactive and reactive), and technical consultants. How do people perceive you and your work environment? Are you approachable? Hostile attitudes, cranky moods, and just being rude can kill a team. You need to maintain a professional relationship with everyone on the development team, so be nice and have fun. Learn diplomacy.

Chapter Summary

- Software programs are very vulnerable to attacks by outside variables. Input validation is very important when securing the application.

- Validating the input request not only checks to see if the parameters are blacklisted, but it also authorizes and authenticates the sender.

- Code encapsulation is the best way to protect data from being tampered with while in transit. Code encapsulation ensures that the properties and values of the object remain unchanged unless access is given through methods called getters and setters.

- Proper exception-handling techniques allow the software to monitor itself and make programmed decisions regarding what to do when something unexpected occurs.

- Don't throw out exception messages that tell anyone who reads them the server name, type, ports, or SQL exceptions with database names and columns. The error messages the end users see on the screen don't necessarily have to be what the programmers see in the log file. Make error messages intuitive and tell the users what they need to do to resolve the issue.

- Self-monitoring is a coding style that puts a lot of decision making in the application's hands. As a developer, you want to sleep well at night and not worry how many times a user tries multiple passwords on your application. Code algorithms and business logic within the software that can cancel user's passwords, log user activity, or send out SOS pages when it detects something peculiar about a user's request or activity.

- Secure third-party access points to protect your applications from attackers sneaking in a third-party JAR file with a malicious logic bomb. This software is so well hidden that it is very hard to detect—make sure no one has access to the directories that are in the server's classpath.

- Know the security advantages or disadvantages of the programming language that is being used on the application. This type of information is a moving target, and you need to stay up to date with the latest versions and features.

- Code the application to debug before you have issues. This style of programming will save hundreds of hours and errors if it is done up front and built in to the code, rather than added after the fact.

- Software diversity means that the software needs to be dynamic enough to change with future requirements. You can anticipate this change by making sure the application is parameter-driven, avoiding limiting methods and other coding conventions, and avoiding spaghetti code.

- The styles in your work habits, personal hobbies, and breaks will help improve the quality of your work. Take time to think about problems, work through designs in your mind, and step away from the PC. Many great concepts and designs will come naturally when the time is right. Don't expect this type of work to disappear the moment you leave the office.

KEY TERMS

blacklist — All values not defined in a whitelist.

buffer overflow — An event that occurs when you put more data into a memory location than it is allocated to hold.

buffer overflow attack — Software attacks to buffer overflows.

compile time — The time when a program language, such as Java, converts ASCII characters into binary (or machine) code. If keywords are misspelled or the code is not per API specification, compile-time errors will occur.

debugs — Style built into the code that assists the programmer in following the application's execution paths and internal definitions.

encapsulation — The process of creating code wrappers around variables, input values, or business logic so that access to properties can be achieved only through the use of the object's methods.

getters and setters — Methods that are used to send or retrieve properties from an object.

JAR file — A Java archive file is a Zip file used to distribute a set of Java classes.

limited code — Code that is written for one purpose only.

parameter-driven software — Software that is coded in such a way that the paths of execution are determined by parameters stored in a table or XML file rather than hard coded.

refactoring — The process of reorganizing the code's structure without changing the meaning or behavior of the software.

run–time error — Errors that occur after the code has been compiled and at the time of execution.

singleton design pattern — A design pattern that guarantees that only one object resides in memory during the time of execution.

SLA (service-level agreement) — An agreement that contractually binds the application support team to service the application in the event of errors, downtime, or other related system problems.

SMS (Short Message Service) — A protocol used for sending messages of up to 160 characters.

software diversity — The ability to design software so that future changes can be easily adminstered and carried out.

spaghetti code — Code that starts in one place but then spawns itself into hundreds of other directions; very hard to maintain.

SQL code injection — An attack type conducted through the use of Web servers where an SQL statement can be substituted for a host variable within an outer select statement.

whitelist — When performing input validation, the set of items that, if matched, results in the input being accepted as valid. If there is no match to the whitelist, the input is considered invalid.

XSS (Cross-Site Scripting) — An attack on Web pages that stores input fields in a database and then redisplays those fields on the Web screen as data. The input fields, however, are corrupted with JavaScript tags that could redirect the user to another Web site.

9

REVIEW QUESTIONS

1. Which of the following is not a style of secure programming?

   a. validating request data

   b. error handling

   c. self-monitoring

   d. self-coding

   e. diversity

2. What three things must be done to validate input data?

   a. authenticate, authorize, and validate

   b. authorize, validate, and cleanse

   c. authorize, validate, and encapsulate

   d. authorize, validate, and filter out

3. _____ values are a list of accepted input values that the application can process.

4. Why is it a good idea to encapsulate data after it is cleansed?

   a. to protect the data from being tampered with

   b. to protect the data from accidental manipulation

   c. to logically group like values together so that code can be well organized

   d. so that data snooping cannot take place

   e. all of the above

5. What are the two types of errors in application development?

6. What is the best thing a developer can do with errors?

   a. Do not code them.

   b. Test applications thoroughly and ask analysts to do the same.

   c. Log all errors.

   d. Code error-handling classes.

7. What type of secure programming style will cancel a user's ID if he or she tried to log on more than three times?

   a. input validation

   b. self-monitoring

   c. error handling

   d. knowing the programming language

8. _____ are Zip files of Java classes that can be called from outside the application's code.

9. Name some social skills listed that will help you write better code.

10. _____ are methods that are used to send or retrieve properties from an object.

11. Which of the following is *not* a characteristic of quality code?

    a. organized

    b. diverse

    c. singleton design pattern

    d. error handling

    e. code refactoring

12. What method(s) are *not* recommended when organizing code? (Choose all that apply.)

    a. You can use the wildcard (*) if you need more than three classes in the same package.

    b. Declare variables at the time that they are needed. That way, code will be grouped together on an as-needed basis.

    c. Because OOP allows objects to call other objects, it is okay to daisy chain programs together.

    d. Avoid spaghetti code.

    e. all of the above

13. _____ is the best way to guarantee that there is only one class that performs a certain function or accesses a certain resource.

14. Which of the following are *not* coding styles for diversity? (Choose all that apply.)

    a. limited options

    b. debugging

    c. dynamic signatures

    d. parameter-driven logic

    e. code refactoring

15. Why is it a good idea to code for debugging even though you might never need it?

16. When a developer has been working for more than six hours on a complicated loop and still cannot figure out how to successfully do it, what is the best thing he or she can do?

    a. Debug it.

    b. Have another set of eyes look at it.

    c. Take a break.

    d. Keep working on it until it is solved.

17. _____ occurs when a variable such as an input field is written to another variable of smaller length in the program's memory.

18. Data validating authenticates the user. True or False?

19. Code refactoring creates more work for the programmer. True or False?

20. Compile-time errors could tell the end user application secrets, such as Web server name, directory structures, and other related information that could be used against the application in an attack. True or False?

HANDS-ON PROJECTS

Project 9-1 Installing the J2EE Web Application

1. Open the "NetBeans.doc file" from the Chapter 9 course data.

   a. Follow the ten-step installation guide to get the application working.

   b. Make a screen print of the welcome page and hand it to the instructor.

2. Review the code from Step 1 and identify the key ingredients for secure code and quality characteristics. Then, tell the instructor where an example of the following styles can be found (for example, Class name):

   ❑ Form validation

   ❑ try{} catch {}

   ❑ Application error logging

   ❑ Use of debugs

   ❑ MVC architecture

   ❑ Input beans as signatures, not hard coded parameters

   ❑ Use of CONSTANTS throughout

Project 9-2 Attacking the J2EE Web Application

The purpose of this project is to provide the reader with some practice time for XSS attacks.

1. Start the J2EE Web application from Project 9-1.

2. Enter *test* as the username and *test* as the password.

3. Click the Refer a Friend link.

4. In the data elements from the Web screen, apply the knowledge learned from XSS to the Comments section.

5. You will validate your result by entering a JavaScript command that alters the message "Hi" when your malicious code is selected.

CASE PROJECT

Look It Up

The purpose of this project is to investigate what SQL and XSS attacks are and how to implement them. This project will reinforce the importance of input validation.

1. Research XSS attacks on the Internet. You might want to try *http://en.wikipedia.org/wiki/Cross_site_scripting* as a starting point.

2. Research SQL code injection attacks on the Internet. You might want to try *http://msdn.microsoft.com/msdnmag/issues/06/11/SQLSecurity/default.aspx* as a starting point.

3. Write a short report in your own words about what XSS attacks are and how they are implemented. Specifically, describe how the attacks are carried out, what technology is affected, and the preferred methods of designing code to defend against them.

4. Write a short report in your own words about what SQL code injection is and how it is implemented. Specifically, describe how the attacks are carried out, what technology is affected, and the preferred methods of designing code to defend against them.

9

CHAPTER REFERENCES

Dupuis, Robert, Pierre Bourque, Alain Abran, James W. Moore, Leonard L. Tripp, and IEEE Society. 2004. Guide to the Software Engineering Body of Knowledge, Version 2004. http://www.swebok.org (accessed February 14, 2008).

Gamma, Erich, Richard Helm, Ralph Johnson, and John Vlissides. 1995. *Design Patterns: Elements of Reusable Object-Oriented Software*. Reading, Massachusetts: Addison-Wesley.

Oaks, Scott. 2001. *Java Security*. Sebastopol, CA: O'Reilly & Associates, Inc.

Olson, Philip. 2007. PHP Manual. http://www.php.net/manual/en/index.php (accessed February 23, 2008).

OWASP. 2006. OpenWebApplication Security Project. Error Handling, Auditing and Logging. http://www.owasp.org/index.php/Error_Handling,_Auditing_and_Logging #Error_Handling (accessed February 23, 2008).

PHP Security Consortium. 2007. PHP Security Guide: Overview. http://phpsec.org/projects/guide/1.html#1.1 (accessed February 23, 2008).

Sun Microsystems. 2007. Reduce Scope. http://java.sun.com/security/seccodeguide. html#gcg3 (accessed February 23, 2008).

10

TESTING FOR QUALITY AND SECURITY

Upon completion of this material, you should be able to:

♦ Understand the basic concepts and definitions of testing

♦ Work with dynamic testing techniques

♦ Use static testing techniques

♦ Test the resiliency of the development process

In this chapter, we discuss various methods and techniques that can be used to test the integrity, confidentiality, and availability for each individual use case as well as the overall application. Testing is a major activity that involves the whole team's participation and the overall guidance and direction of the project manager. This chapter does not create a new methodology for testing; rather, it lists what types of testing need to be done, how testing is administered, and why. After reading this chapter, you will understand what role the developer plays in the testing phase and how to create a repeatable process that looks for common vulnerabilities.

TESTING IN THE INDUSTRY: CONCEPTS AND DEFINITIONS

Testing software consists of running a battery of test cases using multiple techniques against a specific use case and evaluating the results for pass or fail marks. The testing phase of any application is a major phase of the life cycle and should be treated as important as the development itself by the project management team. As a developer, you will play a key role in helping the management team create, execute, and evaluate test cases. Therefore, getting a general idea of what secure testing is and how to administer it will help you contribute more to the success of the project.

The following subsections will help you understand what testing is and how you fit into the overall process:

- What is testing and assurance
- What testing is *not*
- The test plan
- The problems with testing

What Is Testing and What Is Assurance?

Software testing is the discipline of examining the *functionality* of application software to determine whether it meets the requirements (**verification**) and satisfies the need (**validation**). **Software assurance (SwA)** is how effective security is tested and implemented within the software (Redwine, et al. 2007).

During the software assurance process, the development team members must demonstrate their competency with software security testing through the use of artifacts, reports, and tools. It is in this phase that the design and code for each of the misuse cases created in requirements will be executed and thoroughly tested. Testing for both functionality and security requires the execution of the code and the validation/verification of the results.

What Testing Is *Not*

There are some misconceptions that developers have about testing, so this part of the chapter clarifies what testing is *not*.

It Is Not a Security Measure

The application will never be 100 percent secure. Technology, techniques, and business decisions will always affect the vulnerability of the software. Testing has the capability to demonstrate only that an application responds properly when subjected to specific attacks. It can not prove that the software is secure in a general sense.

It Is Not a Quality Measure

For the same reason that testing cannot guarantee security, it cannot prove quality. For example, the testing environment can never be exactly like the production environment, and one test script cannot possibly replicate all the **usability testing** techniques. These techniques include navigation scenarios and combinations of good and bad input data that real world users create. Testing does not generate error-free software. Testing generates software that is acceptable for the user community and that meets the needs of the business.

It Is Not Always Automated

Executing a bunch of shell scripts to emulate users has its purpose in testing but it's just one of many techniques. Most techniques need human intervention so that a wider range of errors can be tested accordingly. What happens when someone shuts down a Web server? How does the system respond when a database is locked? These types of scenarios cannot be automated.

The Earlier Testing Is Done, the Cheaper It Is to Fix

Everyone has heard by now that fixing development errors early in the process is less expensive than waiting until the end of the project. Testing each development iteration, use case, and misuse case will identify major design flaws as early as possible in the life cycle and will catch up to 95 percent of defects rather than waiting for the last phase (McConnell 1996).

The Test Plan

A test plan is created by the project management team and specifies how testing should be performed, who executes the testing, when testing starts and ends, as well as any and all other pertinent data deemed necessary by the project management team. A **test plan** lays out what needs to be tested for functionality and what needs to be protected for security and how the application reacts to specific attacks.

Regardless of which standard, framework, or testing strategy is used on a given project, the following are the common steps that you must take to execute any test plan:

- Define test scripts
- Define the user community
- Identify the showstoppers
- Identify internal resources
- Identify external resources

10

Defining Test Scripts

Test cases are what the developers use to run their tests. Scripts are very detailed, logical steps of instructions that tell a person or tool what to do during the testing. Developers typically play a key role in creating test cases for the software they coded, and the BAs usually lend a hand as well. Test cases define the goals of each feature that needs to be executed. For example, each test case should list the expected result so that the testers will be able to evaluate the outcome.

Functional testing scripts are step-by-step instructions that depict a specific scenario or situation that the use case will encounter as well as the expected result. Functional testing scripts are created for both the human (manual) interface and for automated testing. What is it a tester should do to carry out a test? Which fields are edited and what button(s) are clicked? And, of course, what is the expected result?

TIP Use cases are a great starting point for functional test scripts. Use cases define what the software should do and, therefore, the tester should know how to validate and verify that the software works.

Secure testing scripts are scripts that are specifically created for testing the security of the application. The basis for these scripts comes from the threat models that were generated during the design phase. In the design phase, all areas of an application's weakness (for example, points of input) and attack types were identified. Therefore, a script needs to be created for every possible situation and attack that the program could encounter.

TIP Misuse cases are a great starting point for secure test scripts. It would be very helpful in the maintenance phase if the secure test scripts were added to the misuse case documentation. Misuse cases define what needs to be protected (assets) and what types of attacks can gain access to those assets. Secure test scripts define the acts of carrying out those attacks.

Defining the User Community

Defining the user community helps testers identify acceptable levels of failures and risks. For example, consider the following scenario for data transmission.

As Figure 10-1 shows, a use case states that Internet users will send sensitive data from their clients to the company's Web server from the Internet. Once on the data network, that data will then be transmitted to a company database for internal analysis.

The misuse case in Figure 10-2 shows how attackers could use packet sniffers to trap sensitive information sent from the client. The development team determined it was very possible and rather simple to configure a router to act as a proxy and trap all data elements. As a result, data encryption and SSL would be needed to protect the confidentiality of the data coming from the Internet.

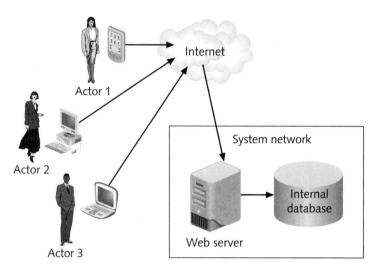

Figure 10-1 User entry use case

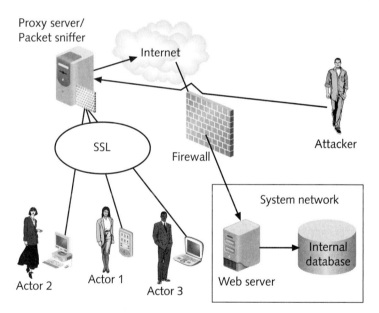

Figure 10-2 User entry misuse case

Therefore, a test would have to be set up using packet sniffers to try to trap the data that goes to the Web server. After that data has made it to the server, it might be transferred to a corporate database in a company's network. Because that data transmission is already considered to be "safe" after it's on the network, testing data encryption to the database will not be conducted. The misuse case considers data on the network to be an acceptable risk because the company encrypts all data on the network.

 NOTE Internal threats should *not* be discounted. While it is probably true that an internal user is less likely to hack into the system, there is probably a greater threat that sensitive data could end up in the wrong hands as a result of an internal user's actions. Trap the information with packet sniffers and try to find what type of sensitive data your application exposes.

As Figure 10-3 shows, the user community in this test case will be the Internet users. The user community will not be the company network or their intranet users.

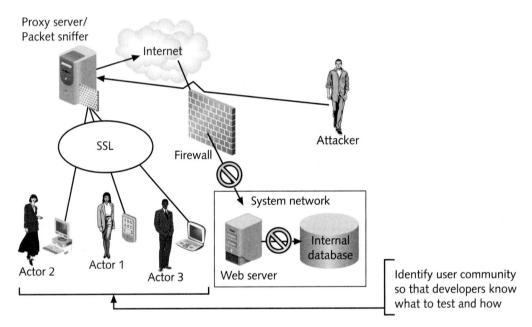

Figure 10-3 Defining the user community

Getting to know who your users are, where they sit (work from), and how they will use the software are very important aspects of testing. Who your users are will help define the types of testing techniques to be used as well as how much testing needs to be done for an acceptable level. If your users are all internal (intranet), you probably wouldn't spend 100+ hours testing for SQL code injections like you would if they were the general public (Internet).

The following is a list of items you need to know about your users:

- From what side of the firewall do they log on? From the outside or from the inside?
- From where do they log on (locales) and when (time)? You need to test software with the same time locations, bandwidth, and other user-specific details.

- What hardware do the users use? Don't test Web screens on a 19-inch LCD flat screen if your users have only handheld devices.

- What other software do they use (for example, OS, browser version)? Test with what you need to support and nothing more. If you don't need to support Microsoft Internet Explorer version 5 or less, then don't.

Identifying the Showstoppers   What does the application need to fulfill the user's request? For example, if the current use case requires collecting product numbers from one table and the product names from another, what happens to the user's request if the product name table is unavailable? Is the name of a product a *must-have* to sell the item or is the model number enough to fulfill the request? In today's object-oriented world, applications are more intertwined and not everything is available when you need it. The test plan should include the must-haves so that the developers can pull the plug on certain entities to see how the application responds.

 Defining must-haves and the "what-if-unavailable" scenarios should be in the use case. If not, a revisit to the requirements might have to happen so that these specifications can be documented.

NOTE

10

Identifying Resources

Far too often, the people who do most of the testing are the same ones who coded the programs, even though all the **PMP resources**, **IEEE** standards, and every other professional testing book available suggests getting other people to test, not just the one who developed it. The reason for not following this advice is simple: money and time. It seems like all applications I've worked on, and the ones I've observed from a distance, pushed testing until the end of the process when time is short and money is tight. Because there is no time to wait for additional resources, testing goes on with the resources available.

The problem with having developers test their own code is that they are too intimate with the program. Have you ever written an e-mail to a bunch of people and proofread your note 10 times before sending it out, yet when you get a response and you reread your message you can pick out typos or the wrong word usage? Testing software has the same effect; the developers are so focused on getting the functionality working, they forget to test different security features such as roles, privileges, and hard-coded comments.

There are two types of resources needed to execute the test case:

- Internal
- External

Internal Resources   Internal resources come from the company's organization, including developers, analysts, software tools, and sometimes even project managers. Who on the team are the security experts for software testing? How did they become experts? What type of training or experience did they have with security features of software? These are just a couple of questions to ask when looking for the internal resources to execute the misuse case/test case. Usually, the best programmers for security testing are the ones who understand hacking techniques (Whittaker 2003).

 It is better to use non-programmers for general testing because they are not familiar with the underlying architecture and code.

NOTE

External Resources   **External resources** are tools or people who are hired on a temporary basis to come into a project, test the application, and report findings. External resources are best suited for security testing because they typically come highly trained in secure programming techniques and they are far removed from the code and any internal politics. If external resources are needed, the test plan needs to state the following:

- What they are going to test?
- To whom will they report?
- With whom will they be working?

The most commonly used practice in the security field is **penetrations testing** (pent test). This is when an outside firm is hired to come in to try to circumvent specific security aspects of an application or use a barrage of attacks and techniques to test the interfaces and code. The use of external resources such as pent testers can have a great impact on the code as well as the development team—especially if they are used early in the development process. For example, after one or two use cases/misuses are coded, call in pent testers to review the code, test the application, and attempt to penetrate the defensive code mechanisms.

When pent testers are called in early enough, the development team can learn from these experts and determine what the team did right and wrong during requirements, design, and development. The learning and training experience that the whole team is exposed to during these tests will greatly enhance all later use cases and applications.

Problems with Testing in the Industry

Testing the application after development has always been challenging. Far too often, the testing activity is the one phase that is shortened because of project overruns, loss of budgets, or lack of resources. There are two features that need to be tested for: quality and security. Much testing is needed to ensure both quality and security goals are achieved in the application.

Testing for security and quality are faced with the following problems:

- Too much reliance on individual skills
- Unpredictable users

- Inconsistent definition of success

Too Much Reliance on Individual Skills

The industry is getting better at testing applications using tools, but it still has a long way to go before you can scan your code once and be done. As mentioned previously, most secure testing techniques are best left to the individuals who know the most about software attacks. Software testing for security relies a lot on individual skill and talent. Automated security tools can find code pointers or invalidated input variables that the developers missed and can alert the team to the vulnerability. Those security tools scan code for specific keywords, classes, and common pitfalls of sloppy code, which helps identify potential defects.

Security code scanners also report a number of **false positives**. False positives occur when code, such as safe input fields, is also reported as potentially dangerous code. False positives aren't necessarily a bad thing, but after sorting through hundreds of them in a project, developers may not look at them carefully.

Unpredictable Users

No one will ever know what an end user will do to the software or how they will do it. After many years of Web development, I continue to be amazed at how some people enter data or just browse reports. From clicking the Refresh button 10 times before the page renders to pressing Ctrl+N to opening up multiple browser sessions, end users will use your software in ways you never would have imagined.

TIP
The problem with testing end-user navigation and usability is that you never know what they will do next. This is when you need to hand the application to other resources (internal and external) and let them try to break it.

Inconsistent Definition of Success   Testing is an arduous task, and at the end of each technique or method a decision needs to be made whether to pass or fail that test. The fact that this kind of judgment is in the hands of testers (usually developers) is a problem. For example, suppose you were asked to code a use case and the coding time went well over the estimated time for development. The project manager (PM) is already upset that it has taken so long. Does the PM really want to hear that the software failed the test case? Would it be easier for the developer to pass that test case and either hope it never happens or take care of it later?

If the tester is the same person who coded the program, the test results can be somewhat subjective. If the tester is not up to speed with the types of attacks that should be tested, how do you know if the code is secure even after the tests are passed?

**QUICK
CHECKS**

The Open Web Application Security Project (OWASP) promotes fighting software vulnerabilities through the use of tools, information, and teaching attacking techniques that are needed in testing.

1. Visit the OWASP Web site and subscribe to any of the mailing lists that interest you. The site is at *www.owasp.org/index.php/Main_Page*.

2. From the OWASP Web site, visit the Getting Started page and list the four items recommended to find out if your code has vulnerabilities. Provide an explanation of each item.

DYNAMIC TESTING IN THE ORGANIZATION

Dynamic testing implies executing the current use case using valid inputs and then comparing the real results with expected results for pass or failures (Redwine, et al. 2007). Every method and technique requires the tester to analyze the results and perform some validation and verification (V&V) on the software and report the findings. For example, each test needs to *validate* that the program satisfies the requirements and *verify* that the program is what the end result should be.

Although a number of separate tools and techniques uniquely address both security and quality, it would be easier to introduce each technique within the three phases of testing:

- Unit testing

- Integration testing

- System testing

Unit Testing

Unit testing is the lowest level of testing a developer can conduct. It is the act of testing an individual method, module, and/or program for V&V. In fact, it is almost impossible to code programs without some sort of lightweight testing by catching **syntax errors**. Compilers will stop the developer from making syntax mistakes or typos.

Unit testing catches errors that compilers won't find. These errors are called **logic errors** and security vulnerabilities. Unit testing is actually conducted while the programs are being written. Unit testing done right includes the following techniques:

- Testing exception handling

- Reviewing error logs

Testing Exception Handling

In Chapter 9, we discussed the importance of proper error handling. In the unit test phase, the testing should deliberately go into the code and cause an exception to happen. Either log in to the application more than five times to see what happens (assuming you coded for a counter) or make an important variable null (null pointer exception). What happens to the software? Does the code manage itself and gracefully take the user to a safe place or does the program crash leaving an awful error page?

Manually going into the source code and forcing an error or attack is called **source-based fault injections** (Whittaker and Thompson 2003). Source-based fault injections can be easy to administer but they require the code base to be altered from the "real" code, which opens the door for more mistakes (that is, leaving the injections in).

Reviewing Error Logs

What does the error log tell the testers? What if the tester caused an exception in the code and the application caught the error and gracefully took the user to a safe place? Is there any trace from that error that the developers could use to prevent this from happening in the future? Every error that the application manages needs to be logged so that developers can analyze those logs for trends and abuses.

Your log files should answer the following questions:

- Who is the user?

- What is the search criterion?

- What method or program caught the error and where did the error occur?

- What type of comments can the developer include to resolve the issue?

QUICK CHECKS

Application error logs offer the best place for applications to hide their secrets. Reading them will be a big part of your job. Do the following activities, which demonstrate how you would use the information supplied in the log file.

1. Open up the log file named "errorLog.txt." It is located in the Chapter 10 course data.

2. From this report, list the following items: Who is the user? What objects are being used? Is the end result good or bad? Can the error be identified?

3. What would you do differently if you had control over what is logged and how?

4. Hand your findings to the instructor.

Integration Testing

Integration testing is when two or more modules, **Web services**, or platforms are linked together and tested. Integration testing requires testing of the whole use case rather than an individual piece of software. As you learned in Chapter 6, interaction diagrams tell the developer which objects to create, which methods to code, and what those methods will take and return. After the interaction diagrams are created, the classes and diagrams are split up among the development team so that coding those objects can be done in parallel. When all the objects are developed, they don't always fit.

Figure 10-4 provides an example of an integration diagram and testing. An application takes form data from the client browser and passes it securely to the Web server. The Web server then validates the data and needs to call another object for further processing.

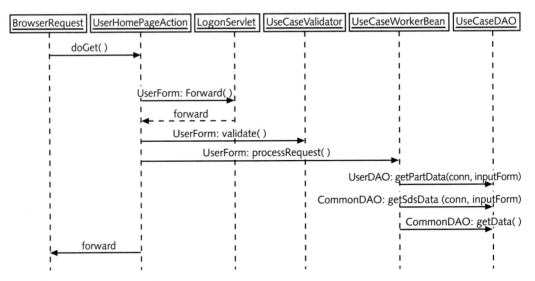

Figure 10-4   Integration test

On paper, the diagram looks good, but as you can see in Figure 10-5, the first problem found is with the method name and signature. If you compare the interaction diagram with the actual code, you will see that not all developers follow directions. Individually, the classes will all compile and run, but when they start to call one another, the classes will not integrate.

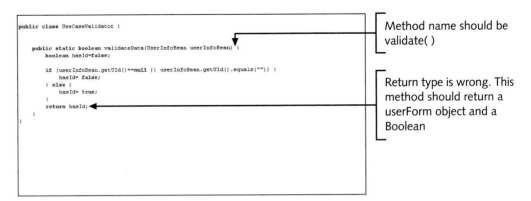

Figure 10-5   Use case validator class

System Testing

After the current use case has been unit tested and integrated with other programs/use cases, the entire system must be tested. A **system test** involves a complete front-to-back execution of the entire application. As each use case is added to the application's architecture, system testing is conducted to make sure that the new programs do not compromise any other element of the system. System testing on a use case basis will catch major errors early and allow the analyst and developers to design better solutions.

Each new use case that is added to the system must be tested for quality features, such as reliability and usability, and for security. The more complexity that is added to the system, the more vulnerable it becomes. Therefore, you need a process that includes automated tools such as load balancers, packet sniffers, and code scanners (analyzers) that can test the application in its entirety.

System testing techniques vary from project to project depending on the type of architecture. For example, system testing Web applications might involve linking to other pages to ensure that necessary session data is being passed around, whereas testing mainframe programs involves running a series of batch jobs and verifying the output files.

The following activities are conducted during system testing:

- Fuzz testing
- Reliability testing

Fuzz Testing

Fuzz testing, or *fuzzing*, is a technique that feeds random input data into applications just to see what happens to the results. Basic fuzz tools generate random characters that can be used as an input file used by the application for processing (Miller, et al. 1995). Fuzzing applications can be done using tools or human methods that simply write garbage data into enterable fields, XML files, or any other inputs to the application.

To carry out a fuzz test, follow these steps for each file or field that feeds into the application:

1. Enter random data or spaces to some part of the input file.
2. Execute the application with that input file.
3. Evaluate results. What broke? What ran as normal? What was expected to happen?
4. Number each test case and report findings to project management.

Reliability Testing

Reliability of an application is when the application produces correct results despite being under attack (Redwine, et al. 2007) or under extreme use. Reliability is just as important to test as confidentiality and integrity. Testing the reliability of the application requires simulation tools that can replicate the number of expected uses, time of day, and software environment as in the real world.

Some tools that can be used during reliability testing include the following:

- *Holodeck*: Holodeck is a unique testing tool that "uses fault simulation to emulate real-world application and system errors" (Security Innovation 2007). This allows testers and developers to analyze and debug error-handling code in simulated hostile environments that can be controlled. This tool is very useful for testing the application for reliability. For more, see Security Innovation at *www.sisecure.com/holodeck/index.shtml*.

- *LoadRunner*: LoadRunner is a simulation tool used to test concurrent users, database connections, and other application resources. This tool monitors code performance and looks for application bottlenecks and other inefficiencies. For more, see the company Web site at *http://www.hp.com/* and search for LoadRunner.

STATIC TESTING IN THE ORGANIZATION

Static testing involves executing methods and techniques to test the code without actually running the application. Static testing does not evaluate the application's performance, but does evaluate what the actual code looks like on paper. Static testing is not always the most exciting work, but it is just as important as dynamic testing. Static testing includes the following techniques:

- Static code analysis

- Code reviews and inspections

- System documentation

Static Code Analysis

Static code analyzers scan (parse) through static code and analyze the code base for security vulnerabilities (such as input fields and buffer overflows). The concept here is conceptually similar to that of an antivirus scanning product: The code checker looks through source code for any series of "known and previously defined problem conditions" (Van Wyk and Graff 2003, p. 164).

A number of static code analyzers are available on the market for both open source and commercial software. Fortify Software, *www.fortifysoftware.com/*, currently leads the pack. Not only does its tools come with sophisticated code parsers, but also they have reporting features that provide metrics, visibility, and policy managers that allow changes for the secure rules of the parsers.

Code Reviews and Inspections

Code reviews are people-intensive verification techniques that are conducted either formally or informally that allow peers to read code statements and look for common security vulnerabilities, such as hard-coded IDs or passwords, and general quality features. Code reviews are one of the most important steps of any development process and, yet, they are the least implemented. A lot of security and quality mistakes can be easily caught while looking at code for problematic areas, but as it stands now, code reviews have a bad reputation in the field as being very subjective and offensive to the person who wrote the code.

Time and money are also key reasons why code reviews are not conducted enough. Timelines are very short and deliverables have to be handed over and code reviews are the last "to-do" on the list. No one has the time to read lengthy code that most likely has already been modified since the programmer printed it out on paper.

Code reviews, if conducted right, should have a very positive effect on the team. Reviewing code as a team is actually a great opportunity for the strongest skilled developers to share knowledge, rationale, and guidance with the entry/mid-level developers.

For a positive experience that creates better code and improves security, follow these steps:

- Have a formal meeting with the right people
- Bring the right supplies

Having a Formal Meeting with the Right People

Code reviews need to be conducted after the developer is done unit testing, integrating, and verifying that the use case and misuse case satisfies the software requirements for both quality and security. Right before the developer tells the project manager that the use case is done, the code review takes place. Code review needs to include the developer who coded the software and two other developers who review the person's code.

These are often called peer reviews because the people who need to attend a review should be people who have knowledge in the computer language and the project. The best people to invite to these meetings are as follows:

- *Individual developer who coded the program*: At this moment, this person knows more about the program and the requirements than anyone else on the team.
- *Lead developer*: This person should be present in the event that rules or guidelines need to be reinforced or created.
- *A third developer from the same project (if one does not exist, ask team members from other projects)*: This person will also be looking closely at the code for issues or concerns.

Code reviews are conducted in a conference room or at someone's desk. IEEE standard for Reviews and Audits, IEEE 1028, states that reviews can take place either formally or informally, but I have found that the more formal the process, the better the results.

The following are the steps to a successful code review:

1. The developer of the use case prints out all the code and makes copies for each participant.

2. At the meeting, each participant walks through the use case, step-by-step, and the programmer talks about each activity.

3. Every code statement is analyzed and reviewed by the participants against a checklist of rules and guidelines.

4. As issues or concerns come up during the meeting, the code is highlighted on the hard copy and notes or instructions are taken.

5. After the meeting, it is determined if another walk-through is needed or if the business analyst needs to be consulted for any questions.

Bringing the Right Supplies to the Code Review

For code reviews to be productive and nonsubjective, the developer has to supply all the relevant material so that reviewers know what to look for.

Code review necessities include the following:

- *Application Guide*: This document prevents any disagreements or subjective advice. Because the Application Guide serves as a contract among the developers, comments like "Don't do that" should be reflected in the Application Guide and all developers should be coding toward team rules.

- *Checklist*: This checklist is a summation of all rules and guidelines documented within the Application Guide.

- *Source code*: Bring handouts of code statements.

- *Highlighters*: Bring highlighters so that you can mark up the code. For example, red means "code must change," yellow means "double-check accuracy," and green means "the code is okay, but change if you have time."

- *Rationale*: Be ready to explain yourself.

 TIP

End code reviews on a positive note. Thank everyone for their participation and tell the reviewers what you have learned from their input. People who feel appreciated will be willing to lend more of their time and skills to you.

Verifying System Documentation

Before you put the test case to rest and go on to the next one, verify that all system documentation is finalized and up to date. System documentation is a lot like life insurance—you might never need to use it after it is finalized, but the one time you need it to be available and accurate, it will be there for you. Verifying that all documentation is complete will make you a more responsible developer, and that level of professionalism will spill into your code and how other team members view you as a colleague.

The following activities will keep the software documentation up to date:

- Verify that the use case documentation says what the software does. Frequently, the code and documentation will be out of sync from the time of requirements to the time of testing. Several iterations and revisions will be made, and it is likely that more business rules will be in the code and not in the use case.

- Verify traceability on the current use case throughout the whole life cycle. Can a use case and misuse case be traced from requirements, design, and testing documentation? Are those requirements visible in the code?

- Verify the current version. Are all the latest documents checked into the version control software?

- Update the Application Guide. Are there any new rules, testing tools, or team standards that were discovered in the testing phase of the use case?

10

TESTING THE RESILIENCY OF THE DEVELOPMENT PROCESS

You have just learned how to create a secure development process. You know how to work and operate in all phases: requirements, design, coding, and testing. How do you know that the process and methods you just learned can be reused or shared? How do you know if you are prepared for a disaster?

Testing will give you a good measuring stick of how good your software is and where the weak areas are, but testing will not tell you if the process in which you created code worked. Despite all the pent testing, code review, static analysis, and fuzz testing efforts, disasters will happen and how you respond and react will make or break your career. Coding for **resiliency** means accepting the fact that something bad will happen and that when it does, you will be ready.

Take a sponge, for instance, and squeeze it, mash it down, and hold it. When that sponge is released, it bounces right back to its original formation and is ready for use. The development process that this book has talked about should be that resilient. If requirements change, the code will be diverse enough so that minor tweaks will handle those changes. If assets are attacked, the software should be smart enough to monitor, log, and alert all necessary parties. Coding for resiliency can be implemented and tested in two ways:

- Knowing how to bounce back
- Knowing how to make something bad happen

How to Bounce Back

Delete a database table, steal and decompile the application code, and take whatever it is the software is supposed to protect and get rid of it. What happened? How did the application respond? How did the application know someone or something stole the assets? This section deals more with testing the policies and procedures that the project management team should have in place. Those policies and procedures need to be tested just as much as the software itself.

What to do when *this* happens, who to call when *that* happens, and **SLAs** (**service-level agreements**) with customers — all these policies should be tested. Just like those fire drills we all had to do in grade school or at the office, testing the resiliency of the application process will identify the areas that need to get better. If the names and numbers on the SLA contact list are wrong, or if the application stops working when no data can be found in the products table, you have a problem. Create an "Are You Ready?" section in the Application Guide that will tell the team what to do when something bad happens.

Are You Ready?

What is the measuring stick for success? How does the project manager determine your success or failure rate as a developer? When an analyst tells you that a secret formula must be protected at all times, how much of the responsibility do you, the team, and the software share if and when that secret is leaked? How can the application find out if someone or something tampered with the software, and how fast can it report this activity to the users? These benchmarks vary from project to project and very few projects go to this level of testing. But as more laws are passed by Congress that force companies to comply with standards that protect sensitive information, benchmarking software will become more responsive to disasters and will become more mainstream.

If a fellow developer was caught e-mailing or copying code from one device to another, how fast can you change the program's encryption logic or the values of the CONSTANT variables? How fast can the application change its defensive layers of protection to continue to provide integrity and availability to all its users?

 TIP   Creating an "Are You Ready?" section in the Application Guide for each project that deals with sensitive information provides managers and stakeholders a way to detail steps that the development team follows when something bad happens.

Making Something Bad Happen

Making something bad happen actually tests the dependencies and resiliency of the software. What must be up and ready for the software application to work? Throughout this book, we have learned how important error handling, coding for diversity, and coding for expected attacks truly are. Making something bad happen will test all those characteristics in one shot.

The following are some bad things you can make happen to test the recovery time:

- *Slam a machine*: How long does it take for a developer to reinstall the OS and all the needed development tools?

- *Stop all Web services that the application calls or offers*: What is the desired effect on the application versus what actually happened?

- *Take out pieces of architecture*: We talked about the principle of separation of layers. What happens when one of those layers is unavailable? For example, if an application server is unavailable, how does the Web server respond? Does the application gracefully exit and invite the user to try again later or does it display the dreaded HTTP error "not found"?

CHAPTER SUMMARY

- Testing software requires a battery of test cases using multiple techniques, tools, and analysis.

- Software assurance will guide how well security is tested within the testing phase.

- Testing software does not prove quality or security. It just proves that it passed the software test case.

- Testing generates software that is acceptable for the user community and that meets the needs of the business.

- A test plan is created by the project management team and specifies how testing should be performed, who executes the testing, when testing starts and ends, as well as any and all other pertinent data deemed necessary for the testing process.

- Scripts are very detailed, logical steps of instructions that tell a person or tool what to do.

- Functional testing scripts are step-by-step instructions that depict a specific scenario or situation that the use case will encounter as well as the expected result. Functional testing scripts are created for both human (manual) interfaces and for automated testing.

- Defining the user community will help testers identify acceptable levels of failures and risks.

- Software tests are conducted by two resources: internal and external.

- The most commonly used external resource in the security field is penetrations testing (pent test). This is when an outside firm is hired to come in and try to circumvent specific security aspects of an application or use a barrage of attacks and techniques to test the interfaces and code.

- Unit testing is the lowest level of testing a developer can conduct. It is the act of testing an individual method, module, and/or program for Validation and Verification (V&V).

- Integration testing is when two or more modules, services, or platforms are linked together and tested. Integration testing requires testing of the whole use case rather than an individual piece of software.

◘ A system test involves a complete front-to-back execution of the entire application.

◘ Fuzz testing, or *fuzzing*, is a technique that feeds random input data into applications just to see what happens to the results.

◘ Static code analyzers scan (parse) through static code and analyze the code base for security vulnerabilities (such as input fields and buffer overflows).

◘ Code reviews are people-intensive verification techniques that are conducted either formally or informally and allow peers to read code statements and look for common security vulnerabilities, such as hard-coded IDs or passwords, and general quality features.

KEY TERMS

code review — A review/inspection of code by its author and/or one or more colleagues (peers) to evaluate its technical content for quality and security.

dynamic testing — The testing of application code by executing the software with valid input fields.

external resources — Human or computer-driven resources used in the software development process.

false positives — An output result from a static code analyzer that highlights valid code, such as an input field, as a vulnerability.

functional testing scripts — A step-by-step process that executes many testing scripts.

fuzz testing — A technique that feeds random input data into applications just to see what happens to the results.

IEEE (Institute of Electrical and Electronics Engineers, pronounced "I-triple-E") — Founded in 1963, IEEE is an organization composed of engineers, scientists, and students. IEEE is best known for developing standards for the computer and electronics industry.

integration testing — The act of testing the whole use case from front to back.

logic errors — Errors within software that are caused by problematic code conditions or faulty If statements.

penetrations testing — A testing technique using qualified personnel to conduct real-world attacks against the application (or system) to help identify and correct security vulnerabilities.

PMP resources — Any project management resource (for example, project plan, minutes, issue logs).

reliability — A test that ensures the application will be up and running under extreme circumstances.

resiliency — The capability to rebound or spring back from an attack.

secure testing scripts — Scripts that are specifically created for testing the security of the application.

SLA (service-level agreement) — A contract between a service provider (application) and a customer that specifies what services and support will be provided and how.

software (security) assurance (SwA) — A software security assurance process judges the effectiveness of how security characteristics and principles are tested and implemented.

source-based fault injections — A testing technique that requires a programmer to physically code an errror into the program to see how the rest of the code reacts.

static code analyzers — Code scanners that identify security vulnerabilities or potential holes by scanning the binary libraries of the application.

static testing — The process of testing application code by inspecting code in its native language and/or scanning binary code for vulnerabilities and quality.

syntax error — A type of error that prevents a code compiler from converting ASCII code into binary.

system test — The act of testing all use cases together as a whole.

test plan — A document created to specify how testing should be performed, who executes the testing, when testing starts and ends, and any and all other pertinent data deemed necessary for the testing process.

testing software — The process of running a battery of test cases using multiple techniques against a specific use case and evaluating the results for pass or fail marks.

usability testing — A technique used to test how the security features of the software affect the convenience of using the application.

validation — A quality check that validates that the final product or service produces the desired result.

verification — A quality check that verifies that the software satisfies the requirement.

Web service — A piece of software that makes itself available over the Internet and uses a standardized XML messaging system.

10

REVIEW QUESTIONS

1. Having a software assurance plan ensures which of the following?

   a. secure code

   b. that a process is in place within the development life cycle that tests for security vulnerabilities

   c. that the software is safe from attacks

   d. that the development team has tested for security vulnerabilities before releasing the software product

2. Which of the following defines a test plan?

   a. a document created by the project management team that specifies what needs to be tested, how to test, and who tests it

   b. step-by-step instructions that depict a specific scenario or situation that the use case will encounter as well as the expected result

   c. step-by-step instructions that are specifically created for testing the security of the application (that is, attacking techniques)

   d. a guide that proves testing has been conducted

3. Which of the following defines a functional test script?

   a. a document created by the project management team that specifies what needs to be tested, how to test, and who tests it

   b. step-by-step instructions that are specifically created for testing the security of the application (that is, attacking techniques)

   c. step-by-step instructions that depict a specific scenario or situation that the use case will encounter as well as the expected result

   d. a guide that proves testing has been conducted

4. Which of the following pieces of information should you know about the user base to ensure accurate testing?

   a. from what side of the firewall they log on

   b. how tech savvy they are

   c. what time zone they use

   d. what other applications they use

5. Why is a piece of software's availability important to define for testing?

6. _____ is the most commonly used practice to test the security of an application.

7. Of the following, which are current problems with testing software today?

   a. too much reliance on human creativity

   b. user actions are never clearly defined

   c. not enough visibility

   d. all of the above

8. _____ implies executing code using valid inputs that test for pass or failure results.

9. In which stage of testing will logic errors and syntax errors be found?

   a. system test

   b. integration test

   c. unit test

   d. all of the above

10. In which stage of testing will input parameters be tested for validation?

    a. system test

    b. integration test

    c. unit test

    d. all of the above

11. In which stage of testing can security features be tested?

    a. system test

    b. integration test

    c. unit test

    d. all of the above

12. Which of the following are techniques of unit testing?

    a. Create an error and test the application response.

    b. Review error logs and debug statements.

    c. Apply stress to the use case to see how many concurrent users will break it.

    d. all of the above

13. _____ is a technique that feeds random input data and/or random input files to the application to test its response.

14. Usability techniques involve the testing of software to see if:

    a. security features affect the performance and convenience of the application

    b. security features affect the integrity of the application

    c. a user has all the privileges needed to perform their tasks and nothing more

    d. all of the above

15. Which of the following techniques can be used to test the development process?

    a. Throw in a last-minute change request and monitor the implementation time.

    b. Pull the plug on all dependencies and test the reliability of the application.

    c. Follow an "Are You Ready" guide.

    d. Use unit testing.

16. _____ scan (parse) through static code and analyze the code base for security vulnerabilities.

17. Code reviews should be conducted with the project management team. True or False?

18. The goal for software testing is to find all bugs. True or False?

19. Testing software cannot guarantee quality software. True or False?

20. Developers should test their own software because they know more about it than anyone else. True or False?

10

HANDS-ON PROJECTS

Project 10-1 WebScarab

1. Open "WebScarab Walkthru.doc" from the Chapter 10 course data.

2. Walk through this tutorial and learn about WebScarab.

3. With WebScarab turned on, go to one of your favorite Web sites and capture your own form data. Print that out and show it to your professor.

4. Write a lessons-learned document and talk about your testing experience from this assignment. Did it give you any new ideas or views on how you use the Web or how attackers might use this information?

5. If you were a developer, what could you do with the code to prevent this type of attack?

Project 10-2 Webgoat

1. Open "Webgoat Walkthru.doc" from the Chapter 10 course data.

2. Walk through this tutorial and learn about Webgoat.

3. Print out a screen shot of a successful cross-site scripting (XSS) attack and show it to your professor.

4. Write a lessons-learned document and talk about your testing experience from this assignment. Did it give you any new ideas or views on how to test software or how attackers might use this information?

5. If you were a developer, what could you do with the code to prevent this type of testing?

CASE PROJECT

Code Review

1. Pair up with two or three fellow students.

2. Open the source code file "SampleCode.java" from the Chapter 10 course data.

3. Using your Application Guide as a reference, how many coding errors can you find with coding conventions, naming conventions, and security vulnerabilities?

4. Can you find any error in the code that isn't mentioned in the Application Guide? If so, update the Application Guide accordingly.

Chapter References

McConnell, Steven. 1996. *Rapid Development*. Redmond, Washington: Microsoft Press.

Miller, Barton P., David Koski, Cjin Pheow Lee, Vivekananda Maganty, Ravi Murthy, Ajitkumar Natarajan, and Jeff Steidl. 1995. Fuzz Revisited: A Re-examination of the Reliability of UNIX Utilities and Services. ftp://ftp.cs.wisc.edu/pub/paradyn/technical_papers/fuzz-revisited.ps (accessed February 23, 2008).

Redwine, Samuel T. Jr., Rusty O. Baldwin, Mary L. Polydys, Daniel P. Shoemaker, Jeffrey A. Ingalsbe, and Larry D. Wagoner. 2007. Software Assurance: A Guide to the Common Body of Knowledge to Produce, Acquire, and Sustain Secure Software Version 1.2. Arlington, VA: U.S. Department of Homeland Security. https://buildsecurityin.us-cert.gov/daisy/bsi/940/version/1/part/4/data/CurriculumGuideToTheCBK.pdf (accessed February 13, 2008).

Security Innovation. 2007. Holodeck Overview. http://www.sisecure.com/holodeck/index.shtml (accessed February 23, 2008).

Van Wyk, Kenneth R. and Mark G. Graff. 2003. *Secure Coding: Principles & Practices*. Sebastopol, CA: O'Reilly & Associates.

Whittaker, James A. 2003. *How to Break Software: A Practical Guide to Testing*. Boston: Addison-Wesley.

Whittaker, James A. and Herbert H. Thompson. 2003. *How to Break Software Security: Effective Techniques for Security Testing*. Boston: Addison-Wesley.

10

11

MAINTAIN YOUR SOFTWARE, MAINTAIN YOUR CAREER

Upon completion of this material, you should be able to:

♦ Sustain a formal development process

♦ Provide software assurance

♦ Keep your career in demand

This chapter is concerned with keeping software secure in the maintenance phase and keeping your career relevant in the industry. Software maintenance projects can be the start of a very long, enriching career—if you handle the opportunity correctly. *Maintenance* used to mean "dead-end career move." Now, it means increasing consumers' interest, meeting the ever-changing security requirements from the business and legal teams, and integrating more software and communication for end users' convenience. Are you ready for the new paradigm?

Chapter 11

SUSTAINING A FORMAL DEVELOPMENT PROCESS

Typically, when software falls into the maintenance category, it seems like all the teamwork, group meetings, and whiteboard drawings fall out of favor. Instead, developers are given individual assignments to be worked on, and once a week the team will meet with the PM for a general status meeting to share information. Whenever this lax approach to software development is implemented, it is easy to let your guard down and produce messy, buggy code all over again.

In order to support the application's operations, everyone on the team must sustain secure software until the application retires. During software maintenance, the software development process that you used when you built the software still needs to be followed and carried out. Every new change request requires a change to the current use case, misuse case, design documents, and test cases. If the code base is changed and the software artifacts are not touched, the design documents that you spent hours creating and maintaining could become worthless.

Whether you're looking at **break/fix** measures, such as fixing bugs, or **enhancement** measures, such as adding new use cases, the drive to sustain secure, quality software should always be present at every level. Sustaining a secure development process during maintenance is easy to administer as long as the developer stays focused on the following:

- Controlling change
- Sustaining security and quality in the code

Controlling Change

If the project management team does not support or condone a formal development process for the whole team, there is not much you can do to sustain the momentum left from the development stage other than hone your own skills. Sustaining secure code with high quality is too much of a responsibility for one person. The developer still needs the support of management, the assistance of the BAs, and the attention to detail with the software artifacts. Without these essential supporting activities, the developer is fighting an uphill battle that he or she will not win.

Project management can help sustain the formality in the development process during maintenance by creating a change control board (CCB). A **change control board (CCB)** is created during the maintenance phase to provide a defined, formal way of reviewing and approving **change requests (CR)** and software enhancements. The main benefit of a CCB is to reinforce management's support for software artifacts and to prioritize the workload. The CCB is made up of members from the project management team as well as BAs and, sometimes, developers.

The CCB meetings have formal agendas where each CR is reviewed and critiqued. As Figure 11-1 shows, if the CR is deemed worthy of development, it is sent to the analysts for further clarification; the CR is then turned into a use case and the iterative SDLC process is started all over again. For example, after a use case is created, the misuse case is documented and the CR is designed into the existing application. When the design documents are completed, coding and testing are done and the CR is complete.

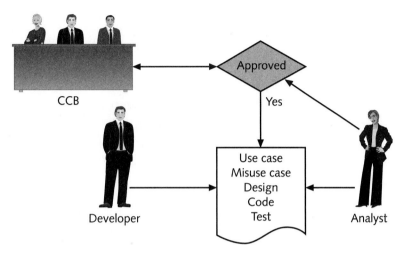

Figure 11-1   Change control board meeting

The benefits to a CCB are twofold:

- Provide a known and methodical decision process
- Sustain security and quality in the software artifacts

Provide a Known and Methodical Decision Process

The CCB holds the project to high standards. Just the mere thought of going to a CCB meeting and presenting a CR to the team forces all the team players involved to formulate their plans, documents, and thoughts about the impact on the software and timelines. Meeting with management, users, and other team players gives you a sense of their priorities, what the hot projects are, and what the security risks are. CCB meetings force the BA to ask the customers the right questions and hold them accountable for their change requests.

Sustaining Security and Quality in the Software Artifacts

Just because the software project is in maintenance mode doesn't mean that the requirement process can be lax with details. The process needs to hold the BAs accountable for use case requirements, misuse cases, and threat analysis. You need to ask for proper software requirements or the BAs will assume that you understood their request. You should apply the basic techniques for understanding software requirements you learned in Chapter 5 to prevent a lax requirement process.

Software is created to achieve organizational goals, and as each goal is achieved, new ones are set. As organizations set new goals through the use of software applications, those goals need to have security requirements (Redwine, et al. 2007). Analyzing each new goal in terms of use case documents and misuse case analysis is the key to sustaining security in each artifact. When a request comes across your table, the best way to avoid new security vulnerabilities or costly mistakes is to stick with the standard SDLC process and use the development methodology that got you to that point.

If the CCB approves a CR, the approval goes back to the analyst where more requirement gathering is done. This process ensures that each request in the maintenance phase is thoroughly documented and analyzed against criteria in the following categories:

- *Use case*: What is the functionality and goal of the CR?

- *Misuse case/threat analysis*: Will any sensitive information be transmitted, received, or updated? If so, who is involved? Why? How? When and where?

- *System design*: How does the new CR affect the current design? Are there any new interfaces or third-party interactions that are being introduced?

- *Testing*: Does the software execute as expected?

To sustain secure software in the maintenance phase, make sure each new CR has a security goal and that each goal can be translated into software requirements. The software environment is undergoing constant change with newly added features, change requests, or software/hardware changes. In the maintenance phase, most of your time and effort will be spent improving the application's efficiency, adding value-added features, and doing basic repairs on bugs. Two of the most common changes to a software application during the maintenance phase are new data flows and new user roles.

New interfaces, input fields, or reports are typical requests that end users make after the application is up and running. It is tempting to want to work on all simple change requests taken from the customer or analyst without going through the CCB process. After all, most people are customer driven and want to work with end users. Bypassing the CCB process sets up a dangerous precedent that opens up new opportunities for security vulnerabilities in the application.

Consider the following scenario: The original use case required a total number of end items in inventory. Now, the user would like to see the details of each end item so that she knows exactly how the total number was calculated. Therefore, a new change request was created to query the inventory data and display each item's detail. Because the developer already displayed the total sum of end items, he should already know how to retrieve the detailed information without any problems. The developer is currently in the middle of fixing bugs and enhancements to the application but determines that he has some free time the next day and that this change request should take only about two hours. He responds with a "no problem" and proceeds to service the request.

In this typical CR scenario, the developer would have proceeded to deliver sensitive information about a person's inventory without considering who was requesting the information (roles or privileges), if encryption were needed to secure the data flow, or if a new query against the table were allowed by the database group. All these items are part of the secure process discussed in the previous chapters, but they are easily forgotten or not thought of during maintenance.

New ways of doing business almost always create the need for new user roles or privileges. Adding new user roles without the appropriate analysis and design could accidentally give more authority to the wrong group of people. Adding user roles and privileges needs to be done so that each user has just enough privilege to do the job required and nothing more.

Sustaining Security and Quality in the Code

During software maintenance, the application's source code will go through revisions, enhancements, and rewrites. If you followed all the rules and examples throughout this text, especially regarding software diversity, the software will already be set up for these types of dynamic changes. For example, each software module should be easily traced to a use case, a misuse case, and design documents. Furthermore, the code itself will be well documented with comments and developed into small, easy-to-understand units of work. Therefore, sustaining security in the code will not be a problem.

The main feature you have going for your code is the consistency of the application. That is, each component, module, subroutine, and file has the same look and feel thanks to the use of the Application Guide. All code looks the same and uses the same objects, naming conventions, and coding conventions. The Application Guide not only ensures these features, it demands them. In addition to the consistency factor, we anticipate diversity in our code, so we develop parameter-driven software that relies on the use of CONSTANTS and other values from database tables.

Overall, the maintenance phase is your opportunity to bask in the sun, work a standard eight-hour day, and enjoy the fruits of your labor. However, you do not want to drop the ball now and fumble away a good job by making costly mistakes during maintenance. To keep doing a good job, pay attention to the following:

- Introducing software upgrades
- Introducing new developers

Introducing Software Upgrades

Updating the supporting operating systems, application servers, or tools can be exciting yet scary. As you already know, each new upgrade brings more risks as well as rewards.

The two action items that need to be carried out after any new upgrade are as follows:

- Regarding the more-testing action, treat any new upgrade as a threat to your architecture. Reexecute the test scripts and plan against the application and test the functionality, performance, responsiveness, and security all over again.

- Regarding the redesign action, remember that new features offer new solutions and a redesign of your application might be necessary to take advantage of this. The best example I can provide is the upgrade to IBM's WebSphere 6.0. from 5.0. One advantage to this upgrade was being able to deploy a smaller portion of the application instead of the whole enterprise application. Because this was a new design factor that my applications weren't set up for, I had to essentially break up the application into smaller components (**WAR files**) so that I could take advantage of this feature. Redesign or rewrite existing deployments to take advantage of any newer technology that would improve the **C.I.A.** of the application. In my example, I was able to deliver an application that is always available.

Introducing New Developers

After a few successful years of secure programming on one assignment, developers are likely to go onto another new project and to reuse the Application Guide and their skills to help other projects get started. After all, that is the ultimate goal for all of us. New teammates typically join the development team during the maintenance phase.

The introduction of new people can be a security risk during software maintenance. When new developers join the team during the maintenance phase, they don't have the background knowledge that the developers who wrote the software do. Therefore, someone needs to help the new team member identify the application's assets. Most of the time, however, no one has the time to do this and, thus, the newbies learn by being thrown into the fire.

To help maintain the software's security, make training part of the development methodology for new hires. For example, if a new person joins the team, have him or her pair-program with a senior developer for the first few weeks until he or she knows the frameworks, assets, and Application Guide. As shown in Figure 11-2, teamwork is essential to sustaining quality and security in the code.

Figure 11-2   New team member

SOFTWARE ASSURANCE: PROVE IT

Software assurance does not mean you have secure code; rather, it means that you have a process in place and a plan of action to ensure that the software that is written is secure (Redwine, et al. 2007). Sustaining a secure process throughout the application SDLC and into the maintenance phase requires checkpoints and procedures to be in place to prevent anything from sneaking in.

How do you know the process is working? How do you see an assurance plan? After all, code is hard to measure, see, and resell. So, how can anything be assured? The collective answer is this: Software assurance can be proven, validated, and substantiated only by the process in place and the artifacts produced from each process. That being said, the following elements need to be in place during maintenance (Redwine, et al. 2007):

- Proactive measures
- Reactive measures

Proactive Measures

Proactive measures are plans and policies created to proactively protect the system. One proactive measure that developers can implement in the development team is sensing. **Sensing** activities involve policies in the Application Guide that define how to use tools to monitor, test, and review code for threats and vulnerabilities and how to report those results to the development team (Redwine, et al. 2007).

Sensing activities can help the code protect itself by analyzing user patterns and resource requests, as shown in Figure 11-3. If a function or service that is requested is out of the norm, the code can gracefully shut down that request or kill the service. For example, a Web site might look at the IP address that you are using to submit requests, and if that IP address isn't what the developers are used to seeing from you, they will not offer you certain services (such as withdrawing money).

The activities inherent to the proactive process are as follows:

- Monitoring and improving error logs
- Scouting for incidents
- Proving your work

Monitoring and Improving Error Logs

In Chapter 9, you learned how to code try{} catch{} blocks within the software to trap and log all application exceptions. During maintenance, your job is to keep the error log free from any such errors and repair the software that is causing the exception. Make it your job to monitor these log files every morning when you start your workday to see if there is anything new that requires your attention. The more errors that are fixed, the more reliable and available the application becomes.

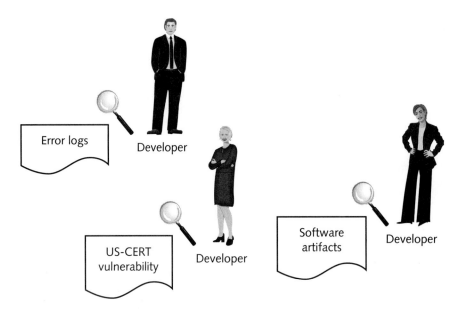

Figure 11-3   Proactive measures

Monitoring error logs and responding to immediate issues is a great way to stay proactive in the secure software process. While you review these log files for errors, you will also get a feel for the type of information that is useful versus the information that is trivial. As you improve the software by fixing the issues, also improve the loggers as needed. I've always found that at minimum, I should have the following information on hand inside the error logs:

- User's ID
- User's role
- User's search criteria
- Name of program that error occurred in
- Name of error and error message

Scouting for Incidents

The Application Guide needs to have rules in place so that everyone knows what to do when a vulnerability is found in the production environment. Typically, when a developer is assigned to the task of monitoring the software components for vulnerabilities, he reads the reports on CERT's vulnerability database or conducts some random Internet searches. If something is found that is deemed a concern, the developer might send an e-mail to the CCB, informing the board of the finding with a request to do testing. The developer tries to simulate the attack on the application, and if successful, an emergency CR is released by the developer and analysts and sent to the CCB or project management team for approval.

Reporting incidents like vulnerabilities or bugs not only makes the software more secure, it strengthens the assurance plan, which provides stakeholders with confidence in your ability to "hold the fort down."

Proving Your Work

If someone were to ask you to prove that your application is secure, how would you respond? How do you know if the application is secure? The bottom line is that you don't know for sure but you have a lot of proof that you did everything necessary to ensure the code is as safe as possible. Your proof will be evidenced in the following:

- *Application Guide*: It provides documentation of the reusable, secure process you have in place.

- *Use case*: Proves that the functionality has been verified and validated. It further details what the system should do and what the system *should not* do. It also proves that the software was written with a goal in mind.

- *Misuse case*: Proves that threat analysis and investigation was done looking for ways to break the software.

- *Code reviews (static and human)*: Prove that a process is in place to scan for bugs, vulnerabilities, and standards in the code.

- *Test scripts*: Prove that testing is a major process in the development life cycle.

- *CCB*: Proves that there is a formal change request process in place to uphold the high degree of standards and ensure the code is secure.

- *Incident reports*: Prove that there is a process in place that proactively monitors new threats to existing software.

Reactive Measures

Reactive measures are plans and policies that outline the proper response to an incident, as shown in Figure 11-4. The duty of responding to attacks is to maintain the security integrity of the software throughout its useful lifetime (Redwine, et al. 2007). During the lifetime of the software application, bugs, vulnerabilities, and attacks will occur. How you contain that information, who you tell, and how you tell it are all part of response management.

The Application Guide needs to establish policies that tell the developers what to do after a software attack occurs. Typically, the developer will not know that one of the assets was attacked or stolen until after the fact. What should that developer do? The two responses that need to be documented are as follows:

- Internal response
- External response

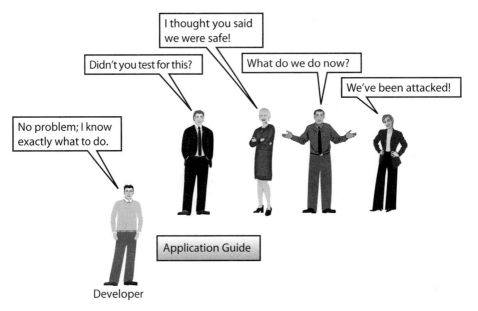

Figure 11-4   Reactive measures

Internal Responses to Attacks

The Application Guide needs to include a managerial policy that the developers will follow to ensure that all other end users of the current software are not harmed in any way as a result of the latest attack. This policy will vary from project to project, but generally, if the software assets were attacked, a formal review of logs, events, and users needs to be conducted. The project managers need to know what was taken, when, and how. The developers also need to know to whom they can talk in these times of crisis because everyone will be asking questions.

Even though everyone on the team will be very upset and stressed during this time, now is not the time to panic. In fact, now is the time to shine because the developer planned for this to happen, each misuse case was tested, and the application was developed to self-monitor itself. Therefore, you should be able to provide as much detail as necessary to find the attacker(s).

External Responses to Attacks

According to the Organization for Internet Safety (OIS), the following five steps make up a threat response process that needs to be part of the software maintenance process (Organization for Internet Safety 2004):

1. *Discovery*: The victim (user) discovers the attack.

2. *Notification*: The victim notifies the organization or application owner of the attack and the organization confirms the incident.

3. *Investigation*: The organization investigates the victim's reports to verify and validate the misuse.

4. *Resolution*: If the attack is confirmed, the organization develops a solution (software patch or change procedure) to eliminate future attacks from the same misuse scenario.

5. *Release*: The organization's management team and victim will coordinate the public release about the attack.

**QUICK
CHECKS**

1. Open the Application Guide you have been building during all chapters.

2. Add team rules that you want your developers to follow when the software is attacked. Please include a specific response process, including the chain of communication and how to report incidents to the management team and to the public.

3. Share this section of the Application Guide with other students. Did they include areas that were not covered in your guide?

11

AFTER THE GLORY: KEEPING YOUR CAREER IN DEMAND

Congratulations, you have learned how to read and write secure requirements, design code using secure principles, analyze that design for threats and misuses, and code and test secure code. During those activities, the working environment was probably extremely intense. Long days and many nights of overtime were spent working with every member of the team, analyzing code for reuse and security features, and programming through iterations of each use case. The BAs were talking to you on a daily basis, customers were helping you test, and the PMs kept tight control of your schedule and availability. Then, after one successful launch and perhaps a "You Did It" certificate, there is quiet.

And just like that, your position goes from the driver's seat to the backseat. The BAs now are spending their time with other people (users, stakeholders), and you see your project management team only in weekly status meeting, if the team attends at all. Your job is still important for break/fix issues, code optimization, and analysis, but the glory is definitely gone.

Even though you might feel you used all the technology that the company has to offer, this is not the time to rest. Maintenance projects are actually quite challenging because the need to make software secure, reusable, and standard is still present, but the drive, support, and determination might be somewhat lax. I call this the "Super Bowl syndrome" because teams that win the championship one year generally come back with a certain entitlement ego that prevents them from working harder the following year.

Three important steps that will keep your software development skills from falling victim to the Super Bowl syndrome are as follows:

- Show initiative
- Improve your estimates
- Create the Application Guide immediately if the team does not have one

Showing Initiative

The reality is that all organizations are doing more with less. There are no hand-holding techniques on the job that will teach you how to code (but hopefully this book has helped show you what you need to do). Mentors exist for career moves, but they will not tell you how to fix your JavaScript errors. Therefore, you have to be willing to practice programming languages, tools, and other technologies at night or on the weekend. Maintenance projects usually bring a more 9-to-5 working lifestyle, so logging extra hours for your own growth should not be too much to ask for; in fact, these days, it's expected.

Showing initiative and figuring things out on your own will bring a lot of benefits to your job. For one thing, you will become more valuable on the team, but, more important, you will also be prepared to solve problems before they happen. Training yourself on different technologies and methods will give you the insight that you need to apply the right solution to the right problem, if and when that problem occurs.

- Learn new technologies
- Network with your peers

Learn New Technologies

There are many tools and technologies that can be helpful in solving a business problem. The more knowledgeable you become with your tools and software, the more you start to develop a prescription list of solutions that can be applied to problems now or in the future. These prescriptions can then be applied or at least suggested to your project management team when the need arises. For example, you might know some special features of the current software programming language, but the current use case did not require them. Keep those features in your back pocket and wait for the right problem to come along so that you can quickly apply solutions when the need arises.

Consider the following Web technologies that offer special features that will not only benefit Web applications, but also update your skills as a Web developer so that you can keep up with current market demands.

Ajax Technologies   **Ajax (Asynchronous JavaScript and XML)** is a Web development technique used to make Web pages interactive and intuitive using XML, DHTML, **style sheets**, and JavaScript. Ajax dynamically changes data while maintaining the current state of the Web page. Ajax is actually an old technology—it has been around since 1998 and supported since Microsoft Internet Explorer 5. However, it wasn't until Google Suggest in

2005 and **Google Maps** in 2006 used AJAX that the technology became the new "must-have" with Web users and developers.

Ajax allows the developer to refresh/build/rebuild a screen's content with pinpoint efficiency without sending all data elements to the server. Ajax, like all programming languages, has its security vulnerabilities and must be used with caution, but it does make applications highly efficient, fast, and user friendly.

Web 2.0 Technologies   **Web 2.0** is a term used to describe the transitional status of today's Web applications. Streaming servers that deliver audio and video content are adding value to business applications worldwide. Companies are realizing cash savings by leveraging the current knowledge base and sharing that data in real time across the globe with their partners and suppliers. From up-to-date training manuals to video instructions or conferencing, Web 2.0 features offer solutions to everyday problems.

The tools that can add instant value to an application in the maintenance phase are as follows:

- **Blogs**: These online Weblogs can be used to share project status of what's new, talk about up-and-coming features, and basically let the people on the outside meet the project team. Personal touches can go a long way in today's isolated world.

- **Wikis**: Wikis are online resources that can be used to define common elements of the application, department, or company. Every company has their own jargon for their parts and products, and the use of online wikis will create a common glossary of terms so that all the items on the Web page are understandable to all.

- **Podcasts**: Podcasts are audio files that can be broadcast to the users to announce or explain certain features or instructions.

- **Webcasts**: Webcasts are online videos that can be used for training, instructions, or demonstrations.

QUICK CHECKS

1. For a real case scenario of how to show initiative on the job, open up the "Cleaning Up Problems with AJAX.doc" file from the Chapter 11 course data.

2. Read the file. Does the introduction of Ajax put the application more at risk to software attacks? Why or why not?

Networking with Your Peers

You will come to find that for such a big industry, there is actually a small network of people. People move from project to project and place to place in this field very quickly, and it is very common to find someone who knows someone whom you know. When you attend conferences and company demos, bring business cards with you and hand them out to people you run into. Some of the most important contacts you will make in your career will be the people you meet for sidebar conversations at these conferences.

Other areas where you can network are bootcamps and advanced training programs. Security University (SU), for example, teaches the fundamentals of secure software programming by providing hands-on workshops and tutorials. While you attend these training classes, you will be working with and meeting people in your field who are interested in the same topic. Get to know them; you never know where your next project will come from.

Improving Your Estimates

I've been in this business a long time, and I am still trying to perfect my estimates on how long a use case should take in development time. Project management, users, and stakeholders will depend more and more on your analysis and opinion if you can provide them with meaningful estimates. The maintenance phase is a perfect time to hone this skill because the application's framework, software, and business rules are pretty much defined at this time. Two ways in which you can sharpen this ability are as follows:

- Keep a daily journal.
- Compare your time with other benchmarks.

Keeping a Daily Journal

Keeping a daily journal of what you did today and where your time was spent will be valuable to your project manager, but will also keep you honest. If you tell the project management team that a certain change request or new use case will take 40 development hours, then track your development time and keep a daily journal of where the full eight hours were spent each day. The truth is, daily sidebar conversations at work with colleagues about what you did last night or over the weekend happen every day, and if you plan your day accordingly, they should not affect the original estimate. It is my opinion that when you provide estimates based on eight-hour work days, plan on developing for six out of the eight hours.

When providing estimates to the management team, give them a very detailed work breakdown list and describe each step and task that needs to be done and how long it will take. This breakdown of tasks needs to be grouped together in eight-hour workdays. At the end of each day, send a status report of where you are at compared with where you *should* be. Then include what you did in that day. By holding yourself accountable each day, you will be able to determine how you work and how long things actually take.

Benchmarking Time

Benchmarking time is a way of looking at the project plan and comparing the estimates with the actual. Then, you use those actual times as the new benchmark for the next use case. Over time, giving estimates will become very easy and, most important, quite accurate. Project managers will use your opinion during decision making and, hopefully, use your analysis abilities to forecast plans or more projects.

Create the Application Guide Immediately

If the organization does not currently have an Application Guide, start one now. It doesn't have to start off as a full-blown contract with the developers out of the gate; eventually it will evolve into one. At first, concentrate on getting the basics defined. These basics include tools and configurations. After that, slowly add the coding conventions and naming conventions as they become defined on the project. The Application Guide could become the best artifact on any given project.

Here is what typically happens on the projects I work on. I start an Application Guide immediately by documenting how my developer machine is configured and where the tools can be found. I then define all frameworks used in the code and when those frameworks are used. After I have documented and tested that much, I share it with the PM and everyone else on the team. At first, it may not be welcomed with open arms, that is, until we have to reconfigure a machine or a new team member comes along and needs to build his or her machine. Once the Application Guide is used and relied on, it saves the organization time, effort, and money. That alone will help you grow in this field.

11

CHAPTER SUMMARY

- In order to support the application's operations, everyone on the team must sustain secure software until the application retires.

- Project management can help sustain the formality in the development process during the maintenance phase by creating a change control board (CCB).

- Software is created to achieve organizational goals, and as each goal is achieved, new ones are set.

- In the maintenance phase, most of your time and effort will be spent improving the application's efficiency, adding value-added features, and doing basic repairs on bugs.

- Each component, module, subroutine, and file in your code should share the same look and feel.

- When new developers join the team during the maintenance phase, they don't have the same knowledge as the current developers.

- Software assurance means that you have a process in place and a plan of action to ensure the software that is written is secure.

- Proactive measures are plans and policies created to proactively protect the system.

- The activities inherent to the proactive process are monitoring and improving error logs, reporting incidents, and proving your work.

- Reactive measures are plans and policies that outline the proper response to an incident.

- Smart developers show initiative and improve their estimates.

Key Terms

AJAX (Asynchronous JavaScript and XML) — A web development technique that allows data elements to be sent asynchronously to the web server without having to submit the whole page.

benchmarking — The act of comparing your work against what other competitors or industry-leading products offer.

blog — A web tool from the Web 2.0 framework that allows individuals to post daily journals of activities of interest.

break/fix — Break/fix mode is a time when the application code is frozen and no enhancement will be implemented. The only way the code can be changed is if there is a bug in the current code baseline.

C.I.A. — Confidentiality, Integrity, and Availability are the three properties that are used to measure software security.

change control board (CCB) — A governing body of managers and other project team members whose purpose is to ensure a formal development methodology during the maintenance phase and to prioritize workload.

change request — A software artifact that end users fill out when they need features in the software modified.

enhancement — A program change to the current code baseline.

Google Maps — Goople Maps is a feature that Google provides for web users that will allow them to view satellite images of a parcel of land and change the direction with the click of a mouse.

podcasts — A web tool from the Web 2.0 framework that allows individuals to post audio clips of activities of interest.

proactive measures — Measures that are taken by the application development team to prevent software attacks and to mitigate issues.

reactive measures — Standard protocol procedures that everyone on the application team follows when a software attack occurs.

sensing — Proactive measures that developers can perform to look for software vulnerabilities.

software assurance — A process/plan of action to ensure that the software that is written is secure.

style sheets — A type of software that allows developers to make every web page look the same within an application.

WAR files — A web archived file, as part of the Java J2EE specification. It is used to represent a web application that belongs to an enterprise of applications.

Web 2.0 — A collective term that describes the next set of client-rich features available in Web applications.

webcasts — Online videos used for training, instructions, or demonstrations.

wikis — A web tool from the Web 2.0 framework that allows applications to self-govern themselves by allowing the user community to post helpful information (i.e., common definitions of terms or FAQs) for other users.

REVIEW QUESTIONS

1. _____ syndrome occurs when a group of people work hard as a team to achieve a lofty goal, but that once it is achieved, their dedication and hard work turns into more of a lax entitlement feeling.

   a. Overachievement

   b. Winner

   c. Super Bowl

   d. Experienced

2. _____ is the phase when software development practices change from new development to break/fix and code optimization.

3. What is the best way you (as the developer) can improve your development skills during software maintenance?

   a. Train yourself on new technologies and keep in good health.

   b. Train yourself on new technologies and work on providing better estimates.

   c. Learn new languages and meet new people.

   d. Work 9 to 5 daily on routine tasks and provide detailed status reports.

4. What are the two ways you (as the developer) can sustain secure code during software maintenance?

   a. Create a CCB committee and conduct threat analysis on each change request.

   b. Go to training for advanced hacking techniques and read weekly journals on security topics.

   c. Work closely with the business analysts with each requirement and continue with peer reviews.

   d. Read weekly journals and Web sites that report on the latest attacks.

5. What is the first item a developer should look for in a change request?

   a. cost

   b. proper documentation

   c. priority

   d. goal

6. During a change request, what type of requirements will most likely increase security risk? (Choose all that apply.)

   a. changes in business logic

   b. changes in data flow

   c. changes in display

   d. changes in user roles

11

7. How can a developer improve his/her ability to accurately provide work estimates?

   a. The developer should look at what his or her peers are doing and how long they take.

   b. The developer should work with the project manager and let the PM decide how long a change request should take.

   c. The developer should rely on past benchmarks for future estimates.

   d. The developer should use an original estimate and compare work done with work estimated.

8. Why should a developer learn new methods and technologies on a maintenance project when there is no current need for newer technologies?

9. How have Web 2.0 features changed Web design?

   a. They provide a refreshing way to add new gadgets to the user community.

   b. They take advantage of reusable communication tools and training techniques.

   c. They provide simpler development methodologies.

   d. They provide better security.

10. Which option will help in the following situation?

    The development team of an intranet application is constantly fielding phone calls from the user community about business rules and definitions.

    a. Provide a wiki so that users can show common words and definitions from the software application.

    b. Provide a podcast of how the software should be used.

    c. Provide a Webcast of how to use the screens.

    d. Provide a group photo of the development team so that the users know who they are talking to.

11. During a typical workday on a maintenance project, Steve, the developer, was busy answering questions from analysts and/or customers, fixing bugs, and investigating issues. At the end of the week, however, Steve did not have a lot of new code written and he had a hard time reporting where each billable hour was spent. What technique can Steve implement to help manage his time better so that he can give more accurate estimates?

    a. Write a status report at the end of the week highlighting all the week's activities.

    b. Write a daily journal of what happened, how long each activity took, and why.

    c. Write daily e-mails to the project management team with updates.

    d. Let the project manager provide the estimates and try his best to meet them.

12. What is software assurance?

    a. a process developers follow to produce secure software

    b. a methodology that provides the framework for secure software

    c. a tool that can be used to produce secure software

    d. a process that proves there are measures in place to produce secure software

13. What deliverables are used to prove a software assurance process?

    a. process logs

    b. error logs

    c. software artifacts

    d. test journals

14. When should software be rewritten? (Choose all that apply.)

    a. when the software's code becomes too complex

    b. when newer versions of software become available that do the same task faster, cheaper, and better

    c. when bugs are found

    d. when it becomes inefficient

15. Introduction of new team members (developers) will pose some risk to software security. True or False?

16. All known breaches of security need to be announced to the user community immediately to attain a high degree of integrity. True or False?

17. The analysts are still responsible for detailed requirements during a maintenance project. True or False?

18. Threat models are used to analyze what new threats can be used against the software. True or False?

19. Software upgrades are the most risky of all enhancements to implement. True or False?

20. Maintenance projects offer great opportunities to optimize code and try newer techniques and tools. True or False?

11

HANDS-ON PROJECTS

Project 11-1 Reaction Time

Users of abc.com recently flooded the company's help center because they could not log in. The help desk forwarded these phone calls to the development team. When the lead developer heard of the problems, he instantly tried to log in to the application himself and found that he could not log in. He then queried the database only to find no records except for one that had been left for him. The one record contained a message stating, "Thanks for the info."

What are the five reactive steps that abc.com must do before communicating this attack to their external users as well as to the general public?

HANDS-ON PROJECTS

Project 11-2 Vulnerability Database

Company ABC uses an Adobe Flash Player Version 8 applet that executes animation on its web site. You have just learned from US-CERT that the Version 8 Adobe Flash Player that you are using is vulnerable to a string buffer overflow that can be used to execute arbitrary code in your application. In response to this knowledge, do the following:

1. Log in to the US-CERT Vulnerability Database at *www.kb.cert.org/vuls/html/search*.

2. Using the search feature, find the long string buffer overflow vulnerability for Adobe Flash Player.

3. What is the remedy for this security vulnerability?

CASE PROJECT

CASE PROJECTS

Response Time Interview

Research several security incidents that have occurred within the last five years. Use news reports as the basis for your research. Here are some questions that will help formalize your research:

1. Did the first notification come from the company itself, or from someone outside?

2. What was the timeline for each part of the response (did the company notify its users immediately or did it wait)?

3. If the first notification was from outside, how did the company initially respond? Did members of management initially try to deny the problem or did they immediately accept responsibility?

4. Prepare a short report of each incident that you found.

CHAPTER REFERENCES

Organization for Internet Safety. 2004. Security Vulnerability Reporting and Response Process, Organization for Internet Safety. http://www.oisafety.org/process.pdf (accessed February 23, 2003).

Redwine, Samuel T. Jr., Rusty O. Baldwin, Mary L. Polydys, Daniel P. Shoemaker, Jeffrey A. Ingalsbe, and Larry D. Wagoner. 2007. Software Assurance: A Guide to the Common Body of Knowledge to Produce, Acquire, and Sustain Secure Software Version 1.2. Arlington, VA: U.S. Department of Homeland Security. https://buildsecurityin.us-cert.gov/daisy/bsi/940/version/1/part/4/data/CurriculumGuideToTheCBK.pdf (accessed February 13, 2008).

Glossary

.NET — The Microsoft .NET Framework and the tools that access the framework.

abuse cases — *See* misuse cases.

active listening — The process of listening in a structured way for meaning. It includes summarizing, paraphrasing, and evaluating body language.

actor — A domain that interacts with the system.

AJAX (Asynchronous JavaScript and XML) — A web development technique that allows data elements to be sent asynchronously to the web server without having to submit the whole page.

analyst — A person who is in charge of ensuring user requirements are documented and translated to the developers.

ANT — A tool that automates common repetitive tasks that developers do every day.

asset — Anything of value to the stakeholders.

association — A relationship between concepts that depicts some sort of meaningful interaction.

attacker — A person who creates and modifies computer software and computer hardware, including computer programming, administration, and security-related items with malicious intent.

bad list — A running list of inputs that have no business requirements; these inputs cannot be trusted by the application.

benchmarking — The act of comparing your work against what other competitors or industry-leading products offer.

best practices — The handbooks of practice, which include administrative rules, guidelines, policies, and procedures that explain the best possible way of doing something.

black box — A term used to describe a process where everything about the process is unknown except for the inputs and outputs.

blacklist — All values not defined in a whitelist.

blog — A web tool from the Web 2.0 framework that allows individuals to post daily journals of activities of interest.

break/fix — Break/fix mode is a time when the application code is frozen and no enhancement will be implemented. The only way the code can be changed is if there is a bug in the current code baseline.

buffer overflow — An event that occurs when you put more data into a memory location than it is allocated to hold.

buffer overflow attack — Software attacks to buffer overflows.

C.I.A. — The three main principles in secure code: confidentiality, integrity, and availability.

change control board (CCB) — A governing body of managers and other project team members whose purpose is to ensure a formal development methodology and to prioritize workload.

change requests — A software artifact that end users fill out when they need features in the software modified.

class diagrams — Software module blueprints that serve as the software specification for a specific module/component.

code editors — Editors that have built-in error handlers that highlight coding errors while the code is being typed in.

code review — A review/inspection of code by its author and/or one or more colleagues (peers) to evaluate its technical content for quality and security.

compile time — The time when a program language, such as Java, converts ASCII characters into binary (or machine) code. If keywords are misspelled or the code is not per API specification, compile time errors will occur.

compilers — Small programs that convert ASCII characters into binary code.

CONSTANTS — A fixed value in a programming language.

CSS — A simple mechanism for adding style (for example, fonts, colors, spacing) to Web documents [w3c.org].

database definition library (DDL) — A schema used by the DBMS to create a physical table, assign keys, and assign definitions to columns.

database schema — A model diagram representing how the database tables relate to each other.

debugger — A small program that steps through the execution of code inside a GUI so that the developer can visually see how the code is being executed and what the current values of each variable are at run time.

debugs — Style built in to the code that assists the programmer to follow the application's execution paths and internal definitions.

decompiler — A tool used to decompile compiled code.

deprecated — A term that describes a software's function or method that no longer encourages the use of a certain method or function that was previously encouraged in early versions or releases.

domain — A business entity or concept with which the application code interfaces.

dynamic testing — The testing of application code by executing the software with valid input fields.

efficient — Making use of application resources and programming logic with optimal performance and speed.

encapsulation — The process of creating code wrappers around variables, input values, or business logic so that access to properties can be achieved only through the use of the object's methods.

enhancement — A program change to the current code baseline.

external resources — Human or computer-driven resources used in the software development process.

fail securely — How the software reacts when the system goes down.

false negatives — When a system reports code as good when it is really susceptible.

false positives — When a system reports code as susceptible when it really is a good piece of code; also an output result from a static code analyzer that highlights valid code, such as an input field, as a vulnerability.

FindBugs — A code analyzer that is used to check binary code (Java) for common software vulnerabilities such as unchecked input parameters and SQ Code injections.

firewall — Security software stored in a device, such as a router, that is configured to permit or deny data requests to and from machines connected to a network.

Fortify Source Code Analysis (SCA) — A static code analyzer that is used to check binary code (C++ and Java) for common software vulnerabilities such as unchecked input parameters and arrays for buffer overflows.

framework — A predefined process or structure which another software project can use or plug into.

functional testing scripts — A step-by-step process that executes many testing scripts.

fuzz testing — A technique used to throw random input data and files to a program to see what happens.

getters and setters — Methods that are used to send or retrieve properties from an object.

GNU — A project that encourages the use and sharing of software programs that are nonproprietary.

good list — A running list of inputs that have business requirements; these inputs can be trusted by the application.

Google Maps — A feature that Google provides for web users that will show users how to view satellite images of a parcel of land and change the direction with the click of a mouse.

GUI — A screen through which users interact with an application.

hacker — A person who creates and modifies computer software and computer hardware, including computer programming, administration, and security-related items with nonmalicious intent.

hybrid methodology — Interbreeding two or more development methodologies so that the process that is ultimately followed adapts to the dynamics and knowledge base of the team members.

IEEE (Institute of Electrical and Electronics Engineers, pronounced "I-triple-E") — Founded in 1963, IEEE is an organization composed of engineers, scientists, and students. IEEE is best known for developing standards for the computer and electronics industry.

indexes — Used by the DBMS to organize the data stored in a table.

inputs — Data elements that come from system events.

integration testing — The act of testing the whole use case from front to back.

interaction diagrams — Diagrams that display interaction activity between the object within a model.

J2EE — A specification created by Sun Microsystems to be J2EE compliant to the enterprise application specification.

JAR file — A Java archive file is a Zip file used to distribute a set of Java classes.

limited code — Code that is written for one purpose only.

logic errors — Errors within software that are caused by problematic code conditions or faulty If statements.

malware — A generic term for a number of different types of malicious code.

memory leaks — A situation when an application or operating system runs out of allocated memory.

messages — Communication links between objects that define input parameters and return parameters.

MIPS (million instructions per second) — The CPU speed of a DBMS.

misuse cases — A document that describes the attack, the pattern of execution, conditions of the surrounding environment, and available tools that must be present for an attack to occur.

object modeling — The process of creating a visualization (using a standard notation) of a software system, design, or component.

open source — Free software created by the public.

open source tools — Tools that are free to use in accordance with the open source license agreement, typically General Public License, such as GNU, and that are owned by the originating authors.

organized chaos — A state of utter confusion in a supervised or managed environment.

outputs — Data elements that come from the application's resources (database, file, code).

parameter-driven software — Software that is coded in such a way that the paths of execution are determined by parameters stored in a table or XML file rather than hard coded.

penetrations testing — A testing technique using qualified personnel to conduct real-world attacks against the application (or system) to help identify and correct security vulnerabilities.

perimeter defense — Drawing a perimeter between two classes of networks, those trusted and those that are not.

phishing — Trying to build a Web site that tricks users into giving up their confidential information.

physical attack — Taking a system off-line without authorization or stealing hardware.

physical theft — The loss of an item (computer, flash drive, and so on) because another person stole it.

PMP — A project management professional who holds a certification from the Project Management Institute. The PMP designation following your name tells current and potential employers that you have a solid foundation of project management knowledge that can be readily applied in the workplace.

PMP resources — Any project management resource (for example, project plan, minutes, issue logs).

podcasts — A web tool from the Web 2.0 framework that allows individuals to post clips.

primary key — A value that must be present to get to the unique data row of a database table.

proactive measures — Measures that are taken by the application development team to prevent software attacks and to mitigate issues.

profiling — The process of defining steps of execution, time of each execution, and memory usage of each step.

proprietary tools — Tools that charge a fee for license(s), either per seat or per server, and that are owned by the company that issues the tools.

prototypes — Small, working applications that provide a user only with the look and feel of the final product.

reactive measures — Standard protocol procedures that everyone on the application team follows when a software attack occurs.

refactoring — The process of reorganizing the code's structure, without changing the meaning or behavior of the software.

Refactoring tools — Automated features that can break down large methods or bodies of code into smaller methods or objects.

reliability — A test that ensures that the application will be up and running under extreme circumstances.

resiliency — The capability to rebound or spring back from an attack.

RUNSTATS — Used by the DBMS to determine how many records and columns exist in a table.

run-time error — Errors that occur after the code has been compiled and at the time of execution.

sandbox — A tightly controlled area for resources to be used by visiting applications. Sandboxes allow for self-contained programs, such as Java applets, to run within browsers.

scope creep — A symptom when original requirements start to spawn off into more, bigger requirements, eventually losing the functionality and focus of the originals.

SDLC documentation — A Software Development Life Cycle artifact, such as requirement documents, design diagrams, code elements, and test cases.

secure testing scripts — A generic term for a number of different types of malicious code.

security policy — Constraints on access to machines for external systems and people. These policies are created by the company, application, or department and are enforced through administration rights and configuration (software installation).

sensing — Proactive measures that developers can do that look for software vulnerabilities.

signature — The method name, the number and type of parameters, and the return type of a specific method.

singleton design pattern — A design pattern that guarantees that only one object resides in memory during the time of execution.

SLA (service-level agreement) — An agreement that contractually binds the application support team to servicing the application in the event of errors, downtime, or other related system problems.

SMS (Short Message Service) — A protocol used for sending messages of up to 160 characters.

software artifacts — Support documentation in the software industry.

software assurance — A process that defines how security is tested within the software.

software diversity — The ability of software to *anticipate* change of requirements, end usage, functionality, or definition.

software engineer — One who approaches the construction of software from an engineering discipline and calculated approach.

software life cycle — The official phases that software goes through while being created from start to finish. Those phases are requirements analysis; design; architectural design; detailed design; coding; testing; installation; acceptance; and maintenance.

software methodology — A governing process that defines and rationalizes the set of procedures and processes that are followed while coding.

software (security) assurance (SwA) — A software security assurance process judges the effectiveness of how security characteristics and principles are tested and implemented.

source-based fault injections — A testing technique that requires a programmer to physically code an error into the program to see how the rest of the code reacts.

spaghetti code — Code that starts in one place but then spawns itself into hundreds of other directions. Very hard to maintain.

spam — Unwanted and unsolicited e-mail.

SQL code injection — An attack type conducted through the use of Web servers where an SQL statement can be substituted for a host variable within an outer select statement.

stakeholders — People who have an interest in a project.

static code analyzers — Scanners that identify security vulnerabilities or potential holes by scanning the binary libraries of the application.

static testing — The process of testing application code by inspecting code in its native language and/or scanning binary code for vulnerabilities and quality.

style sheets — A type of software that allows developers to make every web page look the same within an application.

syntax error — A type of error that prevents a code compiler from converting ASCII code into binary.

system event — An external input event that comes from an actor (user of system).

system test — The act of testing all use cases together as a whole.

test plan — A document created to specify how testing should be performed, who executes the testing, when testing starts and ends, and any and all other pertinent data deemed necessary by the project management team.

testing software — The process of running a battery of test cases using multiple techniques against a specific use case and evaluating the results for pass or fail marks.

unauthorized — The validation process in which requests are denied the permission to use or view an application resource.

Unified Modeling Language (UML) — The notation used for system documentation and object-oriented concepts.

usability testing — A technique used to test how the security features of the software affect the convenience of using the application.

validation — A quality check that validates the final product or service and produces the desired result.

verification — A quality check that verifies that the software satisfies the requirement.

view — A virtual table created by a subset of another physical table.

visualization — An activity used for requirements understanding that allows the developer to think like an application and therefore see the sequence of events from a systematic perspective.

vulnerability — A flaw or weakness in a system design, implementation, or operation that could be exploited to violate the system's security policy.

WAR files — A web archived file, as part of the Java J2EE specification. It is used to represent a web application that belongs to an enterprise of applications.

Web 2.0 — A collective term that describes the next set of client-rich features available in Web applications.

Webcasts — Online videos used for training, instructions, or demonstrations.

Web service — A piece of software that makes itself available over the Internet and uses a standardized XML messaging system.

whiteboard — A drawing board that allows people to use dry erase markers for building visuals.

whitelist — When performing input validation, the set of items that, if matched, results in the input being accepted as valid. If there is no match to the whitelist, the input is considered invalid.

wikis — A web tool from the Web 2.0 framework that allows applications to self-govern themselves by allowing the user community to post helpful information (i.e., common definitions of terms or FAQs) for other users.

wireframes — Static HTML files or screen drawings on paper that depict what the GUIs look like.

XSS (Cross-Site Scripting) — An attack on Web pages that stores input fields in a database and then redisplays those fields on the Web screen as data. The input fields, however, are corrupted with JavaScript tags that could redirect the user to another Web site.

Index